The Office and Philosophy

The Blackwell Philosophy and PopCulture Series
Series editor William Irwin

A spoonful of sugar helps the medicine go down, and a healthy helping of popular culture clears the cobwebs from Kant. Philosophy has had a public relations problem for a few centuries now. This series aims to change that, showing that philosophy is relevant to your life—and not just for answering the big questions like "To be or not to be?" but for answering the little questions: "To watch or not to watch *South Park*?" Thinking deeply about TV, movies, and music doesn't make you a "complete idiot." In fact it might make you a philosopher, someone who believes the unexamined life is not worth living and the unexamined cartoon is not worth watching.

South Park and Philosophy: You Know, I Learned Something Today
Edited by Robert Arp

Metallica and Philosophy: A Crash Course in Brain Surgery
Edited by William Irwin

Family Guy and Philosophy: A Cure for the Petarded
Edited by J. Jeremy Wisnewski

The Daily Show and Philosophy: Moments of Zen in the Art of Fake News
Edited by Jason Holt

Lost and Philosophy: The Island Has Its Reasons
Edited by Sharon M. Kaye

24 and Philosophy: The World According to Jack
Edited by Jennifer Hart Weed, Richard Davis, and Ronald Weed

Battlestar Galactica and Philosophy: Knowledge Here Begins Out There
Edited by Jason T. Eberl

The Office and Philosophy: Scenes from the Unexamined Life
Edited by J. Jeremy Wisnewski

The Office and Philosophy

Scenes from the Unexamined Life

Edited by J. Jeremy Wisnewski

Blackwell
Publishing

BLACKWELL PUBLISHING
350 Main Street, Malden, MA 02148-5020, USA
9600 Garsington Road, Oxford OX4 2DQ, UK
550 Swanston Street, Carlton, Victoria 3053, Australia

The right of J. Jeremy Wisnewski to be identified as the author of the editorial material in this work has been asserted in accordance with the UK Copyright, Designs, and Patents Act 1988.

Designations used by companies to distinguish their products are often claimed as trademarks. All brand names and product names used in this book are trade names, service marks, trademarks, or registered trademarks of their respective owners. The publisher is not associated with any product or vendor mentioned in this book.

This publication is designed to provide accurate and authoritative information in regard to the subject matter covered. It is sold on the understanding that the publisher is not engaged in rendering professional services. If professional advice or other expert assistance is required, the services of a competent professional should be sought.

First published 2008 by Blackwell Publishing Ltd

1   2008

Library of Congress Cataloging-in-Publication Data

The office and philosophy: scenes from the unexamined life/edited by J. Jeremy Wisnewski.
    p. cm. — (The Blackwell philosophy and popculture series)
  Includes bibliographical references and index.
  ISBN 978-1-4051-7555-5 (pbk.: alk. paper)   1. Office (Television program: United States)
2. Office (Television program: Great Britain)   3. Philosophy.   I. Wisnewski, Jeremy.

  PN1992.77.O34O34   2008
  791.45′75—dc22

                                                          2007046026

A catalogue record for this title is available from the British Library.

Set in 10.5/13pt Sabon
by Graphicraft Limited, Hong Kong
Printed and bound in The United States of America
by Sheridan Books, Inc., Chelsea, MI

The publisher's policy is to use permanent paper from mills that operate a sustainable forestry policy, and which has been manufactured from pulp processed using acid-free and elementary chlorine-free practices. Furthermore, the publisher ensures that the text paper and cover board used have met acceptable environmental accreditation standards.

For further information on
Blackwell Publishing, visit our website at
www.blackwellpublishing.com

Contents

Contents

Introductory Memo

A Note to Our Suppliers in the US and the UK: Support Philosophy, It Uses Lots of Paper!

To: Wernham-Hogg, UK and Dunder-Mifflin, USA
From: J. Jeremy Wisnewski, philosophy enthusiast and paper connoisseur
RE: The importance of philosophy (for paper companies)

I have a business proposition for you. From a paper production and consumption standpoint, it makes oodles of business sense, as I'm sure you will see. I am part of an enterprise that requires ample use of paper: we write and revise, speak and argue, and then revise again. The only thing we actually need to complete our work is paper, something to write with, and a trash can (and some in my line of work don't even bother with the trash can). We are *thinkers*, and because writing is a form of thinking, we are *writers. And we use paper*. Paper, gentlemen.

And so we need you. But you need us too! Philosophy is important. It refuses to let us rest our minds with comfortable conclusions or flaccid, empty ideas. It acts as a constant impetus to revisit our views, and to take seriously our own fallibility. But we matter to you guys more directly, too. You see, most of what gets said in the name of philosophy is incomplete, and a lot of it is just not right—it is incredibly interesting, and it is even important, but it just isn't right. And so we keep writing and thinking, and we keep using more paper. *More paper*, gentleman. More paper.

We've been doing this for two and a half millennia, and I don't envision it ending anytime soon. And that spells continuous investigation, and more paper than even you can imagine. Even when we think we've nailed something down—perhaps something about the nature of knowledge, or value, or self-deception—there will always be clarifications that need to be made, criticisms that need to be met, and additional questions to be considered. And besides, there will always be some schmoe who will claim that what we've said is wrong, or misses the point, or doesn't go far enough, or is nonsense, or trivial, or something else.

So philosophy will always need paper. We can support your offices. I ask in return that you also support *ours*. In the following pages you will find some of the things we do, and I hope you will agree that, even if we aren't coming up with final answers, we are nevertheless doing something of great importance—we are exercising our minds, exploring assumptions, and doing our best not to let dogma get in the way of what matters. And we're using paper to do it. Paper, gentleman.

We will be there for you great paper companies. And perhaps you could even learn something about the workings of your own organizations from what we have to say here. Perhaps, Michael and David, you'll even learn something about yourselves in the process. And paper will be there. Paper.

Spread the word about philosophy, boys! It's the key to the future of paper, and maybe even to the future of civilization. And if you don't buy that, at least think of all the philosophers who need employment! Are either of your guys hiring, by the way?

A Note to Bitter Brits and Confused Americans . . .

Some of you are unhappy, and others are confused. The bitter Brits are clenching this book tightly, wondering why there are so many chapters on the *American* version of *The Office*, when the British version was what started it all. These Anglophiles are grinding their teeth and shaking their fists. "The British version," they are thinking, "is the superior version of the show, not some cheap knock-off. The book should have been only on the British version of the show!" And then there are the confused Americans, puzzling over some of the chapter titles, wondering "Who is this David Brent, and what's he got to do with *The Office*?" You see, they didn't even know there was a British version of the show.

Bitter Brits, meet Confused Americans. Confused Americans, meet Bitter Brits.

There will be no placating some of the Brits, and no clarifying things to some of the confused Americans. It's true, *The Office* did originate in Britain, and the British version is excellent in every respect. But it's also true that the American version now has a life of its own—it isn't a cheap knock-off. And, for you Anglophiles out there, I want to remind you that Ricky Gervais (co-creator of the show, with Stephen Merchant, for any confused Americans not familiar with the name) has done some writing for the American *Office*, and is routinely credited as a producer. So pooey on your elitist cynicism! If Ricky Gervais approves of the show, so can you! This book is dedicated to doing philosophy on *both* sides of the Atlantic, in Slough and in Scranton.

And besides, we love both versions of the show enough to spend a good deal of time investigating them carefully and critically. The same can't be said for every version of *The Office*. We make no mention (other than the one coming up) of the French knock-off (*Le Bureau*), the German knock-off (*Stromberg*), or the French-Canadian one (*La Job*). If you Brits think you're angry, you should see the rest of the world!

The Dundies: Some Awards for Making this Book Possible

Paper, I love thee. Without you, where would I be? From birth certificates to parking citations, you allow me to organize my life. Without you, I would have no grocery list, no "to-do" list—probably no lists of any kind. For this, you deserve the most prestigious of the Dundies: the Michael Scott Award. You make things *happen*. Admittedly, they're not always the greatest things—I could do without death certificates and notices of eviction—and they're never entirely rational, but you do get things going . . .

Scrantonicity kept me pumped while working on this book. Kevin's drumming and vocals are superb, and the cover songs the band does are incredibly well executed. If ever I'm in the Scranton area, in need of some live music, you can bet I'll be hiring Scrantonicity. And you should too! (Call 555–Rock, or just look up Kevin in the local phone book.) For the groove and the inspiration, you guys get the Old Rocker Award. Thanks for keeping The Police alive.

I'd also like to thank everyone who wrote for this book. You guys have produced wonderful work here, and have really managed to do the show—and philosophy—justice. Working with you guys (or all but two of you, anyway!) was a real joy. For the two of you who gave me headaches, I've reported you to corporate, and you'll be written up for your behavior. Unfortunately, this means absolutely nothing, as there isn't really a corporate, and if there were, they sure as hell wouldn't give me any power. So, really, never mind that last bit. We'll give you guys the Philosophy Award (I'm going to stop giving out awards and just start saying thanks, I think. Clearly, my creative energies have been exhausted. And I don't want to face the wrath of an angry Michael Scott . . .)

I'd like to thank my colleagues at Hartwick for talking to me about the show, and encouraging me to pursue the project in its early stages. I'd also like to thank Bill Irwin, the series editor, and Jeff Dean, of Blackwell, for their help and support in executing the project. It's been great working with you guys. I hope you're taking my recent proposal to branch out into the paper business seriously.

Lots of folks read parts of the book, providing comments, corrections, and criticism. Even more have talked with me about the ideas in these pages. Thanks to those students of mine who read chapters of the book—and there were *lots* of them. In particular, I'd like to thank Nick Forst and Meg Lonergan. Meg, who acted as my Faculty Research Assistant and deserves special thanks, is perhaps the most dedicated fan of the show in the world. She read the entire manuscript more than once, hunting down errors of all kinds, double-checking quotations and references, and being an all around delight to work with. Way to go, Sparky.

As a family guy who spends a good deal of time in the office, I also want to thank my wife, Dorothy Wisnewski, for her continued support. You're the best thing since paper. Thank you for everything you do for me. I also want to thank Audrey Wisnewski, simply because I can. She is wonderfully capable of keeping my spirits where they should be.

Hartwick College provided me with funds to support my work on this book. I'd like to thank the institution for its generous support. I am grateful for this, and for the opportunity to work in such a nice environment. There are others I could thank, but I'll leave it at this.

The real measure of appreciation, after all, is the Christmas bonus.

MEMO 1

PAPER THIN MORALITY

1

Screws and Nails: Paper Tigers and Moral Monsters in *The Office*

J. Jeremy Wisnewski

We're Screwed

The problem with doing what's right is simple: there are too many ways to screw it up, and usually only one way to nail it. From the moment I get up in the morning, I'm ready for something to go wrong—and I don't have to wait long for it to happen.

The odds are just against us. Given all the things that might happen in a day (and there's a *lot* that happens every day), the likelihood that those things will not involve somebody screwing up in some way are just abysmally small. Even given the number of things that *I* do in a day—the number of possibilities I have to choose from—the chance that I'll pick the thing that isn't messed up is pretty much negligible. So, I'm screwed—but so are you—and for some reason, knowing that makes me feel better. I see vindication for my view everywhere—especially in *The Office*. No matter how much people try to get things right, no matter what their intentions are, things are always screwed up; no one seems to nail decency.

We fail to be decent for different reasons. Philosophers generally consider three categories of moral failure: evil (wanting to do wrong), weakness of will (not being able to stop yourself from doing wrong), and ignorance (not knowing that what you're doing is wrong). Knowing *the ways* we mess up, philosophers often contend, might help us limit our propensity to screw things up so completely.

But there's an important category of moral failure missing from this list—one that *The Office* helps us see clearly. This is the category of *moral blindness*. Even when we *want* to do what's right, and know what rules we should follow, and have the strength of will to follow these rules, we still botch things up in tremendous ways. My solitary piece of evidence for this category of moral failure is found in one place: the manager's office at Dunder-Mifflin, and his name is Michael Scott.

Getting to Know Yourself: Some Species of Moral Failure

The rather despairing view of our daily lives that I've been painting (we'll call it the "we're screwed view") has prompted some great work in moral philosophy—the branch of philosophy that is fundamentally concerned with the nature of right and wrong, good and evil, and with our capacity to engage in one sort of action rather than another. Indeed, our most famous moral theories are dedicated to telling us what we can do to *guarantee* that we won't screw things up.[1] Plato (c. 427–347 BCE), for example, thought that all moral failure was the result of ignorance. The reason people fail to do what's right is just that they do not *know* what's right. Once you know what the right thing to do is, you can't help but do it.

Other philosophers have taken darker views of human motivation, recognizing that some people are just downright *malicious*. No amount of moral education will ever enable such people to do the right thing. There are a couple prime candidates for this kind of moral failure in *The Office*: Creed and Andy. Creed is routinely weird, but he's also often surprisingly creepy, and sometimes in a downright malicious way. When Pam begins to dress less conservatively in the office, for instance, Creed loiters at her desk, staring at her chest for several moments. Pam is obviously distressed by Creed's lustful looks, and she asks him to go back to his desk. He ignores her request, continues to ogle her breasts, and says "in a minute . . ." ("The Coup").

In certain respects, Stamford's Andy is even worse. It's Andy, after all, who essentially engineers Dwight's short-lived departure from the office. After botching up a sales call, Andy continues an attempt to convince Michael that Dwight is utterly worthless:

Andy: So sorry man. I really screwed that up.
Michael: Oh, don't worry about it.
Andy: I really Schruted it.
Michael: What?
Andy: I Schruted it. It's just this thing people say around your office all the time, like when you really screw things up in a really irreversible way: you Schruted it. I don't know where it comes from though. Think it comes from Dwight Schrute?
Michael: I dunno. Who knows how words are formed . . .
("Traveling Salesmen")

Earlier in the same episode, Andy had compared the staff to the "Superfriends," insisting that in this regard Dwight was the odd man out: "It's like everyone has their own special skill, you know, just like the superfriends . . . except for Dwight, who's more of a super dud. I mean, he'd be a superfriend if there was a superfriend whose superpower was always being late."

When these first efforts at bad-mouthing Dwight fail to get Michael's attention, Andy ups the ante: he breaks into Dwight's car, looking for something he can use against Dwight. He finds a receipt from a New York City toll booth, and uses this to convince Michael that Dwight is attempting another coup. This is obvious malicious self-service: Andy wants Michael's affection to further his own career, and wants to ruin Dwight because Dwight stands in his way (and, well, because he's *Dwight*).

Fortunately for us, malice is not the most common cause of inappropriate action. Much more common is our inability to refrain from acting on our desires. The term philosophers often use for such weakness of will is *akrasia*: when one's desires overpower one's rational decision-making. *The Office* is bubbling with *akrasia*—it occurs here and there in most of the characters on the show. Some of the more striking examples of this are Jan's consistent giving in to her desires for Michael. She admits that he's bad for her, that there's something idiotic about him—but she nevertheless goes home with him time and again, reason be damned. (Eventually, of course, Jan decides to simply stop fighting her irrational and self-destructive desires for Michael, on the advice of her therapist.)

Meredith is an even more striking example of akratic action. Despite a decision to be done with alcohol, she repeatedly comes back to it. As the office is spring cleaning, for instance, we see her throwing out an empty bottle of vodka that she had been keeping in her desk ("The Secret"). Likewise, when alcohol is brought to an office party, she quickly gives in to her temptations, despite her decision to stay on the wagon.

The last of the common trio of moral failure is ignorance. Sometimes we fail morally because we just don't know what the right thing to do is, either because we don't have all the information, or because we don't know the relevant moral principles. We see this kind of moral failure in "Christmas Party," when Pam chooses to take a video iPod from Michael instead of Jim's heartfelt gift (a teapot full of personal affects, intended only for Pam). Pam isn't malicious. She has no desire to hurt Jim. Likewise, she's not just giving in to her desire for a video iPod, despite Jim's feelings. Rather, she doesn't *know* how much Jim has put into his gift for her, and so she initially opts not to take it. The key evidence that Pam's failure is ignorance, of course, is that she trades Dwight her iPod for the teapot as soon as she realizes what's going on. In any instance where new knowledge will change one's behavior substantially, it's likely that the cause of one's moral failure is ignorance.

But the really interesting examples of moral failure—from my philosophical vantage point, at any rate—are *not* when we are evil, or when we give in to our desires, or even when we are ignorant of all the facts, or of the relevant moral rules. The really fascinating moral failures are failures to *see* that there is even a moral issue at stake.[2] It is this kind of failure, I contend, that we see in Michael Scott.

Knowing But Not Seeing

Does Michael understand what it means to be offensive? In one respect, the answer must be "no." Everyone who has even casually watched *The Office* will be quick to recognize that Michael is a master of the art of unintentional offense. But *why* is this so? Is it simply that no one has taught Michael what's offensive, or is it something deeper? I'll call this one like I see it: no number of rules will ever help Michael. The problem isn't failing to know the rules. The problem is a failure to see when the rules are relevant.[3]

Deciding what Michael's problem is turns out to be a thorny task. In many cases, he really seems just plain ignorant: he doesn't seem to

6

know what's going on, or what he's saying, or how it relates to other things in the world. When Michael decides to run his own diversity day, for example, he immediately kicks Toby out of the meeting for making a joke. "This is an environment of welcoming, so you should just get the hell out of here!" ("Diversity Day"). It's as though there is a short-circuit between the words Michael utters and his ability to comprehend those words—after all, one doesn't need a PhD in philosophy to recognize that kicking someone out of a welcoming environment is contradictory! A welcoming environment is one where you welcome people!

In other contexts, Michael attempts to justify his actions by analogy —by relating what a decent person would do in other contexts. Once again, he seems oblivious to what a decent person *would* do. In these situations, it looks like Michael is ignorant of the rules of the moral life. In trying to justify his email forwards to his employees, Michael claims that he doesn't come up with these jokes. He just delivers them, and "you wouldn't arrest a guy who was just delivering drugs from one guy to another" ("Sexual Harassment"). When Toby tells him he shouldn't send out inappropriate jokes, regardless of their source, Michael replies that "there's no such thing as an appropriate joke. That's why it's a joke." When Jan tells Michael that there will be downsizing, Michael doesn't see the point of letting the gang know about the possibility of losing their jobs. "As a doctor, you would not tell a patient if they had cancer" ("Pilot"). Things only get worse when Michael has people wear tags with particular races on them to encourage awareness of diversity ("Diversity Day"). Michael wears a tag that says "Martin Luther King, Jr.," apparently not recognizing the difference between a *person* and a race. Michael explains why he has not included some groups among those named: it would be "explosive" to include Arabs in a diversity exercise, "no pun intended . . . [pauses] . . . Maybe next year. The ball's in their court." In attempting to encourage awareness of diversity, Michael brazenly invokes the very stereotypes he supposedly wants to overcome.

Episodes like this make Michael seem downright idiotic. He just doesn't seem to *know* what doctors should do, or what the law says, or what races are, or even that jokes can be offensive. But, I'll confess, I don't think simply listing some rules would help Michael navigate the murky waters of the moral life. Michael knows *plenty* of rules. His problem isn't that he can't recite what the moral rules are.

7

His problem is that he has no idea what they mean, or how they apply, or what the hell to do with them. As a way of dealing with diversity issues, for example, Michael's first idea is to talk about the diverse people you might want to screw!

> *Michael*: You know what? Here's what we're going to do. Why don't we go around and everybody . . . *everybody* . . . say a race that you are attracted to sexually. I will go last. Go!
> *Dwight*: I have two . . .
> *Michael*: Nice.
> *Dwight*: . . . white and Indian.

Although Michael quickly realizes this isn't the best route to diversity training, his later ideas are nowhere near representative of the real issues in dealing with diversity in the workplace. Michael claims, for example, that he's "2/15ths Native American Indian." When Oscar says this fraction doesn't make sense, Michael claims that it's painful for him to talk about! He *recognizes* (on some level, anyway), that we should be sensitive concerning race—that we should not say things to make people of other races self-conscious, or that might lead them to suffer. This recognition of a general moral principle comes out clearly when Michael talks to Oscar about his status as a Mexican-American:

> *Michael*: Let me ask you . . . is there a term besides Mexican that you prefer? Something less offensive?
> *Oscar*: Mexican isn't offensive.
> *Michael*: Well, it has certain connotations . . .
> *Oscar*: Like what?
> *Michael*: Like . . . I don't . . . I don't know.
> *Oscar*: [getting irritated] What connotations, Michael? You meant something.
> *Michael*: Now remember . . . honesty . . .
> *Oscar*: I'm just curious.
> *Michael*: . . . empathy, respect . . .

Michael appeals to a general principle to avoid using offensive terms, but he's got no idea what counts as offensive. He then appeals to certain virtues (honesty, empathy, and respect) while at the same time violating these very values! He cites honesty at the very moment he refuses to be honest about the connotations he thinks the term *Mexican* has! Indeed, the very *cause* of diversity training (Michael doing an offensive impersonation of Chris Rock) is totally lost on Michael. While he recognizes, in some abstract way, that diversity and tolerance are important—even essential—to the moral life, he simply does not see that his own actions might violate the respect he owes to his fellow human beings. He's unable to take diversity training seriously, but yet he knows that diversity is important (in some sense of the term "know"). His problem results from an inability to *see* the morally salient features of a situation.

Thus, even though his employees were offended enough to call corporate to complain about Michael's antics, Michael fails to recognize that he ought to be more sensitive. Instead, he mocks the very idea that he doesn't know the importance of diversity. Reading the contract corporate forces him to sign, Michael is obviously oblivious to the issues that underlie his employees' complaints:

> I regret my actions. I regret offending my co-workers. I promise to bring my best spirit of honesty, empathy, respect and openmindedness . . . Openmindedness? Is that even a word? . . . into the workplace. In this way, I can truly be a hero. Signed . . . [Michael holds up the contract] "Daffy Duck" [cackles].

This is not simply a failure to know the rules. If we were to give Michael a multiple choice test on issues of diversity, he would be able to identify some core things to avoid (provided we worded the test the right way!). He would know, for example, that we should promote tolerance, that we should avoid racism, and that sexual harassment was utterly unacceptable in the office. Yet his actions show that regardless of the knowledge he has—regardless of the sentences he would affirm on our imagined multiple choice test—he suffers from a kind of moral blindness. He doesn't see that some actions conflict with the very things that he says he values. When Michael intervenes to defend Phyllis during one of Todd Packer's sexually explicit stories, he displays his moral blindness in classic *Office* style:

> *Michael*: You know what? I love Phyllis. And you know what else? I think she is gorgeous. [kneels down beside Phyllis, wrapping his arms around her] I think she is an incredibly, incredibly attractive person. [To Phyllis] Come here. Give me a kiss. C'mon [kisses Phyllis on the cheek].

9

Phyllis: [smiling and laughing] Michael, come on. You don't have to worry. I'm not . . . I'm not gonna report you to HR.
Michael: I'm not worried! You know what? The only thing I am worried about . . . is getting a boner [Phyllis looks distraught].

Michael's heart is probably in the right place—but, as usual, his mouth is not. In trying to defuse a pending sexual harassment issue, Michael actually engages in sexual harassment. He is utterly blind to the offense (and disgust) his action causes Phyllis, while also being fully aware of the rule that sexual harassment is morally reprehensible.

In another case, Michael is explaining to Ryan (who's having his first day at Dunder-Mifflin) that he is a friend first, a boss second, and an entertainer third. He then calls Pam in, presumably to reveal what a fun-loving guy he is. The conversation is unforgettable:

Michael [to Pam]:   As you know, there's going to be downsizing, and you have made my life so much easier in that I am going to have to let you go first.
Pam [shocked]:   What? Why?
Michael: Why? Well, theft. And stealing.
Pam: What am I supposed to have stolen?
Michael: Post-It Notes.
Pam: Post-It Notes? What are those worth, like 50 cents?
Michael: Yeah. If you stole 1000 Post-It Notes at 50 cents then you've made a profit . . . margin. You're going to run us out of business Pam.
Pam: Are you serious?
Michael: Yeah. I am.
Pam: Oh, wow . . . I can't believe this. I mean, I've never even stolen so much as a paper clip and now you're firing me.
Michael: But the best thing is . . . uh . . . we're not going to have to give you any severance pay because [puts hand over mouth to cover any smile] that's gross misconduct and, uh . . . just clean out your desk. I'm sorry.
[Pam covers her eyes and begins to cry]
Michael [now smiling]:   You've been x'd punk! Surprise! It's a joke. We were joking around. Ok. He was in on it. He was my accomplice [pointing to Ryan, who shakes his head no]. It's kind of a morale-boosting thing . . . and we were showing the new guy around . . . kinda, kinda giving him a feel of the place. Wow! We totally got you!
Pam [in tears]:   You're a jerk!

Michael: Uh . . . I don't know about that.
[Pam leaves. Michael looks awkwardly at a fax Pam brought in, then
     tries to get Ryan to look at it. Ryan refuses.]

A friend first indeed! It is his blindness to what matters morally in
concrete situations that leads him to fail (morally speaking) again
and again. When he orders lunch at Hooters, for example, he says "I
will have the chicken breast, hold the chicken" ("The Secret"). He is
utterly incapable of keeping Jim's secret, blurting out Jim's affection
for Pam. When he wants to engage in conflict resolution in the office,
he tells Toby (probably the nicest guy in the office) that he's in no
position to resolve conflicts: "What do you know about conflict
resolution? Your answer to everything is 'get divorced'" ("Conflict
Resolution"). And the list goes on.[4]

A Few Cases of Getting Things Right:
Getting Unscrewed

But Michael has his good moments too. He's no moral monster. In
fact, he's more like a paper tiger: he looks ferocious far away, but
up-close he's fragile—and laughable in his attempts to be more than
he is. After a dispute with Dwight (involving a trip to the dojo, no
less!), Michael tries to make up with Dwight by promoting him from
Assistant to the Regional Manager to Assistant Regional Manager
(though he insists that the promotion be kept secret). He then
confides to the cameraman his motivations: "I told Dwight that
there is honor in losing—which is completely ridiculous. But there is
however honor in making a loser feel better, which is what I just did
for Dwight" ("The Fight").

   Michael has no idea what he's talking about. He's trying to make
himself look good by talking abstractly of virtues like honor. What's
interesting here, though, is that Michael *did* do the right thing. He
has upset Dwight, and he steps in to rectify the situation. The same
thing happens in "Drug Testing," when Michael asks Dwight for his
urine ("I want him to have all the urine he needs," Dwight admits).
After Dwight resigns as a volunteer deputy sheriff, Michael recognizes that Dwight has been hurt by the entire affair. As a way of

making it up to him, Michael decides to make him "the official supervisor of security" (learning that he cannot have a gun, Dwight replies: "Ok. I'll have to bring my bo staff."). Finally, Michael shows a truly humane side when he goes to Staples to ask Dwight to come back to Dunder-Mifflin. Again, though, he seems to misconstrue what he is doing. ("It takes a big man to admit when he makes a mistake," Michael says, "and I'm that big man.")

What these examples show, I think, is that knowledge isn't all that important for the moral life. When Michael has knowledge, it doesn't help him do the right thing (he knows that sexual harassment is wrong, but he tells Phyllis she'll give him a boner). When he lacks knowledge, it doesn't hurt him that much (he thinks he's done something special whenever he tries to right the wrongs he's committed, when really he's just done what any decent person would). What's important is responding to others in the right ways—seeing what's required when it's required—and no knowledge of rules will ever enable us to acquire this kind of sight. Much like studying theories of art won't teach you to paint beautifully, so too studying ethical theory (or ethical rules) won't help you to act morally. What is required is much more basic: it is *seeing* what a situation requires.

Despite my claim that Michael is a prime example of moral blindness, I do admit that he has his moments (Michael's support of Pam's art in "Business School" is unforgettable)—and the other folks in the office have their moments too. Pam, for instance, is particularly sensitive to the emerging (and continuing) relationship between Dwight and Angela—so much so that she goes out of her way to protect their secret. When Dwight gets a concussion and has to go to the emergency room, Pam makes a point to tell *Oscar* that Dwight will be ok, making sure that Angela hears what she's saying.[5] Pam knows that Angela is worried about Dwight, but she also knows that Angela is trying to keep her relationship with Dwight quiet. Pam is sensitive to *both* Angela's concern for Dwight *and* her desire to keep that concern a secret ("The Injury"). And Pam doesn't screw things up. She finds a way to respect Angela's concern, as well as her desire to keep this concern a private matter.

In this same episode, Jim shows some real decency as well. When Dwight collapses on his desk, Jim jumps to the rescue. He insists that Dwight needs medical attention, ignoring Michael's ridiculous crying about his foot:

Jim [sees Dwight collapse, walks over to him]:   Ok, I think we need to take him to the hospital. I'm pretty sure he has a concussion.
Dwight [barely coherent]:   No, no, no, no.
Michael [on crutches, foot wrapped in bubble-wrap]:   Oh, now you feel some compassion *for him*.
Angela: He needs to go right now, and you're his emergency contact. I think you should go with him.
Michael: Why don't you go with him?
Angela: I barely know him.
Dwight [moaning]:   I want Michael to take me.
Michael: I can't take you. I don't have my car and yours is all vomity.
Meredith: You can take my van!
Michael [irritated]:   Oh, ok. That's great. No. I can't drive. Jim, why don't you drive?
Jim: Fine.
Michael: We'll go. I'm still recovering so let's just . . . Ryan, will you get my coat please?
Jim [holding Dwight up]:   Slowly, slowly . . . let's just get to the elevator
[Dwight begins to make helicopter sounds.]
Jim: What are you doing?
Dwight: Vietnam sounds.

Jim steps up to the plate, while Michael doesn't even know what game is being played! On the way to the car, Michael calls shotgun. When Jim replies that Michael should sit in the back with Dwight (to make sure he's ok), Michael responds with indignation. Later, talking to the cameraman, Michael explains his indignation *by citing the rules of shotgun!* "The rules of shotgun are very simple and very clear. The first person to shout 'shotgun' when you're within sight of the car gets the front seat. That's how the game is played. There are no exceptions for someone with a concussion" ("The Injury"). On the way to the hospital, Jim keeps Dwight's best interests in mind (while Michael just sits shotgun, ignoring the severity of Dwight's injury), eventually getting him to the hospital for treatment, and making sure to keep Michael in check on the way (by squirting him in the face with a water gun).[6]

Jim also rescues Michael on occasion: he steps up to the karaoke mic when Michael is stuck singing alone, even though Michael has shown up to a party uninvited. Rather than letting Michael make a fool of himself, or sink to new lows of self-esteem, Jim croons along to "Islands in the Stream" ("Email Surveillance"). In another case,

Jim recognizes how painful the annual Dundie jokes about Pam's long engagement are. Rather than confront Michael about hurting Pam's feelings (which Michael likely wouldn't understand), Jim gets Michael to tell another joke by pandering to his comedic sensibilities. "Using the same joke every year," Jim says, "just looks lazy." Jim sees what a situation requires, and effectively orchestrates a *different* Dundie award for Pam: she wins "the Whitest Sneakers Award" rather than "the Longest Engagement Award"[7] ("The Dundies"). I'm certain that her joy in getting the award was helped by her alcohol consumption (she drank so much, you'll recall, that the manager banned her from the chain!)—but it certainly wasn't *just* that. Once again, Jim made someone's life a little less messed up.

Having the Patience of Toby: A Lesson About a Vagina

Is there a moral hero in the office? Well, there are certainly no moral saints. No one nails decency with every action on every day. Nevertheless, there are some downright decent moments in *The Office*—moments when folks aren't utterly self-absorbed, and see the needs of those around them. Consider what happens when Toby announces that he will answer any questions that the office staff might have. Dwight comes to him, very seriously, with a problem (presumably misunderstanding that Toby was volunteering to answer questions about Dunder-Mifflin's sexual harassment policy):

> *Dwight* [entering Toby's office]:   Hey Toby.
> *Toby*:   Hey Dwight.
> *Dwight*:   You said we could come to you if we had any questions.
> *Toby*:   Sure.
> *Dwight* [long pause]:   Where is the clitoris? [pauses again] On a website it said, "At the crest of the labia." What does that *mean*?
> [Toby looks at Dwight. Dwight looks back.]
> *Dwight*:   What does the female vagina look like?
> [Scene cuts to Toby, talking to cameraman]:   Technically, I am in human resources, and Dwight was asking about human anatomy. Umm . . . I'm just sad that the public school system failed him so badly.
> [Scene cuts back to Toby, talking to Dwight in his office, clearly in the middle of whatever conversation ensued following Dwight's

initial questions]: You know, maybe when you get really comfort-
able with each other, you can ask for that.
Dwight: Good. And . . .
Toby [slowly and nicely]:   I . . . should get back to work.
Dwight: Ok.
("Sexual Harassment")

This respect and patience is the most we can ask from anyone.
Despite not being friends with Dwight, not having sex ed as part of
his job description, and having plenty of other things to do, Toby
responds to Dwight's needs—even though Dwight has not been
particularly nice to him. If we could all be more like Toby, I think,
we'd be nowhere near so screwed.

NOTES

1   Immanuel Kant (1724–1804) and John Stuart Mill (1806–1873) both
thought they could identify moral actions by applying their respective
theories to particular cases. Kant claimed that a moral action was one
done from duty, and that we could check our intentions to determine
whether our actions were so motivated by using his "categorical imperative." Mill claimed that we could determine what course of action was
appropriate by asking what actions would increase the total amount of
pleasure over pain for all affected by a given action. For Aristotle, who
bears some resemblance to the view defended here, see chapter 5 of this
volume.

2   The notion of moral perception is discussed in a wide variety of places.
See, for example, Iris Murdoch, *The Sovereignty of the Good* (New York:
Routledge, 1970); Lawrence A. Blum, *Moral Perception and Particularity*
(Cambridge: Cambridge University Press, 1994); John McDowell, *Mind,
Value, and Reality* (Cambridge, MA: Harvard University Press, 1998);
and Maurice Mandelbaum, *The Phenomenology of Moral Experience*
(Glencoe, IL: Free Press, 1955). For an argument for the importance of
this notion, see J. Jeremy Wisnewski and Henry Jacoby, "Failures of
Sight: An Argument for Moral Perception," *American Philosophical
Quarterly*, 44:3.

3   Dwight has a similar problem. He routinely cites laws and rules as a way
of saying what *ought* to happen—but his slavish adherence to the letter
of the law often leads him to miss its spirit entirely.

4   A failure to see is, of course, a failure to know *in some sense*. This might
lead folks to suspect that moral blindness is just a species of ignorance.

I have no real problem with this, provided we know what we're saying! The kind of ignorance involved in moral blindness is not the kind of ignorance that can be cured by the simple assertion of sentences. The kind of ignorance we've been talking about, however, can. If I don't know the meaning of a word, or the square root of −2, or the time of my next class, a simple sentence that conveys this information would cure me of my ignorance. Moral blindness is importantly different. Simply telling the morally blind person that they should be sensitive to racial differences won't do any good. Something else is needed to cure this kind of blindness (art, literature, and even pop culture can often get people to see things much more clearly than argument). So, we can call moral blindness ignorance, if we like, but we should know exactly what we mean by this. It isn't the same kind of ignorance as the kind we cure by, say, reading biology textbooks.

5 Recall that Dwight gets a concussion when he crashes his car. The car crash is the result of trying to quickly speed off to pick up Michael, who has burnt his foot by stepping on a George Foreman grill. (He really likes to wake up to the smell of bacon!)

6 Compare this to Michael's antics in the same episode: he tries to convince the doctor that his foot injury is more serious than Dwight's head injury!

7 Both Pam and Jim have their weak points too, though. There are occasions when they're just downright mean. Think, for example, of all of the pranks Jim plays on Dwight. He even tries to get Dwight to quit at one point! ("The Fire").

2

Flirting in *The Office*: What Can Jim and Pam's Romantic Antics Teach Us About Moral Philosophy?

Mark D. White

Ah, Jim and Pam, Pam and Jim, sigh . . . Sitcom audiences just love romance, and the more tortured the relationships, the better. We had Sam and Diane, David and Maddie, Frank and Hot-Lips, Michael and KITT . . . the list goes on and on. But there weren't just sparks (or spark plugs) in these hot couples. They also had something else in common—they worked together. (That's why I didn't mention Ross and Rachel—*Friends* is finished, people, get over it!)

Of course, Jim and Pam haven't actually dated—at least not when I wrote this chapter. (And I haven't watched since then—don't tell me what happens!) They certainly each know how the other feels, and they've even kissed, but mostly they flirt, flirt, and then flirt some more. (And then date other people.) But again, it's not just flirting, but flirting in the office—*The Office*, to be precise.

Is this a problem? In the real world, workplace romances are a sticky issue, and for many reasons. Obviously, there's the issue of other relationships—for instance, Pam flirting with Jim while engaged to Roy can be considered infidelity to some degree, though people will disagree about how serious it is. (And we know how Roy feels about that, don't we?) But that issue isn't specific to workplace flirting and dating, so we won't worry about it here. (Roy, however, will—you can count on that.)

When considering workplace dating in particular, the most serious problem is sexual harassment, especially when a superior is involved (or wants to be involved) with someone he or she supervises. (Think of Jan and Michael—or Michael and Ryan!) Considering everybody's favorite Dunder-Mifflin couple—no, not Angela and Dwight—we have to remember after all that Jim is Assistant Regional Manager. Another issue is the effect of such romantic canoodling on the company itself. We know that other Dunder-Mifflin employees have noticed Jim and Pam's flirting, which can affect morale, especially if they see Pam favored by Jim in assigning work. And that points to a more basic issue—what if Jim favors Pam, or evaluates her less harshly than he otherwise would? Dunder-Mifflin's profitability could be affected if Pam were a horrible receptionist but were allowed to stay because of Jim's feelings for her.

In this chapter, we'll examine these issues in light of several prominent theories of ethics: act utilitarianism, rule utilitarianism, and deontology. What relevance does each of these concepts have to the issue of office flirting and dating? We'll hear from most of the Dunder-Mifflin Scranton crew along the way—a little *too* much from Kelly, but you know Kelly! Now into the conference room, everybody, because it's time to start, and don't worry—Michael did not prepare a movie or a rap video.

Someone Get The Lights (Oh No . . .)

One group of ethical theories would say that office flirting or dating is bad if it lowers total happiness or "utility." These theories are known generally as *utilitarianism*, but utilitarianism comes in many different varieties—just like paper products.[1] (True fans know that *The Office* is not about the people who work there—it's about the paper. Paper rules.) Versions of utilitarianism that focus on individual actions and their effect on utility are called *act utilitarianism*. Other versions that focus on rules or guidelines for action, and their general effects on utility, are known as *rule utilitarianism*. There are pros and cons to each, as we will see when we apply each to the most pressing ethical issue of our time: workplace nookie.

If Jim and Pam were to reflect on the morality of their flirtation, they might ask themselves—after asking if there's any way to use philosophy to torture Dwight[2]—how their flirting affects the well-being or utility of those affected by it. Presumably, they themselves enjoy it, so that's a plus. (Viewers obviously enjoy it too, but let's not break the fourth wall here!) But, as we mentioned before, it may affect their co-workers, or even Dunder-Mifflin itself, negatively—that's a minus. In act utilitarianism, the balance of the good and bad determines the overall effect of Jim and Pam's carrying on.

So what Jim and Pam will have to do is go around the office and ask each and every one of their co-workers—even Dwight—how their, uh, special friendship affects him or her. (For instance, Kelly would squeal with glee, Creed would ask for pictures, and Toby would just cry.) And then they have to examine all the ways their flirtation may affect the Dunder-Mifflin bottom line—go to corporate, meet with Jan, bring in a few consultants . . .

Ugh—this is really hard.[3] Doesn't seem to have much to do with right and wrong, does it? And isn't that what ethics is supposed to be about? "This seems more like, uh, math!" Yes, Kelly, it does—the effects of an action on utility can be a matter of intense computation if they are wide-ranging and uncertain. There are also issues of quantifying the utility changes—how do we compare the tender feelings of Jim and Pam to the adverse effects on Dunder-Mifflin's stock price? Given that there is no easy way to do this, Jim and Pam could always claim they are *so* happy with their odd, Zen-like state of togetherness-without-being-together that it exceeds all negative impact of it on anyone else. And how can we prove that it doesn't?

Who Likes Rules? (Put Your Hand Down, Dwight!)

For these reasons, and many more, most philosophers shy away from act utilitarianism like Pam avoids thongs, and adopt some version of rule utilitarianism, which side steps the problem of assessing each individual action and instead judges a general practice or institution. For instance, act utilitarianism is often criticized for condoning punishment of the innocent, such as framing an innocent man for an unsolved murder if it would help deter future murders. Common sense would say that couldn't possibly be right, but artful manipulation of the costs and benefits would easily justify such an act by demonstrating an increase in utility. (A more realistic example may be torturing a terror suspect in hopes of extracting information that could save thousands of innocent lives.)

But surely a government that practiced such actions would be reviled, and would likely result in widespread disenchantment, civil unrest, and perhaps revolution? While one instance of punishing the innocent may increase utility, adopting the practice of doing so would not. Rule utilitarians prefer this sort of reasoning, because it avoids the case-by-case, detailed examination of costs and benefits, and instead evaluates the general practice of the action in question.

This is the approach that most businesses take to problems such as office dating. They realize that not every instance of office dating will be harmful, but in general they feel that it lowers morale, weakens the chain of command, and may even lower profits. Jim and Pam could appeal to the human resources department (skipping Toby, for obvious reasons), arguing that none of these negative effects would occur in *their* relationship. But HR would likely reply, "that's the policy—sometimes we block harmless relationships, but if the policy results in more harm than good, then the policy works." In other words, the rule maximizes utility across all the instances of workplace dating, even though some great relationships are wrecked along the way.

The fact that rule utilitarianism comments on practices in general and not particular acts lends it the flavor of distinguishing between right and wrong that we "want" from our ethical systems. Or does it? Well, rule utilitarianism doesn't actually say that, for instance, office dating is always bad, just that it tends to be bad more often than not, and for that reason the company forbids it. So if we're looking for definitive statements on right and wrong with all the authority of Michael—or even more—rule utilitarianism may not give it to us.

Another problem with rule utilitarianism is that despite all its good intentions, act utilitarianism tends to rear its ugly head. Let's suppose that Dunder-Mifflin forbids office dating, and corporate explains the rationale so that everyone seems fine with it. But then Jim and Pam make a case that while they agree that office dating in general is bad, their relationship is good—their co-workers don't mind, morale won't suffer, there are no sexual harassment issues, and since Jim doesn't evaluate Pam or assign her duties, there's no favoritism to threaten the bottom line. Their case to corporate would be: prohibiting office dating completely may increase utility over allowing it freely, but prohibiting it while making an exception for Jim and Pam would increase it even more.

I Think We've Got A Problem . . . Don't Tell Ryan!

The general problem for a policy justified by rule utilitarianism is this: How do you handle exceptions that would clearly increase utility? If the government followed a policy of not punishing innocent persons, but then came across an instance in which making an exception to that policy would definitely increase well-being, what then is the rationale for sticking to the policy? In that instance, adhering to the policy would lower utility. One of the benefits of rule utilitarianism is that it eliminates the need to make case-by-case evaluations of acts, but that doesn't mean we can't, or that it makes that evaluation irrelevant when the results are obviously positive. So it's not at all inconsistent for Jim and Pam to say, "we understand the policy against office dating, we agree with it in general, but we should not be subject to it because we know our relationship will increase utility."

Rule utilitarians can argue that exceptions destroy the value of a policy—in other words, a rule subject to exceptions isn't truly a rule. If Michael enforces a Hawaiian dress code at Dunder-Mifflin Scranton, but lets Pam out of it because she says she's allergic to macadamia nuts, and then lets Stanley out of it to show Michael's solidarity with African-Americans, and then Angela because she was offended when Michael said "we're all getting lei'd," and so on . . . Well, it's not much of a policy if Michael and Dwight end up the only ones following it. To some extent, the utilitarian value of a rule or policy depends on how strictly it's enforced, so even if there are exceptions which would increase utility by themselves, they would reduce the value of the rule by more, and therefore lower overall utility. But this still allows for cases when the exception is so beneficial, it would outweigh the harm done to the institution, and we're back at the beginning.[4]

We could also consider issues of authority—even if Jim and Pam are right, they do not have discretion to disobey a policy from "above." Even if their relationship were harmless, and it would not endanger the anti-dating policy itself, they would be flouting the authority of the company leaders to set policies regarding allowable interactions among employees. This would be another sort of disutility that would speak against even the best relationships—but still, if the relationship would provide enough benefit, well, anything is possible (or permissible).

21

When you get down to it, in the end—don't say it, Michael—any sort of utilitarianism is the process of adding up benefits and harms, pleasures and pains, and seeing whether the total is positive or negative. Some may feel that such a process—highly contingent on the particular characteristics of any one ethical decision—does not reflect the strength and universality of true morality. Such scholars favor a general type of ethics known as deontology—

"Deontology—oh, right, like Tom Cruise? I love him!"

No, Kelly, deontology is—

"Not as much as Ryan, of course, but I mean, like, if Tom Cruise asked me out, I'd be like, totally, what about Katie? But then I really wouldn't care—I mean, it's Tom Cruise, and he's so gorgeous, and rich—HE'S SO RICH—we wouldn't have to go to Chili's all the time, and . . ."

(Poor Ryan. No wonder he usually made Toby look giddy in comparison.)

Anyway, a deontological approach judges an act by properties intrinsic to the act itself, rather than any consequences the act may have. For instance, because of the inherent dignity or rights of persons, punishing the innocent is simply wrong to a deontologist. A deontologist would hold that no considerations of utility would ever justify punishing an innocent person. Likewise, deontologists usually forbid telling lies or breaking promises, no matter how beneficial doing so in *this* case would be. This is not because such practices are generally harmful (though they may be), but because doing these things is wrong, a judgment based on the actions themselves—the consequences, good or bad, play no role in deontological statements of right or wrong.[5]

So if a deontologist decided that office dating was wrong, that's it, end of story—you just don't do it.[6] Jim and Pam can't appeal to the personal happiness their union would create, nor do they have to dispute the possible harm done to their co-workers or Dunder-Mifflin—none of this matters to a deontologist. But that still leaves the question—would a deontologist have a problem with office dating?

Well, it doesn't help that there are many understandings of the term "deontology." In an article exploring the topic, philosopher Jerry Gaus found *ten* different (and not entirely consistent) meanings of "deontology."[7] But most of them focus on some sense of obligation or duty that transcends any consideration of utility or well-being, such as a duty to tell the truth even when the truth may hurt somebody. (Examples: "Kevin, your band Scrantonicity probably won't be offered the opening slot on The Police reunion tour," or "Dwight, you're assistant *to* the regional manager," or telling Karen *anything* about Jim and Pam's past.) Since they can't be based on consequences, these duties or obligations are often based on rights, which are themselves grounded in various ways, such as human dignity, equal treatment or respect, or legal/political convention.[8]

So can we find any duties that would be threatened by office romance? Well, the easiest would be the duty of an employee to obey company policy, based on the agreement he or she made when the job was taken, but that doesn't provide a rationale for the policy itself. And I'm going to assume that sexual harassment violates deontological ethics, based on its violation of personal dignity and equality. What we need is a justification for denying one employee the right to hang out at another employee's reception desk for half the day, planning oh-so-cute practical jokes on other employees (usually with names that rhyme with "night").

This is more difficult than it may seem. (Thanks to Michael, I can no longer use the word h-a-r-d-e-r. Sadly, spelling the word seems to get around this problem.) Based on ideals of equal treatment, an employee such as Jim has a duty not to show undue preference toward some employees with regard to evaluation or work assignments based on personal feelings. But if Jim is careful not to do this, or removes himself from situations where this may be a problem, then that duty would not be endangered by his relationship with Pam. Along similar lines, Jim has a duty to perform his own job responsibilities without undue distraction (for instance, if Pam ever wears the clothes she bought online while he was in Stamford). But again, if he is careful, this won't be a problem.

Let's approach this from the other direction—might there be deontological arguments *supporting* employees' right to make goo-goo eyes at each other? Do Jim and Pam have a valid moral right to their flirtation? In one view, it really comes down to a right to privacy, which most philosophers believe is not absolute. Privacy rights grant people the right to do anything not forbidden by duties to the contrary, or that interfere with other people's rights (which in turn generates a duty not to do such a thing). In that view, since we were unable to support any firm duties against office dating, we would conclude that employees do have such a right. But that seems like shaky ground to support a right, since it is only valid as long as no one provides a duty to contradict it.

So Who Wins? Somebody's Gotta Win, Right?

In the end,[9] it would seem that in the absence of sexual harassment issues—the reason behind many corporate office dating policies—there is little deontological rationale for forbidding flirting or dating between co-workers, or for giving employees the right to date co-workers. We may have to dip back into the utilitarian punch bowl to settle the question of the pros and cons of office dating, and that opens the door to all of the objections covered earlier.

Does this speak against deontology as a general approach to addressing ethical issues? Not at all—remember, there are many varieties of deontology, and many concepts other than rights to support them (as well as many concepts of rights themselves), so one or more of them may fit this issue. Plus, even if deontology doesn't help with office dating, there are—seriously—other, possibly more pressing moral issues in the world, such as bringing strippers to the office for bachelor and bachelorette parties, or distributing vacation photos of your semi-nude boss over the company email system. (Not to mention terrorism, world hunger, and the continuing popularity of *American Idol.*)

So Jim and Pam, you two crazy kids go ahead and flirt until 5 p.m. every day like you always do. The deontologists cannot stop you. Just be on the look-out for nasty, vengeful utilitarians—or Roy. Or Angela. Or Toby. (Mark my words, someday that guy's gonna snap, and it will be just like Milton at the end of *Office Space*–oops, wrong "office.") Mind you, we didn't touch other areas of ethics, like virtue ethics, but we'll leave that for *"Jim Loves Pam" and Philosophy*, the follow-up book covering the best spin-off ever! (And no, I didn't forget *Joey*—though I wish I could.)

NOTES

1   The "classic" utilitarians include Jeremy Bentham, John Stuart Mill, and Henry Sidgwick. For modern debates over utilitarianism (or the more general theory of consequentialism), see J. J. C. Smart and Bernard Williams, *Utilitarianism: For and Against* (Cambridge: Cambridge University Press, 1973) and Samuel Scheffler (ed.), *Consequentialism and Its Critics* (Oxford: Oxford University Press, 1988).

2   Then they'd giggle, Jim would give one of his innocent "who me?" looks to the camera, and they'd part, only to succumb to their irresistible mutual attraction after the next commercial break. But you know that, or you wouldn't be reading this book.

3   "That's what she said" (Michael Scott, 2007).

4   For a comprehensive summary of arguments for and against rule utilitarianism (or, more generally, rule consequentialism), see Brad Hooker's entry on "Rule Consequentialism" at the Stanford Encyclopedia of Philosophy (www.plato.stanford.edu/entries/consequentialism-rule/).

5   Major deontological thinkers include Immanuel Kant and W. D. Ross; see note 7 for a recent paper surveying the subject.

6   Just between you and me, there are always exceptions. Kant made room for apparently conflicting duties (I say "apparently" because duties can never truly conflict in Kantian ethics, but obligations can), and Ross wrote only of *prima facie* duties, which can conflict with others. Both of these ideas open the door for exceptions, but not nearly as easily as utilitarianism does.

7   Gerald F. Gaus, "What Is Deontology? Part One: Orthodox Views," *Journal of Value Inquiry* 35(2001), 27–42.

8   For an excellent introduction to rights, see William Edmundson's cleverly titled *An Introduction to Rights* (Cambridge: Cambridge University Press, 2004).

9   Nothing? He must not have gotten this far . . .

3

Can Michael Ever Learn?
Empathy and the
Self-Other Gap

Andrew Terjesen

Michael Scott may just be the most clueless person on the planet. You would think he would realize that having an online dating alias of "littlekidlover" is not the best way to let potential dates know (in his words) "where my priorities are at" ("Take Your Daughter to Work Day"). And you would definitely expect a boss to have a better handle on his employees' feelings. He should at least recognize when his choices of motivational activities, like the Dundies or a Booze Cruise, are not actually motivating his employees—but are, in fact making them uncomfortable (as when handing out Dundies like the Spicy Curry Award to Kelly and Hottest in the Office Award to Ryan). One might wonder if Michael will ever learn to act more appropriately and with a greater regard for the feelings of others. (In a deleted scene from "The Dundies" episode, Toby even confronts Michael about how uncomfortable Ryan is with the award he received—but Michael dismisses Toby.)

To ask the question "*Will* Michael ever learn?" is to miss the point. After all, from a comedic point of view, Michael's cluelessness adds many opportunities for humor. It would be more productive from a philosophical point of view to ask the question, "*Can* Michael ever learn?" In philosophy, our aim is to understand the meanings of various concepts, not to predict the future of our favorite sit-com. With this in mind, let's examine the nature of Michael's lack of regard for the feelings of others and whether it is something that he has the potential to overcome (putting aside the question as to whether he will ever exercise that ability). Exploring this philosophical question will help us to clarify our understanding of the extent to which people in general can understand each other. Michael may be an extreme example of cluelessness, but we have all had our inconsiderate moments. If Michael has the potential to be more considerate, then so do we. And since we have the potential, we have a certain moral responsibility to exercise it whenever possible.

How Clueless is Michael? Ping, Yankee Swap, and the "Faces of Scranton"

Much of Michael's clueless behavior involves inappropriate and insensitive comments. A classic example of this is the "Ping" impression Michael does at every Dundies ceremony. In a deleted scene from "The Dundies" episode, Oscar and Kelly talk to Michael about Ping and try to convince him not to perform the routine. Michael's response to this is twofold. First, he states that Ping is based on his delivery person (he seems to think it's ok either because he's making fun of a particular person or because it's based in truth). And secondly, Michael says to Kelly and Oscar, "neither of you are Chinese, so why do you care?" Michael clearly believes that a joke is only offensive if it is actually heard by and offends a person it is about.[1]

Of course, part of the reason that Michael may not make a distinction between offensive and inoffensive humor is that he doesn't see one. As he says at one point, there is "no such thing as an appropriate joke—that's why it's a joke" ("Sexual Harassment"). Because he doesn't make the distinction between an inappropriate and an appropriate joke, Michael thinks it best to make everything funny—with disastrous results. Consider what he says about AIDS jokes: "AIDS is not funny, believe me I tried . . . I hope to live in a world where someone can tell a hilarious AIDS joke, it's my dream" ("Casino Night"). Such a desire would strike most of us as misguided, but notice that what motivates Michael is a desire to make everyone laugh. What he fails to recognize is that not everyone will find it funny.

Michael's insensitivity is not limited to tasteless jokes. In numerous situations, especially when dealing with the women in his life, Michael says and does things that upset people (without ever really understanding why). He sees nothing wrong with sending out a Christmas card that Photoshops himself into a scene with his girlfriend Carol and her two kids, taking the place of Carol's ex-husband. As Jim remarks, "It's a bold move to Photoshop yourself into a picture with your girlfriend and her kids on a ski trip with their real father, but then again Michael is a bold guy. Is bold the right word?" ("A Benihana Christmas, Part I") Boldness would indicate courage in the face of fear, but Michael has no comprehension of how Carol might be disturbed by this action (or his planning of a Christmas getaway for the two of them without consulting her). In fact, he is stunned when these actions lead Carol to dump him. Similarly, Michael doesn't seem to realize that when he institutes "Yankee Swap" at the office Christmas party because he is unhappy with the homemade gift he got from Phyllis, that Phyllis will be deeply offended ("Christmas Party"). He doesn't even seem to realize that the reason he instituted "Yankee Swap" is obvious to everyone in the room.

A classic example of Michael's cluelessness also illustrates why we might find him endearing. He doesn't seem to really hate women or people of different ethnic groups, nor does he seem not to care about his employees. Instead, his problem seems to be an inability to appropriately match situations and emotional responses. A classic example of this (and one which is not actually offensive) is the video that Michael makes for his presentation to corporate entitled "The Faces of Scranton" ("Valentine's Day"). Michael makes this video—showcasing various employees while U2's "With or Without You" plays in the background—the centerpiece of a presentation designed to prevent downsizing. In a commentary to this episode, Mike Schur remarks that "'With or Without You' is perfectly wrong—the song isn't about anything related to what he's talking about—it's a great Michael Scott choice—it's emotional, but it's emotional in totally the wrong way" ("Valentine's Day"). And that perfectly sums up the problem with Michael. While Michael's offensive jokes and insensitive remarks might be what attracts attention, they are really reflections of a deeper problem.

HERO: The Key to Curing Michael's Cluelessness

According to Mr. Brown (from Diversity Today), the key to a comfortable workplace is to follow the acronym HERO: Honesty, Empathy, Respect, and Openmindedness ("Diversity Day" and "Gay

Witch Hunt"). People who routinely do wrong, such as psychopaths, are said to lack empathy. In the case of a moral wrong like racist or sexist speech, it seems obvious that one cause could be a lack of empathy. However, while there appears to be some truth to this claim, it is complicated by the fact that "empathy" does not have a universal meaning. In general, it's difficult to pin down the meanings of words that refer to things that are not publicly observable— such as beauty, justice, pain, and love. We can't just direct someone's attention to what we're talking about—instead, we have to gesture towards it and hope they get the idea. When it comes to the word "empathy" things are especially complicated because "empathy" was a word invented in the twentieth century to serve as a translation of the German word *Einfühlung* (literally "feeling in"). Over time, "empathy" has been used in place of "sympathy," but that has only further served to confuse the issue.

There are two main things that people could be referring to when using the word "empathy." One is the understanding we have that someone is in pain, love, or any sort of emotional state. This is a popular usage among psychotherapists. Such understanding is nothing more than the belief that one has concerning someone's mental states. Because it focuses on the beliefs we have about others, this form of empathy is referred to as cognitive empathy. The other thing that people could be referring to with the term "empathy" is the actual experience of pain or love that we feel when we see someone in pain or love. Because this kind of empathy involves actually feeling something, it is referred to as affective empathy.

In everyday language, people tend not to discriminate between the kinds of empathy. But philosophy is about being careful with words so that we do not confuse our concepts and get misled about our conclusions. For example, one would normally say that a psychopath does not have empathy. This is somewhat misleading, since a psychopath who lacked cognitive empathy would be very frustrated. After all, if his goal were to harm or torture people, then he wouldn't know whether or not he was doing it right! It would seem then, that if he lacked anything it was affective empathy—he doesn't truly feel the pain he is causing. So, we need to ask ourselves, what kind of empathy does it take to be a HERO? The answer is both, which then raises the question: What kind of empathy does Michael have?

Not Totally Clueless: Oscar, Phyllis, and the Client

To suggest that Michael is totally clueless is to miss what it is about him that keeps him from getting fired. For example, Michael didn't offer the "Faces of Scranton" video as the only part of his presentation—he had prepared reports on the profitability of his branch. Michael's problem was that he thought the video should be what swayed the board as opposed to the economic data. In general, Michael couldn't have been a good salesman if he didn't have some understanding of what people were thinking and what would motivate them to buy from Dunder-Mifflin. Consider "The Client," in which Michael lands a large account with the county by wining and dining a Lackawanna County official at Chili's. Although Michael's actions seem inappropriate, he seals the deal. Similarly, when Michael goes on a sales call with Andy, he uses his understanding of how other business people think—and he only fails because of Andy's cluelessness ("Traveling Salesmen"). Ironically, Michael's comments about Andy suggest that even he recognizes when someone else has crossed the line. As Michael says, "I don't understand how anyone could have so little self-awareness" ("The Return"). Although one might wish Michael had a little more self-awareness, he does have some other-awareness: he recognizes how much Andy ignores negative feedback about his behavior.

Michael was successful as a salesman, so it's no surprise that he's able to make use of empathy when making a sale. But even as a manager, it's clear that Michael understands the importance of empathy— even if he rarely seems to make good use of it. After learning that Ryan had predicted the failure of Dunder-Mifflin in class, Michael scolds Ryan, but doesn't fire him. According to Michael, "A good manager doesn't fire people. He hires people and inspires people. People, Ryan. And people will never go out of business" ("Business School"). Sometimes Michael really lives up to that standard—as when, later in the episode, he goes to Pam's art show (and is the only one other than Oscar, who dismisses her work as "motel art") and tells Pam how proud he is of her and even buys a picture of the office building that he proudly displays in his office. Michael recognizes the need to understand people as a manager and usually tries to do so, though he often fails. One thing that might explain his frequent failure is his inability to draw clear boundaries—as when he dismisses Ryan's apology that the prediction was nothing personal and tells Ryan, "Business is always personal. It's the most personal thing in the world" ("Business School"). Clearly, Michael doesn't see the world the way most of us do, and so it's not surprising that he often misreads people's moods and expectations when it comes to things other than sales.

In situations where Michael has been made aware of how people might be offended—notably, Oscar's feeling about being outted in "Gay Witch Hunt" and the effect of Todd Packer's jokes—Michael reacts and even tries to comfort the offended parties. For example, when Packer tells a joke in front of Michael that is offensive to Phyllis, Michael jumps to her defense and even tries to say things that might make her feel better—such as "You know what? I love Phyllis. You know what else? I think she's gorgeous. I think she is an incredibly, incredibly attractive person. Come here, give me a kiss" ("Sexual Harassment"). However, even in his attempts to comfort and defend her, Michael fails to act appropriately. After all, he disciplines Kevin for laughing at the joke, not Packer for telling it. And he definitely crosses the line while hugging Phyllis when he says, "The only thing I am worried about is getting a boner."

To understand why things go awry with Michael, it helps to understand how cognitive empathy probably works. According to Bertrand Russell (1872–1970), we understand what goes on in other people's minds by way of an analogy between their behavior and our behavior. For example, when you see Michael hopping around screaming and holding his foot, it seems analogous to the time that happened to you (although there was no George Foreman Grill involved in your case, I hope). When it happened to you, you had just dropped something on your foot and felt excruciating pain. Making the connection between Michael's behavior and yours, you realize that Michael must be in pain. This act of cognitive empathy relies on your ability to make such analogies. In Michael's case, the limited cognitive empathy might be the result of the limitations in his ability to make analogies between himself and others. Thus, when Oscar returns to work, Michael tries to make him feel that he needn't worry about homophobia—but Michael focuses on the homophobia issue and neglects all similar forms of discrimination, as is evident when Michael tells Oscar, "Your gayness does not define you, your Mexicanness defines you" ("The Return").

So, why does Michael get it so wrong in some cases, but not others? Well, when he gets it right, Michael seems to be dealing with people much like himself—especially in the world of sales. But when he gets it wrong, Michael is trying to deal with someone whose life experiences are radically different from his (or someone who just doesn't see the world the way he does—remember how he thinks about business). In effect, while he can do simple analogical reasoning, he has difficulty with complex acts of imagination since they require him to feel something he doesn't normally feel. Usually, this is where affective empathy might come in and bridge the gap between self and other. However, in Michael's case there seems to be a lack of affective empathy—but why is that? And can he overcome it?

That's What She Said: A Catalogue of Kelly's Lack of Consideration

In order to appreciate the root of Michael's problem with affective empathy (and consequently the root of his cluelessness) let's look at another member of the office who exhibits similar traits—Kelly Kapoor. Admittedly, Kelly doesn't usually say things that are deeply offensive, but she does exhibit a complete lack of empathy (both cognitive and affective) in some situations. For example, when Kelly is talking she doesn't really seem to care what her conversation partner says or thinks. In fact, when Jim is jinxed (and hence not allowed to talk), and Kelly must do all of the talking, she says, "We're having the best conversation ever" ("Drug Testing").

Not only does Kelly talk incessantly without any consideration for what others might want to say, she is not always aware of who it is she is talking to. As a result, when she complains to Toby about Ryan, she doesn't recognize that he is the Human Resources person and is treating this as a complaint—because she thought she was talking to a friend (even though Toby would never identify himself as Kelly's friend) ("Conflict Resolution"). And in her interactions with Ryan, Kelly seems to be totally focused on what she wants out of the relationship and not at all concerned with what Ryan wants. She even seems oblivious to his obvious discomfort with how she treats him in the relationship.

A classic example of Kelly's obliviousness (and how it can be offensive and hurtful) is what she says to Pam at Phyllis' wedding. After Pam says that she is ok with the fact that Phyllis' wedding is a complete copy of Pam's wedding plans (down to the hiring of Scrantonicity to perform), Kelly says to her, "There's no way it's fine. I'm sorry. If I was you, I'd just freak out, get drunk, and tell someone I was pregnant" ("Phyllis' Wedding"). Kelly is rubbing salt in a wound, refusing to allow Pam to come to terms with what has happened to her.

So how do Kelly's and Michael's cluelessness parallel each other? They are both rooted in extreme egocentrism. There is no denying that both Michael and Kelly are very self-centered people. That leads them to view every situation in terms of how they see it and no one else, which leads them to say and do things that don't take others' feelings into account. In Kelly's case, there are some mitigating factors—her status as an Indian woman in American society might make her more aware of discrimination. (Hence, she confronts Michael about Ping.) But in the end, she is acting out of her feeling that she would be offended if the joke were about *her*. When she does act on behalf of others it's because something is connected to her.

The Root of Michael's Problem: Firing Devon, Kevin's Skin Cancer, and Dwight's Concussion

Michael's cluelessness is rooted in his egocentrism. For example, even when Michael has some sense that what he's doing will hurt someone's feelings—such as when corporate ordered him to fire someone—his sense of the harm seems completely out of whack. When pretending to be the employee getting fired, he says, "Arggh . . . I'm going to kill myself and it's your fault. I'm going to kill you for firing me" ("Halloween"). He can't help but see things through his own eyes, even when pretending to be someone else. (His attempts at Improv—where everything immediately jumps to dramatic gunplay ("Email Surveillance")—and at screenplay writing ("The Client") illustrate this very well.) For someone like Michael—for whom his job is everything—being fired is the end of the world. But when he finally fires Devon, Devon is upset to the point of smashing a pumpkin on Michael's car, but not nearly to the extent Michael expected.

Arguably, Devon is more offended by the offer of a Chili's gift certificate to ease the pain of being fired—which was Michael's feeble attempt to remain friends with the employee he fired (another indication that Michael makes everything about himself).

Michael's egocentricity is very clearly displayed in his response to the revelation that Kevin may have skin cancer. Upon hearing of Kevin's plight, which is revealed on Michael's birthday, Michael responds, ". . . sorry that's terrible news . . . terrible news for both of us" ("Michael's Birthday"). Michael isn't able to separate Kevin's plight from how it affects him personally. Thus, when Michael says, "it's not brain cancer, we can still have fun," his concern is not with comforting Kevin (since that isn't very comforting); rather, his concern is with getting everybody in the mood to participate in his surprise party (that he planned for himself). To see how this egocentricity is the source of much of Michael's insensitive behavior, let's return to the "Yankee Swap" incident. Michael is upset with Phyllis' gift because he only sees it in terms of his own desires. Michael describes the intent of the oven mitt as follows: "Phyllis is basically saying: hey Michael, I know you did a whole lot to help the office this year, but I only care about you a homemade oven mitt's worth" ("Christmas Party"). Michael is offended, because he can't understand Phyllis' intentions as someone who is not as well paid as he (he was the only one to get a bonus) and who also is not viewing the $20 Secret Santa gift as a statement about anybody's personal worth. Nor does he place much value on the time and energy that go into such a homemade gift.

As the contemporary philosopher Robert Gordon notes in his article on the role of simulation in moral judgment, the key to good moral judgments is the ability to decenter one's ego and see things from the perspective of the impartial observer.[2] Gordon is continuing the ideas of the eighteenth-century philosophers David Hume (1711–1776) and Adam Smith (1723–1790). Both Hume and Smith thought that morality was based in our sentiments and that the key to learning to be moral was to be able to enter into the feelings of an impartial spectator. Impartial does not necessarily mean dispassionate—in fact, if you think that emotions are key to moral behavior (as Hume, Smith, and even some contemporary neuroscientists do), then to be impartial is to have the right kinds of feelings—the feelings that take into account the community's perspective.

The question then becomes: How does one move from an egocentric view to a more group-centered view? After all, someone like Michael seems very resistant to getting outside of himself. A classic example of this is when Oscar expresses frustration at Michael's attempts to show that he is ok with Oscar being gay. Oscar finally explodes and says, "I don't want to touch you. Ever consider that? You're ignorant. And insulting. And small" ("Gay Witch Hunt"). While this is pretty much true, Michael is hurt by Oscar's response, but rather than recognize that Oscar's frustration is a response to the poor way in which he has handled the situation, he places Oscar in a position where he needs to make up with Michael—as if Oscar were the only one who had done anything wrong! To an extent, this makes sense: if Michael's problem is his egocentrism, he can't just decide not to be egocentric—something needs to pull him out of himself.

Who Has Two Thumbs and Is Michael's Friend: This Guy!

Hume and Smith were well aware that people did not immediately have the ability to see things from other people's perspectives. Instead, they argued that the natural contact between people would force them outside themselves. They appealed to a kind of proto-empathy referred to as "emotional contagion." Contagion is not a process that is in our conscious control—so we can't prevent it from happening. An example of contagion is when a very nervous person enters the room and other people get nervous just by being around that person. Close contact with your family and friends presents situations where the needs of people other than yourself infect you. Over time, you can't help but be pleased by the things that make your friend happy. This unconscious transmission of what it feels like to be someone else is complemented by the fact that anyone who wants to have a healthy relationship with friends and family needs to pay attention to their concerns. So, the initial feelings sneak into us through contagion, and then we build on them out of a desire to maintain these relationships.

The problem for Michael is that he is a very lonely man. Without people around him to care about, he has difficulty thinking about things from anyone else's perspective. Consider his best friend, Todd

Packer. This friendship seems entirely one-sided, as Michael himself makes clear when he says, "Todd Packer and I are total BFFs, Best Friends Forever. We came up together in sales. One time we went to a bar and met this set of twins. And Packer said that we were brothers. One thing led to another, and we took them to our hotel room . . . And Packer did *both* of them! It was awesome!" ("Sexual Harassment"). Todd Packer is even more egocentric than Michael. Packer is about taking whatever he wants and is not sorry if someone points out that he has done something to hurt someone. Michael, on the other hand, awkwardly expresses remorse.

Michael's only other real friend is a subordinate who can't stop sucking up to him. Although Dwight may serve as Michael's confidant, he will always defer to Michael. In doing this, Dwight is not a real friend. Michael, of course, doesn't seem to mind this relationship. "I don't want someone sucking up to me because they think I can help their career. I want them sucking up to me because they genuinely love me" ("The Return"). Although this reasoning enables Michael to recognize the unhealthy nature of a friendship with Andy, it also highlights the problematic aspect of his relationship with Dwight. Dwight's friendship will not help Michael get outside himself, since it's always focused on what Michael wants.

The problem of finding a real friend to help Michael grow as a person is compounded by the fact that Michael's whole life seems to revolve around the office. He can't really be friends with his employees. As Ed Truck points out to Michael, he "can't be their friend—they'll always see you as the boss" ("The Carpet"). To his detriment, Michael's entire world is designed to feed into his egocentricity since (at least in the workplace) it really is all about him.

There is a glimmer of hope for Michael. Jim doesn't seem to view Michael solely as the boss (especially when he was away from Scranton—and since his return with promotion his status is even closer to Michael's). Jim has acted to help Michael out—for example, when he was embarrassing himself singing karaoke ("Email Surveillance") and when he threw an otherwise unattended party at the Mid-Market Office Supply Convention ("The Convention"). Jim has also served as a check on Michael's egocentrism—for example, when he told him the joke about Pam's long engagement was "lazy" ("The Dundies") or when he told Michael that the Benihana waitress was not "the one," she was just a rebound ("A Benihana Christmas,

Part II"). If Michael is ever going to get outside himself in a major way he needs that kind of corrective feedback. The bond that he forges with Jim, when Jim confesses his affection for Pam on the Booze Cruise is another step in the right direction, as this kind of sharing of feelings and trust can serve as a conduit for the kind of emotional contagion that would drag him away from his own concerns. Of course, Michael blew that trust almost immediately in "The Secret" and that put a damper on his attempts to bond with Jim. Still, if Michael could nurture a friendship with Jim or someone like Jim, then he could build on that connection and learn to be more sensitive and considerate—though probably it would take a long time. (But hey, he was right about Jan, so maybe we should bet on him after all.)

NOTES

1   Interestingly, on the commentary to this episode, it is mentioned that Steve Carell apologized to the Asian family that had been in the background when they were filming at Chili's—even though it should have been clear that this was a television show that was filming.
2   Robert Gordon, "Sympathy, Simulation and the Impartial Spectator," *Ethics* 105:4, 1995, 727–742.

4

Leaving the Dice Alone: Pointlessness and Helplessness at Wernham-Hogg

Wim Vandekerckhove and Eva E. Tsahuridu

What bothers me about this job? Wasted talent.
(David Brent, episode 1, series 1)

Wernham-Hogg is in the paper business, an industry everyone knows exists but most people know very little about. Still, the office life at Wernham-Hogg could be any office. It could be *your* office, or *our* office. We can relate to life there—and to the staff as well.

Tim "is the person most sensible people are supposed to relate to, yes. And along with Dawn he's the moral conscience of the show."[1] Tim appears to think morally. He talks about people with dignity and compares such people with his colleagues, finding the latter wanting —or rather wacky. He is looking for meaning in his life, yearning for purpose and authenticity, and thus intends to go back to university. To his credit, Tim respects Dawn's choices and the fact that she is in a relationship (until the last episode of the second series, anyway), despite his feelings toward her.

But Tim isn't a saint. He asks Dawn out, he hasn't gone to university, and he hasn't left Wernham-Hogg. He doesn't respect Gareth, and he uses his superior intelligence to belittle him. Nothing unusual here. Most of us live our lives with such moral contradictions most of the time. Sometimes we succeed in living our lives according to what

38

we know we ought to do—and sometimes that coincides with what we want or can do. Other times we engage in activities that go against our values and our intentions. It's here that Tim is so useful: he reminds us that we're always weak enough to avoid doing what we know we should.

What if Everyone Threw a Stapler Out the Window?

There are a number of reasons why we relate to Tim more than anyone else in the show. To start with, Tim seems to stand above the mediocrity that surrounds him. He's always one step ahead of Gareth, for instance. When they fight over a stapler, Tim turns every argument around on Gareth. He's also able to keep David at an appropriate distance, one moment joking along with him, the other making him embarrassed about having scribbled down quotes from philosophers that he recites to unsuspecting employees in order to impress them.

> *Tim*: Are you reading this?
> *David*: Am I what?
> *Tim*: Reading the quote?
> *David*: Sort of.
> *Tim*: What does . . . [Tim looking at David's papers] Confucius, oh, Bernard Shaw.
> *David*: It's not who said it first, I am passing on my wisdom to you.
> *Tim*: Cool.
> *David*: And don't tell [pointing at the door] those I've been reading these.
> *Tim*: I'm not going to.
> *David* [clearly annoyed]: I'll put it down there if it's obvious.
> (2:2)

Tim's aware of the pointlessness of his work but, unlike his cohorts, he's got a backup plan: to go back to university to study psychology. Throughout the series, for Tim, the job at Wernham-Hogg is but a temporary thing. He doesn't have to care if things go terribly wrong because it doesn't really affect his life or what he'll be doing next. In short, Tim seems in control of his own person. In moral philosophy we would say that Tim is an autonomous moral agent. He is an agent with the capacity to know what is moral and also with the capacity to *behave* morally.

Immanuel Kant (1724–1804), one of the most influential of all moral philosophers, developed an ethics based on the premise that morality is rational and therefore the same for all rational beings. Just as we can all understand the rules of mathematics, we can also understand the rules of morality. Rational morality will then provide principles that both can and ought to be held by all persons, regardless of circumstances, and be consistently obeyed by all rational agents at all times.[2] These principles are captured in what Kant calls the categorical imperative. It goes as follows: "Act only according to that maxim through which you can at the same time will that it should become a universal law." Ouch. We'll explain this shortly.

In the very first episode, a fight over the use of Gareth's stapler ends up with Tim throwing it through the window. Gareth wrote his name on the stapler to ensure that it was *only his* stapler—and Tim threw it out of the window in an attempt to get through to Gareth that he was being very silly and unreasonably possessive about a piece of office equipment.

Gareth: Give it back.
Tim: I'm just using it for a second.
Gareth: It's got my name on it: "ga-reth" [pointing at the Tippexed "Gareth" on the stapler]
Tim: Yeah it says "ga-ret" actually but . . .
Gareth: Ask if you wanna borrow it.
Tim: You always say "no," mate, so what's the point.
Gareth: Perhaps that's why you should ask.
Tim: Gareth, it was just there, ok.
Gareth: That's his home, leave it there.
Tim: Ok [picks up the stapler from Gareth's desk and runs to the window, holding the stapler outside the window]. I'm going to let this go unless you stop acting like a fool.
Gareth [hesitates]: Well, you won't, so.
Tim [drops the stapler]: Well I have, so.
Gareth: What if that killed someone.
Tim: Oh, they'll think you're the murderer. It's got your name on it.
Gareth: Why would a murderer put his name on a murder weapon?
Tim: To stop people borrowing it.
Gareth [turns]: David.
Tim: I hate the fact that you've brought me down to this.
[Gareth walks away]
Tim: You bring me down to this, mate.

Has Tim behaved morally? To assess this, Kant contends, we need to know *why* Tim has done what he's done. Presumably, Tim is trying to make a point about the silliness of certain disputes. To determine if this is an acceptable thing to try to do, Kant asks us to imagine a world where *everyone* is trying to do exactly what Tim is trying to do. This is a way of testing the "maxim" (the principled policy someone is acting on—the reason why they do what they do) of an action. If a maxim can hold universally (if everyone could have that maxim without any kind of contradiction), then that maxim is morally permissible.

Whether a maxim passes the test of universality or not is independent of particular results. Gareth's comment that Tim might have killed someone—a consequentialist argument—is irrelevant here. It does not lead to a contradiction (we can wear helmets!). Neither is the argument of effectiveness—does it stop Gareth's silliness?—relevant here (it doesn't in fact stop his silliness).[3] What matters is just whether or not everyone could consistently act on the same principle. If they can, then that maxim doesn't violate the moral law. Or so says Kant, anyway. Because there's no contradiction in throwing staplers out of windows in order to make a point, it seems Tim's in the clear.

"It is the Wackiness I Can't Stand"

One of the reasons we relate to Tim is that he seems to be in control. Tim isn't whatever people want him to be. He has an identity. He doesn't go along with whatever is happening. For instance, he doesn't join in Gareth's "Mana Mana" song (first episode), as the others do. And on red-nose day (2:5), he refuses to join in "with someone else's idea of wackiness." He has an idea of what he wants in his life and it's not Wernham-Hogg: "I feel a little bit like I'm wasting my time . . . I'm 30, I wanna retire with some stories to tell" (2:2).

In short, Tim has an identity. He says that "it is the wackiness I can't stand" and yearns for people with quiet dignity. But we also see Tim on the same episode entering the wackiness by kissing Gareth for a pound, hiding Gareth's possessions to collect money, and finally holding the check for comic relief with Dawn in the car park, while David is dressed as a bird.

In episode two of the first series, for example, someone cut and pasted David's head onto a porn picture. The whole team saw this and David gets Gareth to find out who did it. Based on nothing but his own bias, Gareth concludes that Tim's the one who did it. Tim, despite the fact that he wasn't responsible for this, doesn't immediately tell who pulled the porn joke. It's only when he's accused in front of Jennifer (head office) and supposedly gets sacked, that he argues that David's conclusion has to be wrong—"you put your best man on the job"—before revealing that it was Finchy (David's friend) who pulled the trick on his computer.

Tim gives an account of why he has put his dream on hold when he gets promoted to Senior Sales Rep:

> If you look at life like a rolling dice then my situation now . . . it may be only a three . . . If I cash that in now, go for something bigger and better . . . yeah I could easily role a six . . . no problem, I could role a six . . . I could also role a one. So . . . I think sometimes just leave the dice alone. (2:6)

Indeed, one doesn't gamble with one's life.

Unfortunately, Tim's promotion seems to have gone to his head, telling Dawn to do her job properly and putting Lee on the spot (2:1). But, on the other hand, he's just being professional about the responsibilities that come with the job. He takes those seriously, wearing a suit and tie, telling someone in a supportive way they haven't done their job properly (2:1):

> Ok, listen, I suggest we put this down as a lesson. You have this off over to me by three o'clock today . . . Three o'clock, please . . . all right? Then we'll say no harm done.

But Tim doesn't seem to be constant about it. There are moments when he just goes with the flow. For instance, while being culturally literate—Tim knows about literature and film—he has nothing better to do than to go out with David, Gareth, and Finchy. He's aware of the silliness of their idea of "a good night out" because he's sometimes cynical about it (1:5). And yet he *does* go out with them. Consider too the ease with which he accepts the promotion at the end of the first series and lets go of his intention to hand in his notice. Then there are the numerous occasions when Tim is left speechless at the stupidity of others—mainly Gareth. Tim knows a situation is unacceptable, but he fails to see how he could bring about a change. He is left helpless with his "moral conscience."

Dripping Boredom

The term for helplessness in moral philosophy is anomie. Anomie is not the opposite of autonomy (self-rule), but the *absence* of rule. It denotes a lack of purpose, identity, or values in a person. In philosophy, anomie is described as moral lawlessness where there is no freedom.[4] The sociologist Emile Durkheim (1858–1917) called it a state of amorality—not immorality!—resulting from society's inability to provide a normative framework.

Later, philosopher Karl Polanyi (1886–1964) linked anomie with a lack of embeddedness of the economic activity of the market. Erich Fromm (1900–1980) further suggested that experiences in industrial societies limit the possibility for leading meaningful and self-directed lives and make individuals experience powerlessness and paralysis, leading to alienation in organizations and society.[5] Industrial societies, Fromm argued, provide the socialization that strips people of their ability to take initiative. Wernham-Hogg is a paper business, but no one in the office knows or cares what the paper they sell is used for. When Tim gets promoted his focus on himself leaves the rest even more alienated: "I've been made Senior Sales Rep which is a great opportunity for me, as people now are comin' in from Swindon which is a new and exciting sort of venture for me" (2:1).

It seems working at an office is fully self-referential. It's just about keeping the office going, not about what is actually produced. And that's why office life is mainly the same everywhere, as long as it's an office. The sociologist Robert K. Merton (1910–2003) reformulated the notion of anomie and made it apt for organizational analysis.[6] For Merton, anomie results from a lack of regulation in goal achievement with no reference to the appropriateness of the goals themselves. Based on that formulation, we can distinguish organizational anomie from anomia at work. Anomie is an organizational state, while anomia refers to the individual's state of mind. Management promotes organizational anomie when it fails to live up to workplace norms,[7] such as norms relating to racism and sexual harassment, but also norms about leadership and motivation.

David is a remarkable example of anomic management behavior. He tells a racist joke at the welcome reception for the Swindon people (2:1), and he puts people down for expecting more from life than what Wernham-Hogg has to offer during the appraisals (2:2). He's terribly insensitive to what matters to other people, and he fails to motivate them. In a brilliant scene in episode six of the first series, David tells his team that there is good and bad news about the planned redundancies. The bad news is that some of them will have to go and those staying will move to Swindon, but the good news is that he's been offered the job of national manager. He says it all with the same excitement, and when one of the team explains that they're disgruntled ("David, there is no good news"), he really doesn't get it.

Boredom drips from the shots between scenes where we see people sitting at their desks staring at their screens. In episode two of the second series, the Swindon lot complains to David that they're not expected to work hard, that there is no dynamism in the office, that they're bored and that "people could get away with murder here." David's management style has everything to turn those working at the office into anomic drones.

Tim's Struggle

The anomic person does not see and does not want to know. It's all too big and complicated, and besides what can be done?[8] This gives ground to cynicism both toward the organization and toward management commitment.[9] No one on David's floor seems to be very serious about their job or about Wernham-Hogg as a business. The office at Wernham-Hogg is filled with cynicism, as is office life in general. Still, the people in *The Office* are not anomics. The situation has everything to let them slip into complete anomie, but we see each of them struggling with it. Tim's struggling even has physical repercussions (he keeps some indigestion tablets in his pen tidy).[10] But, more significantly, Tim's blatant awareness of the pointlessness of his job at Wernham-Hogg makes him grab every opportunity to give his life some meaning.

Throughout series one, Dawn is his ray of sunshine. He flirts with her every time he passes the reception desk and teams up with her to play tricks on Gareth. He welcomes every new face—Ricky and Donna—with hope that they might make conversation at the office a bit more bearable. The way he lets his promotion go to his head (2:1) and getting together with Rachel (series two) are also attempts to find any tiny bit of meaning that comes along.[11]

The anomie is daunting, but his moral consciousness always raises its head. Sadly, though, he's never able to fully carry out what he knows he should be doing. Tim's not an anomic, but he's not completely autonomous either.

To Quote Lennon . . .

When, in the final episode of series one, David asks Tim why he's thinking of leaving, Tim answers: "I'm not thinking of leaving, I *am* leaving." Yet he doesn't leave. We could've known that even before he accepted his promotion. Right after the talk with David, we see Tim talking to the camera crew. He says: "It's like an alarm clock has gone off and I just have to get away." That's his consciousness peeping up. He even quotes Lennon: "Life is what happens when you're making other plans . . . and that's how I feel."[12] Tim wants to be in control of his own life. But he immediately adds: "Lennon also said I am the Walrus, so I don't know what to believe." And by the time episode six ends, the promotion he gets offered pulls him down again. The "slight change of plan," as he explains to Dawn, is actually a U-turn. And for what? More of the same. To be precise—and it is striking that Tim uses the same language, intonation, and even mannerisms as David—"500 quid guaranteed a year and if I do a bit of networkin' there's a real chance I'll be in David's chair in three years, so . . ."

So even though Tim has the capacity for autonomous action, he seems to lack courage or conviction to behave autonomously. Tim's dream of going back to university and leaving Wernham-Hogg is hardly an issue in the second series, except for the final episode, when he refuses to replace David as the regional manager. When Neil offers him the job and asks him to do it just temporarily, Tim answers, "I thought that about this job too." It seems Lennon's line

45

runs through his mind again. Tim refuses the management job because he feels that if he takes it, he'll be stuck at Wernham-Hogg forever.

Sadly, in the Christmas special, set a year after the final episode, we find Tim still at his same old desk. Tim is indeed the moral conscience of the show, but he's not a moral hero. He keeps up his struggle against anomia, but at the same time he lacks the strength to act as his autonomous will dictates. Such is Tim's character—and it is a rather *common* one. Most people have a will that is unstable and that fluctuates, fades, or even surrenders under pressure. Maybe, then, most of us relate to Tim not because he is the moral conscience of the show but because—like most of us—he is no moral hero. Like most of us, in fact, he is rather weak-willed.

To Roll or Not to Roll

Tim tries hard, but life's a bitch. It's a constant struggle to keep ourselves from being sucked into that anomic swamp that *is* office life (and Slough life generally). It's simply too hard to actually do what we have to do whole-heartedly. So we cling to anything that might give us some meaning in life, like a silly promotion, or a job title—"something they give you to do things they don't want to, for free" (Tim to Gareth on his team leader title in episode one of series two).

But our conscience is stubborn. It doesn't give in. It has this silly idea that we're free and that if we really want to, we can change things. And so, perhaps even only once in a lifetime, we really go for it. Most of the time, it's not job-related stuff, but something we call love. Just like Tim in that moment at the end of the final episode. There he is, explaining to the camera crew: "Under different circumstances something might have happened. But she's going away now and you can't change circumstances." And then it hits him, a full flash of moral consciousness—now or never! He rushes out to Dawn . . .

Flashes rarely come to two people at once. Dawn is too far in with Lee. Tim goes back to his desk, having dumped Rachel, having refused the management job, and having gotten a "no" from Dawn.

Sometimes it's better to leave the dice alone.

NOTES

1 This was what Ricky Gervais and Stephen Merchant said in reply to a question asked by Dominic Green of Gloucester on the BBC "The Office" website (www.bbc.co.uk/comedy/theoffice/). The question, of course, was "Tim represents the viewer, right?"

2 See A. MacIntyre, *After Virtue: A Study in Moral Theory*, 2nd edn. (London: Duckworth, 1993).

3 The contradiction we're looking for can be a contradiction of conception or a contradiction of will. Either one annuls the maxim to be a moral duty and, as we will see, the maxim of the stapler incident results in both contradictions. A contradiction of conception is when everyone trying to act according to that maxim makes everyone's ability to do so impossible. If everyone could make objects over which there is a dispute about their use disappear, they wouldn't be able to make use of those objects anymore. The implication is that there wouldn't be any more disputes about the usage and thus one couldn't make those objects disappear. It seems far fetched, but that is where the contradiction of conception or logical contradiction leads us to. The contradiction of will is when we can think of a world where everyone acts on the maxim, but we cannot consistently will such a world. We cannot will that everyone makes objects over which there is a dispute about who can use them disappear because it would make it impossible to get anything done. We wouldn't get any more stapling or hole punching done, for instance.

4 S. I. Benn, *A Theory of Freedom* (New York: Cambridge University Press, 1988).

5 E. Fromm, *The Sane Society* (New York: Fawcett Premier Books, 1955).

6 For a discussion about the relation between organizational climate and anomie at work, see E. E. Tsahuridu, "Anomie and Ethics at Work," *Journal of Business Ethics* 69 (2), 2006, pp. 163–174.

7 R. Hodson, "Organizational Anomie and Worker Consent," *Work and Occupations* 26 (3), 1999, pp. 292–323.

8 C. Hampden-Turner, *Radical Man: The Process of Psycho-Social Development* (Cambridge: Schenkman Publishing, 1970).

9 Research into role stress and anomie among police executives has shown this link. See J. P. Crank, R. Regoli, J. D. Hewitt, and R. G. Culbertson, "Institutional and Organizational Antecedents of Role Stress, Work Alienation, and Anomie among Police Executives," *Criminal Justice and Behavior* 22 (2), 1995, pp. 152–171.

10 See Tim's desk on the interactive map at www.bbc.co.uk/comedy/theoffice/map/.

11　But everything he tries wears thin after a while. He tries several times to rationalize staying where he's at: the "new and exciting sort of venture" that the merge with Swindon entails, the "I'm 30, time to grow up basically, it's that simple" (2:1) or "I could roll a six . . . I could also roll a one. So . . . I think sometimes just leave the dice alone" (2:6)

12　Tim's quote is inaccurate. It should be ". . . *busy* making other plans."

5

The Virtues of Humor: What *The Office* Can Teach Us About Aristotle's Ethics

Sean McAleer

Early in the very first episode of *The Office*, David Brent is mugging for the camera as he introduces Dawn Tinsley, the receptionist. "Ah, Dawn," he muses. "I'd say that at one time or another, every bloke in the office has woken up at the crack of Dawn." Dawn is mortified (as is the viewer, on her behalf), while Brent cackles with delight at his own "wit." We're mortified not because the joke isn't funny (though it isn't—or at least hasn't been since junior high) but because it's so inappropriate. Its inappropriateness isn't just a matter of bad taste or a failure of etiquette (as is Brent's t-shirt and ball-cap ensemble at his presentation on "motivational techniques" in episode four of series two). The joke is *morally* inappropriate. As such, it tells us something about David Brent's character. Jokes can be funny that way.

Given the centrality of character and virtue to the ethics of Aristotle (384–322 BCE), it's not surprising that Aristotle can help us understand what's wrong with David Brent. But Aristotle can also help us understand humor generally. For Aristotle, ethics is not a matter of duty or promoting good outcomes, it's about being a certain sort of person—the sort of person who lives a life expressive of the virtues. In this, Aristotle's thought differs from most modern moral philosophy, which tends to take either notions of duty or the notion of a good outcome to be fundamental.[1] A *virtue ethics*, such as Aristotle's, takes the virtues—traits such as courage, wisdom, temperance, honesty, generosity, kindness, and the like—to be morally fundamental. Instead of defining virtue in terms of duty by saying that a virtuous person is someone who does her duty, a virtue ethics would define duty in terms of virtue, holding that an action is my duty

49

if and only if a virtuous person would perform that action in the circumstances. If this were a treatise on moral theory we might want more precision or complexity in our account of virtue ethics, but this should do just fine for our purposes. To any professional or amateur philosopher inclined to disagree, I can only say, having gotten in touch with my inner Brent, "Exsqueeze me."

Virtues and Vices

So what *is* a virtue, for Aristotle? Aristotle speaks of the virtue*s* or *a* virtue rather than virtue. The word *virtue* can have a quaint, Victorian ring that seems closely tied to chastity, which isn't Aristotle's sense at all (though sexual temperance is *a* virtue). Our English word *virtue* translates the Greek word *arête*, though a better translation would be *excellence*, since a virtue for Aristotle isn't essentially moral. The English word *virtuoso* retains this non-moral connotation. While David Brent isn't exactly a virtuoso guitar player, he's actually not bad—and he's certainly a better guitar player than he is a music video crooner. If you don't know this by now, you will never never never know this.

For Aristotle, a virtue is a state that enables its possessor to achieve its function or purpose well. The function of a knife, for example, is to cut. To cut well, a knife needs to be sharp: that's the state or condition that enables the knife to perform its function well. Thus dullness would be its vice, since a dull knife can't cut well. Presumably, those knives one sees advertised on late night infomercials, the ones that cut through cinderblocks and still slice tomatoes paper-thin, are about as virtuous as knives can get. The function or purpose of a regional manager of a paper merchant is more complex, but ultimately perhaps it's to increase profitability. Many virtues will be needed if the manager is to succeed; but among them will be honesty, discipline, reliability, prudence, resourcefulness, loyalty, genuine concern for the staff and customers, clarity of vision, integrity, and the kind of toughness that is consistent with compassion and that enables a manager to make hard choices.[2] I'll leave it to the reader to decide whether David or Neil more fully embodies the virtues of a manager.

Our virtues, then, are the states that enable us to think and act well. When we are functioning well, we are *eudaimôn*, which is usually rendered as *happy*, though *flourishing* is a much better translation of that Greek word. Happiness (*eudaimonia*), for Aristotle, is not a pleasant, transient psychological state or mood. It is not the result of hot love on the free love highway, for example, because happiness is not a mere result at all, but rather an activity. People, no less than rosebushes, can flourish; it's just that the conditions of human flourishing are rather more complex than the conditions of rosebush flourishing.[3] Here's Aristotle's official definition of a character virtue from his most important and widely read work on ethics, the *Nicomachean Ethics*:

> Excellence, then, is a state that is concerned with choice, lying in a mean relative to us, this being determined by reason and in the way in which the man of practical wisdom would determine it. Now it is a mean between two vices, that which depends on excess and that which depends on defect. (1106b36–1107a3)[4]

Aristotle is telling us that every virtue of character has *two* vices opposing it, not just one. Cowardice is not *the* opposite of courage, but *an* opposite. The courageous person faces danger, feels no more fear than the situation warrants, and is able to act appropriately. The cowardly person is excessively fearful in the same situation, and is thus unable to act appropriately. But what of the person who fails to appreciate how dangerous a situation is, and takes unnecessary and unreasonable risks? This is the rash person, who, on Aristotle's view, also fails to display virtue. The virtue of generosity is a mean between profligacy and stinginess, the virtue of proper pride is a mean between vanity and excessive humility, and so on for the other character virtues. (The intellectual virtues do *not* have this mean-between-extremes structure, by the way: *epistêmê* or knowledge, for example, is not a mean between knowing too much and knowing too little.)

Aristotle's doctrine of the mean is *not* a doctrine of moderation. He is not saying that the good-tempered person, for example, feels a moderate amount of anger in all situations, while irascible and meek persons feel too much and too little. The good-tempered person does not feel the same moderate anger when she discovers her best friend has betrayed her and when someone accidentally steps on her foot in a crowded elevator. Finchy's anger at losing the quiz is excessive not by some absolute standard, but because it's out of proportion to the cause, trivia quizzes being by nature trivial, and because he and Brent lost fair and square. Neil's anger at David's mocking him in front of the staff, is by contrast, appropriate, not just because Neil's level of anger is appropriate to the circumstances—his authority has been undermined, and by someone who himself exhibits the qualities in question (*"just want to be as popular as the new boss . . . oh love me!"*)—but also because its expression is appropriate: he expresses it in private, it's controlled, and it doesn't last longer than it should. And notice that it expresses a healthy self-respect: "I don't let anyone talk to me the way you just did—not my staff, not my boss, no one— certainly not you." Finchy's, by contrast, expresses the petulance of a rather fragile ego dressed up in macho bravado. Someone with proper and healthy self-respect won't feel the need to seek revenge when they haven't been wronged. Virtue is not a one-size-fits-all thing for Aristotle, but rather is a matter of acting and feeling appropriately in the given circumstances, where what's appropriate is determined by the virtue of practical wisdom:

> The man who is angry at the right things and with the right people, and, further, as he ought, when he ought, and as long as he ought, is praised. For the good-tempered man tends to be unperturbed and not to be led by passion, but to be angry in the manner, at the things, and for the length of time, that reason dictates. (1125b31–35)

The lesson here is that although Aristotle often discusses virtue and vice in quantitative terms, the virtues are best understood *qualitatively*: they are dispositions to act and feel in ways that are appropriate in the circumstances. It turns out that this is a mean between extremes of excess and deficiency, but virtue is really about acting and feeling appropriately.[5]

Wit and Virtue

That a good sense of humor is an Aristotelian virtue tells us something interesting and important about Aristotle's conception of morality—namely, that it's broader than is typical of modern moral philosophy. If we think that morality is primarily about rights and duties, then we'll probably write off wit as a matter of personality rather than morality and regard it, like punctuality and dressing well, as largely immune to moral evaluation, for it seems obvious that no one has a duty to be funny or a right to a good joke—though perhaps people who aren't funny have a duty not to try to be (this means *you*, Carrot Top).

Aristotle, in contrast, is concerned with human flourishing, and there are more ways to flourish or live well than to conscientiously discharge our duties to others. So when Aristotle asks what it is to be virtuous, he's really asking what it is to be an excellent person, and he doesn't limit the scope of his inquiry to moral excellence. He is interested in the excellence of the whole person. This holistic approach is one of the things that attracts many contemporary philosophers to Aristotle's approach to ethics.

Since we are naturally social creatures, according to Aristotle, the scope of human excellence must extend to our social interactions. Moreover, we need relaxation and amusement, if only to recharge our batteries for the serious business of life, so there are virtues with respect to this sphere of social interaction, since one can interact well or poorly when it comes to amusement, just as one can act well or poorly when it comes to truth-telling. As is obvious to anyone who's watched *The Office*, David Brent tends to not act excellently when it comes to amusement. How exactly does he go so wrong, so excruciatingly, hilariously wrong?

To begin, here's what Aristotle says about wit and its corresponding vices in Book IV, Chapter 8 of the *Nicomachean Ethics*:

> Those who carry humor to excess are thought to be vulgar buffoons, striving after humor at all costs, and aiming rather at raising a laugh than at saying what is becoming and at avoiding pain to the object of their fun; while those who can neither make a joke themselves nor put up with those who do are thought to be boorish and unpolished. But those who joke in a tasteful way are called ready-witted. (1128a5–10)

Since here and elsewhere Aristotle employs quantitative terms such as *excess* in distinguishing virtues from vices, it's important to remember that the crucial difference between wit, buffoonery, and boorishness—and between virtue and vice generally—is qualitative, not quantitative. It's not that the buffoon is too funny, the boor not funny enough, or that the buffoon jests too much, the boor too little, and the person of wit just the right amount. And the qualitative difference is not really that the witty person's jokes are just qualitatively better—though they probably are. The difference is that the witty person's jesting is *appropriate* to the circumstances, while the buffoon's is inappropriate and the boor fails to jest when jesting would be appropriate (or at least not inappropriate). Consider the first episode of series two,[6] when "the Swindon lot" are now members of the Slough branch. Neil, formerly the manager at Swindon and now David's boss, gives a light-hearted welcome speech, with gentle barbs for one and all, including himself:

> Hello everyone. For those of who you don't know me, I'm Neil Godwin. For those of you who do, keep stumm! I'm a man of simple pleasures. I don't need lovely houses, beautiful girls and classy restaurants, so it's a good job I moved to Slough! . . . I know David is feeling a bit worried about taking on these new staff, because as manager it's going to mean a lot more responsibility: he'll now have to delegate twice as much work.

It's clever and appropriate, and it's appropriate largely because it's aimed at putting everyone at ease, at making an awkward situation less awkward. David, by contrast, isn't trying to welcome the new staff, he's trying to put on a show, as his brief remarks to Neil before the meeting starts indicate: "Don't be nervous. Just keep it short, bring me on, and enjoy the show." Moreover, his "routine" just isn't funny:

> Welcome to Slough, to the new people. My name's David Brent, and I've always been in the paper industry, haven't I? Yeah. My parents owned a paper shop . . . until it blew away . . . [*No laughter*] It was made of paper . . . I'm not used to public squeaking. I piss-pronunciate a lot of my worms.

It goes downhill from there (though the Basil Fawlty impersonation is pretty darn good). He gets angry when people don't laugh, and is especially peeved and puzzled by the thought that Neil is funnier than he is. He's doing a bad comedy routine, not making a witty and appropriate welcoming speech. For him, it's an occasion to be the center of attention. His intention isn't to put the staff at ease or make them feel welcome; his intention is to be funny—or, more accurately, to be thought funny.

With this understanding of what Aristotelian wit is, let's explore its nuances, using the characters who most embody its structure: David Brent, buffoon; Tim Canterbury, wit; and Gareth Keenan, boor. My apologies to those sad souls who've seen only the American version of *The Office*, for my discussion will focus exclusively on the British version (even though Michael Scott, Jim Halpert, and Dwight Schrute embody an analogous Aristotelian structure).

David Brent: Regional Manager, Chilled-Out Entertainer, Buffoon

Not only is David Brent a buffoon, he's a buffoon *par excellence*. Indeed, he looks like what the word *buffoon* sounds like. The hallmark of the virtuous person in general is that her actions and feelings are appropriate in the circumstances; knowing where the mean is, she acts accordingly. David's actions and feelings are anything but. The problem isn't his erroneous self-conception of funny man *and* great boss, the problem is his overweening need to be thought to be funny. He's a buffoon because he is "the slave of his sense of humor" (1128a33–34). He's unable not to try to get a laugh, even when doing so is inappropriate, just as a drug addict is unable not to take drugs, even when doing so is harmful.

To get a sense of this, consider the last episode of series one, in which the office is in a state of anxiety about the rumored redundancies. Malcolm, older than the rest and quite concerned about losing his job, is puzzled about David's hiring a new secretary in light of the looming redundancies or layoffs. He wants to speak seriously about this situation, but David is incapable of being serious when seriousness is what's called for. Rather than listening to Malcolm's concerns and thinking creatively about a solution or being caringly direct about Malcolm's plight, David makes squeegee noises on Malcolm's bald head and does a rather bad Kojak impersonation.

There are times when humor is just what a heavy situation calls for, and the witty person can tell what those situations are and what they're not, because he or she possesses the virtue of practical wisdom. Practical wisdom is a kind of insight or intuition into what a situation calls for, rather than a deductive, discursive process. There is no computer-like decision procedure that can determine where the mean is. As Aristotle sees things, where the mean is "is not easy to determine by reasoning ... the decision rests with perception" (1109b21–23).

This feature of Aristotle's ethical thought—that knowing what one ought to do is not a matter of following an abstract decision procedure but is rather a matter of seeing the world in a certain kind of way (as the virtuous person sees it)—is mirrored in the virtue of wit itself, for having a sense of humor is not a matter of grasping abstract universal principles and applying them disinterestedly, it's about seeing the world in a certain way. Most of us have probably found ourselves trying to explain why something is funny to someone who does not find it funny. Indeed, David reports just this phenomenon in episode three of series one: "We'll be doing a bit of shtick and we'll be cracking up, and people watching will go, 'why is that funny?' and we'll tell them why."

Mark Twain once said, "Show me someone who knows what's funny and I'll show you someone who knows what's not." Surely what Twain means is that genuinely having a sense of humor—possessing the Aristotelian virtue of wit—involves knowing when humor is inappropriate and when it isn't. In describing the properly witty person, Aristotle tells us that "there are . . . jokes he will not make" (1128a29). Ironically, David is at least intellectually aware of this. In the first episode of the series, Tim has (once again, it seems) ensconced Gareth's stapler in jello ("jelly" in British English). "The thing about practical jokes," David says, "is that you've got to know when to stop as well as when to start." The person of practical wisdom *does* know this; he or she can discern when a joke, practical or otherwise, is appropriate and when it's not, when a joke is funny and when it's cruel. But the episode ends with David playing a cruel, extremely unfunny joke on Dawn (and doing so in front of Ricky, the new temp, to boot), pretending to terminate her for stealing Post-It Notes. The "joke" is a complete bust, with Dawn in tears and Ricky in stunned, mortified silence. A person of practical wisdom would know that such a joke is out-of-bounds, but David, despite some cognitive awareness that "there are limits to my comedy," is unable to act on that awareness. In particular, he's unable not to make a joke, even when joking is inappropriate. The problem is that buffoons strive after humor at all costs. It's not that they value humor, it's that they value it too much. In the third episode of series one, David *says* that "there are limits to . . . comedy; there are things I'll never laugh at," but he's not able to recognize these limits in action. He says he'd never laugh at the handicapped, because "there's nothing funny about them." But this suggests that what restrains him isn't the thought that one shouldn't make sport of the handicapped because doing so would be hurtful and cruel. Rather, what restrains David is the mere lack of comic potential that the handicapped present.

The buffoon's willingness to do anything to raise a laugh shows us that he has no sense of shame. While the virtuous person will act properly, she is not, on Aristotle's view, restrained by a sense of shame, which Aristotle regards as "a sort of fear of disrepute" (1128b10–11). She is, rather, motivated by her desire to act in a way that embodies what is fine, noble, and beautiful—what is, in Greek, *kalon*. A person who is still learning to be virtuous might be motivated by a desire to avoid what is shameful or disgraceful. But the virtuous person, who loves what is noble, will not even be tempted to act disgracefully, even if doing so is to her material advantage. A positive motivation, the love of what is *kalon* (rather than the negative motivation of avoiding what is shameful), explains the virtuous person's actions and choices. The buffoon, by contrast, doesn't even have this negative motivation. Unable to tolerate not being the center of attention, he'll do anything to claim it— even if this involves ruining a training session not only by refusing to let Rowan, a specialist in such matters, be in control, but by hijacking the session with his guitar. Buffoonery, thy name is David Brent.

Gareth Keenan: Assistant (to the) Regional Manager, Territorial Army Lieutenant, Boor

Boors, Aristotle tells us, "can neither make a joke themselves nor put up with those who do" (1128a8–9). Now, strictly speaking, this doesn't perfectly fit Gareth, for he tries to joke, and probably regards himself as having a good sense of humor.[7] Our very first encounter with Gareth involves his jokey macho posturing about his drinking plans for the evening: "That'll be a quiet night at the library . . . not!" I'm not sure if "*x* . . . not!" jokes were ever funny, but if they ever were, their time came and went long ago.

In the very first episode we see Gareth satisfying the second component of Aristotle's definition of the boor, for he's unable to put up with Tim's jello-stapler practical joke. Rather than being a good sport, Gareth officiously claims to be "more worried about damage to company property." It's not just his not being able to take a joke that makes Gareth a boor. He's a boor because he's oblivious to the fact that he's being joked with, usually by Tim and Dawn. Their wind-ups of Gareth typically involve spoofing his homophobia: "Could you give a man a lethal blow? . . . If he was coming really hard? . . . Could you take a man from behind?" (I.3), and they're funny precisely because Gareth is so oblivious to them.

Why is Gareth a boor of the oblivious variety? The answer is that he is a literalist, and having a good sense of humor requires not taking things just as they are but recognizing the absurdity of the ordinary. Literalists are just not able to do that. Gareth takes Tim's questions at face value, even though he should be well aware of Tim's tendency to wind him up, because he's incapable of not taking things literally—just as David is incapable of not trying to be funny. Indeed, Tim and Dawn's name for this activity—"winding Gareth up"—describes it perfectly, because Gareth, like a wind-up doll, is incapable of not taking things literally. Like a computer, he's incapable of departing from his literalist programming. It's easy to forget what a complex achievement getting a joke is—and how difficult (if not impossible) it would be for a computer to "get" a joke. When we think of all the background, context, and subtlety that goes into getting a joke, it's no wonder that literalists—and computers—have such trouble getting jokes.

One of the funniest examples of Gareth's literalism occurs at Chasers, the lame nightclub to which the Wernham-Hogg crew repair after a long day of not getting very much done. Donna, the daughter of David's best friend, whom he's recently hired, tells David that she wouldn't sleep with Gareth, not, as David suggests, because he didn't go to university, but because

Donna: He's a little weasel-faced ass.
David: Don't call my second-in-command an ass-faced weasel.
Donna: I didn't. I called him a weasel-faced ass.
David: Same thing.
Donna: No, it's not. [To Gareth] Would you rather have a face like an ass or a face like a weasel?
Gareth: A weasel, probably.

Poor Gareth. He can only take things at face-value. We can well imagine how Tim would respond. And even though Finchy would respond in a predictably lowbrow and misogynist way, he would not take the question literally.

Gareth's literalism, and hence his boorishness, is rooted in his taking things—himself most of all—too seriously. His self-seriousness is most apparent in his regularly regarding himself as "team leader" and "assistant regional manager," in his leading the investigation of the source of the pornographic photo of David, of his annoyingly shredding documents rather than throwing them in the trash, lest competitors come upon them. Perhaps the best example of his self-seriousness is the "Health and Safety Seminar" he conducts for the benefit of Donna. The "fun game [he's] made up" about safe placement of coffee mugs is anything but, and it's plain that Donna doesn't need to practice properly lifting boxes: it's not that hard to grasp.

It's crucial to distinguish being *self-serious* from being *self-important*. The latter implies an arrogance and pomposity that needn't be present in the former, which implies rather an overestimation of the level of concern and care that certain activities merit. Gareth takes the safety seminar too seriously, regarding it as more important than it is, and while he takes himself more seriously than he should, he doesn't regard himself as better than others in virtue of who he is, which is the hallmark of the self-important person.

Consider the difference between Gareth and Simon the computer guy in the fourth episode of series two. Not only is Simon a literalist —Bruce Lee did not fight Chuck Norris in *Enter the Dragon*, he fought him in *Way of the Dragon*—he's a self-important prat: humorless, pedantic, gassing off about his Formula One-worthy go-kart driving. Neither Gareth nor Simon picks up on Tim's quip, "those cats were fast as lightning," but while we loathe Simon in his brief appearance (he's perhaps the least likeable character in the entire series), we have a soft spot for Gareth that isn't explained just by his being familiar to us—that, proverbially, can breed contempt. Gareth is a bit of a fool (as are we all), but he's not vainly self-important—or no more than most of us, anyway.

Though he regularly makes sport of Gareth, Tim recognizes Gareth's seriousness as a virtue (though one that can become a vice when taken to excess), and suggests to Neil that Gareth, not himself, should be David's interim replacement:

> I think you should give it to Gareth. Seriously, I do. He takes things seriously. He's conscientious. He works hard. He's responsible. He knows this place inside and out. Genuinely, I think he might be the man for it.

He's sincere, and it's genuinely touching. Of course, in the background we hear Dirty Bertie, the annoying boner-man, which undercuts Tim's claims a bit (but not enough to dissuade Neil from offering the job to Gareth).

Tim Canterbury: Senior Sales Clerk, Unrequited Lover, Ironic Wit

This brings us at long last to Tim, who embodies the Aristotelian virtue of wit. As we noted earlier, the crucial difference between wit, buffoonery, and boorishness is not quantitative but rather qualitative. It's not that the person of wit tells a moderate number of jokes while the buffoon tells too many and the boor too few, but rather that the genuinely witty person jests appropriately. When Aristotle tells us that "the well-bred man's jesting differs from that of a vulgar man" (1128a20–21), he has not only that in mind, I think, but also the way in which the witty person jests.

We've already noticed that Tim's jesting with Gareth often involves practical jokes and wind-ups, but much of his jesting occurs via detached, understated irony. When Jennifer puts David's call on speaker-phone and thus reveals to all that he isn't firing Chris Finch, Tim's response is a deft, "Does anybody have the right time?" When David is going on and on in his Brently way during a training session about wanting to know what it would be like to live forever, Tim says, to no one in particular, "I think I'm starting to know what that's like." Or consider this exchange, also from the training episode:

> *Rowan*: Gareth, quick trust exercise: [what's your] ultimate fantasy?
> *Gareth*: Hmm?
> *David*: We're just doing the ultimate fantasy, we're all doing it.
> *Gareth*: Two lesbians, probably sisters. I'm just watching.
> *Rowan*: Ok. Um. Tim? Do you have one?
> *Tim*: I'd never thought I'd say this, but can I hear more from Gareth please?

Dawn also displays an ironic outlook on life. Sharing this outlook with Tim helps to explain the affinity between them. Only someone able to get some ironic distance on her own life could tell the story Dawn tells of Lee's proposal of marriage to her:

> He proposed on a Valentine's Day, although he didn't do it face to face, he did it in one of the little Valentine message bits in the paper. I think he had to pay for it by the word, because it just said "Lee love Dawn, marriage?" which, you know, I like, because it's not often you get something that's both romantic and thrifty.

What's striking about Tim's sense of humor—especially in contrast to David's—is how responsive it is to the subtle particularities of the situation. It's not shtick or regurgitated bits from a *Monty Python* episode, as David's so often is. Aristotle tells us that "those who joke in a tasteful way are called ready-witted, which implies a sort of readiness to turn this way and that; for such sallies are thought to be movements of the character" (1128a9–11). Wit is nimble and responsive and suggests both intelligence and a sense of the absurd. David is "the slave of his sense of humor" (1128a34), while Tim is the master of his, not least because he lets the situation dictate whether humor is appropriate (and if so what kind). David, on the other hand, seeks out occasions for displaying his humor, and all too often thinks he's found an occasion when he really hasn't. Sometimes the situation calls for smuggling a pink dildo onto David's desk while he's meeting with Neil; other times the situation calls for gentle wit that puts others at ease—and involves subtle commentary on England's lingering class divisions. We see this when Tim is leading the new employees from Swindon on a tour of the warehouse:

> Ok now guys, we're about to enter a warehouse environment now. I'll just warn you that some of the people in here will be working class. So there may be some arse cleavage. Just find a partner, hold hands and don't talk to anyone.

"The ridiculous side of things is not far to seek" (1128a12–13), Aristotle tells us. No one knows this better than Tim, who only has to look across his desk at Gareth or listen to David to get in touch with the ridiculous.

Though David professes to know what the person of practical wisdom knows—that there are limits to comedy, that some things just aren't funny, or that they aren't funny in these circumstances—it's clear from his actions that he doesn't. Tim, by contrast, has just this practical wisdom. He knows intuitively, for example, that Finchy's mimicking sex with Dawn in front of Dawn—inexplicably inspired by the famous homosexual rape scene from *Deliverance*—is outrageously inappropriate. Tim isn't even tempted to laugh, because it's just not funny; David, of course, cackles uncontrollably.

Indeed, Tim's reaction to the forced humor of Comic Relief Day provides us with both his philosophy of humor and his most characteristic mode of jest, irony:

> Don't get me wrong, I've got nothing against this sort of thing . . . um . . . it's a good cause, but I just don't want to have to join in with someone else's idea of wackiness. It's the wackiness I can't stand. It's like . . . um . . . you see someone outside as they're collecting for cancer research because they've been personally affected by it or whatever, or . . . I don't know . . . an old bloke selling poppies, there's a dignity about that. A sort of real quiet dignity . . . [Cut to his officemates, led by David, hooting and howling as they wrestle a co-worker to the floor and pull his pants down to photograph his privates] . . . and that's what today's all about: dignity, always dignity. [Cut back to Tim, smilingly shaking his head in disbelief]

Tim reacts with incredulity rather than harsh judgment at his colleagues' making no effort at "avoiding pain to the object of their fun" (1128a7). It's as if Tim intuitively recognizes that "most people delight more than they should in amusement and in jesting" (1128a13–14) and, presumably, that the mean is hard to hit and easy to miss.

Lessons Learned

The Office has much to teach us about Aristotle's ethics, for its major male characters illustrate the structure of a character virtue as a mean between extremes. The uncodifiable nature of humor mirrors the uncodifiable nature of morality. There are no explicit rules that a person without a sense of humor can follow to make or appreciate a joke or jest, no step-by-step guides. One can profitably read *Living*

Gluten-Free for Dummies, *Breast-feeding for Dummies*, even—gulp
—*Philosophy for Dummies*, but one cannot profitably read *Having a
Sense of Humor for Dummies*, which explains why there is no such
title. This isn't to say that there isn't helpful advice one can get or give
regarding writing jokes, or that one can't be brought to see the humor
in a situation, but rather that one already has to have a sense of
humor for the advice to make any difference. Just as someone
without a sense of humor—or without a particular kind of sense
of humor (the right one)—can't understand why *The Office* is funny,
someone who lacks the kind of moral vision the virtuous person
possesses can't see what a situation calls for morally. Ludwig
Wittgenstein (1889–1951), one of the greatest of all philosophers,
once said that a serious work of philosophy could be written entirely
as a series of jokes.[8] I'm not sure if he's right about that. But I think
he was on to something when he said:

> So in the end when one is doing philosophy one gets to the point where
> one would like just to emit an inarticulate sound.[9]

I think it's safe to say that when thinking philosophically about *The
Office*, the inarticulate sound the philosopher makes—or even the
ordinary viewer—is a howl of laughter. Or at least a smile.[10]

NOTES

1   For example, the ethics of the great German philosopher Immanuel
    Kant (1724–1804) centers on duty, while the utilitarianism of the
    great English philosopher John Stuart Mill (1806–1873) centers on
    outcomes.
2   For an excellent discussion of an Aristotelian, virtue-based approach
    to business ethics, see Robert Solomon, "Corporate Roles, Personal
    Virtues: An Aristotelian Approach to Business Ethics," *Business Ethics
    Quarterly* 2 (1992): 317–339.
3   Many philosophers, ancient and modern, agree with Aristotle that the
    virtues are morally fundamental. Aristotle's teacher Plato (429–347
    BCE), for example, also had a virtue ethics, as did the great Scottish
    philosopher David Hume (1711–1776 CE). One way in which their
    virtue ethics differ is their differing accounts not just of what the virtues
    are, but of how the virtues are structured.

4   This is the standard way of citing Aristotle. It means that the quote begins on line 36 of the right ("b") column of page 1106 of Aristotle's Greek text as compiled by Augustus Bekker of the University of Berlin in the nineteenth century and ends at line 3 of the left ("a") column on the next page, page 1107. This way of referring to texts that have many translations or editions will be familiar to readers of the Bible, Koran, Shakespeare, etc. (e.g., "Isaiah 53:3" refers to the same passage, regardless of the page number of the translation you happen to be reading). The translation here is W. D. Ross's, as revised by J. O. Urmson, in J. Barnes, ed., *The Complete Works of Aristotle* (Princeton, NJ: Princeton University Press, 1984). Most translations of the *Nicomachean Ethics* will have these "Bekker numbers" (or "Berlin numbers," as they're sometimes called) in the margins.

5   For an excellent discussion of this topic, the interested reader should consult Rosalind Hursthouse's "A False Doctrine of the Mean," *Proceedings of the Aristotelian Society* 81 (1980/81): 57–72, reprinted in Nancy Sherman, ed., *Aristotle's Ethics: Critical Essays* (Lanham, MD: Rowman & Littlefield, 1999).

6   What Americans would call "season" two.

7   It perhaps fits Dwight K. Schrute even better. He never jokes, unless he's had a head injury.

8   Norman Malcom, *Ludwig Wittgenstein: A Memoir* (New York: Oxford University Press, 1958), p. 29.

9   *Philosophical Investigations*, 3rd edn. (Oxford: Blackwell, 1967), §261.

10 I am grateful to my friends and colleagues Erica Benson, Geoffrey Gorham, Mary Novaria, and Stuart Rachels, and my editor Jeremy Wisnewski for their very helpful comments on earlier versions of this essay. And, of course, to Ricky Gervais and Stephen Merchant for creating *The Office* in the first place. Or, as David Brent would say, "Wank you very much."

MEMO 2
KNOW THYSELF!

6

Pam and Jim on the Make: The Epistemology of Self-Deception

Stefanie Rocknak

You might think that with all of its confessional moments—those times when the characters are interviewed alone with the never-seen "documentary team"—that *The Office* would be a half an hour of scathingly honest self-evaluation. Hardly. Instead, we are treated to a brilliantly exaggerated display of self-deception. Realistically, the show is mostly about the way we lie to ourselves. For instance, we might insist on telling ourselves that we work at a meaningful job, when we *don't*; think of the office staff's glorious employer: *Dunder-Mifflin*. Or, we might fool ourselves into thinking that we are powerful and important, when we *aren't*; think of Michael and Dwight. Or, we might tell ourselves that we've fallen in love with the right person, when we *haven't*; think of Jim, Pam, Kelly, and Toby. And so on.

But as much as I'd like to talk about *all* of the various instances of self-deception that plague *The Office*, including the almost endearing cloud of delusion that hangs over Michael's head, or Dwight's malignantly inappropriate self-image, I just don't have enough room (my editor is bitching enough as it is). So instead, I'll focus on the self-deception that concerns Pam and Jim, those misbegotten love-pigeons. But I'm not so much concerned with a psychological, or even cognitive approach. Instead, my interests are "epistemological."[1] So, I'll decipher just what it means to say that at one level, Pam appears to *know* that she's in love with Jim, while at another level, she vigorously insists that she *knows* she's not, largely because she thinks she's supposed to be in love with Roy (seasons 1–2). And, for most of season 3, probably much to the audience's malicious delight, the tables are turned: Jim appears to *know*, at least at some level, that he's still in love with Pam, but at another level, he insists that he *isn't*. Instead, he occupies himself by diligently going through the motions of dating Karen. So, the epistemological problem we've got on our hands is: How can you simultaneously know and *not* know?

Epistemology 101: A Crashed Crash-Course

I initially wrote a seven-page introduction to epistemology for this chapter, but the editors slashed it. Maybe because they thought I went on too long, or possibly because they thought you couldn't hack it— you'd get bored, or you just wouldn't understand it. So you're just going to have to live with the fact that, ala a nifty chart, I'm going to *stipulate* distinctions among knowledge, hypotheses, mistakes, and opinions. Keeping these distinctions squarely in mind will help us to sort through our problem (how can you simultaneously know and not know?):

Different kinds of claims

Knowledge	Mistake	Hypothesis/Theory	Opinion
Confirmed by the evidence, empirical and/or rational[2]	Discounted by the evidence, empirical and/or rational[3]	*Might* be confirmed by the evidence one day (empirical and/or rational)[4]	Will *never* be confirmed or discounted by the evidence, empirical and/or rational[5]

Damning the Evidence

How very much in love they are: everyone knows but Pam?

Although the pilot episode takes place well after Jim and Pam started working together, we can bet that Pam started cheating on her fiancé Roy the minute she met Jim. At least in her head. The reason is pretty straightforward. Jim, unlike the simple-minded, but somehow brutishly attractive Roy, *gets* Pam. In fact, Roy—Pam's boyfriend since high school—really has no clue about what makes Pam tick. Maybe it's because he has such a hard time listening to her, both in terms of what she actually says and in terms of reading her body language. But the *evidence*, both empirical and rational, is there for the taking. It's just that Roy doesn't really seem to be interested in *knowing* who Pam is, or is incapable of processing the evidence. Pam seems to think that it's the former when she barks in the Chili's parking lot (in regard to some issue we aren't privy to): "If you [Roy] would have *asked* me that, you'd *know*" ("The Dundies").

So it's no surprise that Roy has no idea that Pam deeply despises her job at Dunder-Mifflin. But the audience *knows* that Pam *really* wants to be an illustrator, simply because she presents us with the appropriate evidence—she *tells* us that: "Most little girls don't dream about growing up to be a receptionist" (confessional moment; Pilot Episode). But *we're* not the only ones who know this. Jim does too. Evidently, Pam told him or he just figured it out, using *common sense*. In fact, Pam tells us in the same confessional session that Jim not only "thinks [my illustrations] are good," but "he's *onto* me"— he *knows* me. Obviously, Jim's been carefully, if not obsessively, collecting all the evidence he can get on Pam. Meanwhile, Roy tells Jim's season 2 girlfriend, Katie, that Pam "was totally Miss Artsy Fartsy in high school—she wore a turtleneck and everything" ("Booze Cruise"). Right—so much for understanding and respecting Pam's talent and self-image.[6]

But *Jim* listens to Pam, he *knows* Pam (he's "onto" her), and, more importantly, Pam *knows* he *knows*. Think of Jim's teapot-gift to Pam, which was stuffed with trivia pertaining to her more intimate likes and dislikes ("Christmas Party"). Jim may as well have scrawled on the outside: "*See*, I understand you and am fascinated by the smallest detail about you." Ironically though, this is part of what seems to matter in wildly emotional affairs of the heart; presenting evidence—carefully acquired through rational thought and/or empirical data—that confirms that each partner truly gets the other one. And, equally importantly, *accepts* what they get, if not occasionally thrills in it.

Not surprisingly, Pam isn't frightened by Jim's interest and understanding, his *knowing* her. Rather, there are moments where it's pretty clear to both Jim and the audience that Pam *likes* it that Jim gets her. In fact, it's not until the third episode of season 1, "Basketball," that we see Pam smile at *anyone* besides Jim. Up until then, her facial responses to Roy are almost identical to those she gives to Michael; reflecting what we—in light of the evidence—can surmise are her feelings of "who is this stupid %$#ing moron who doesn't get me?"

So it's no real surprise that Pam's as fascinated with Jim as he is with her. They are "onto" each other. But the evidence for Pam's fascination with Jim is much more covert; after all, she's "committed" to her fiancé Roy. Regardless, thanks to the stealthy "documentary" crew, we see Pam eagerly listening to Jim's every word and laughing at all of his jokes. And when they're not chattering away about plots to humiliate Dwight, we see Pam intently watching his every move from the safety of her battleship of a desk. Even more condemning, the camera crew catches her examining Jim's bedroom during an after-work office party, carefully and quietly cataloguing every detail about Jim's most intimate personal space ("Email Surveillence"). Pam's in love, and the audience *knows* it. So does Jim. And this isn't just a hypothesis, or worse still (you irritating postmodernists), an opinion, we *know* this, based on the evidence, based on *common sense*.

By season 2, the rest of the office (with the exception of the perpetually oblivious Michael)[7] *knows* it as well. Everyone, it seems, is "onto" the Pam and Jim love connection. In fact, even prickly Angela indulges herself in a private game called "Pam Pong," which consists of keeping track of how many times Jim sidles up to Pam at her desk ("Office Olympics"). Roy also knows, and pretty much attacks Jim in "Diversity Day" and "The Alliance," when he catches the two at one of their many intimate over-the-desk chats.[8] And at Jim's party during the "Email Surveillance" episode, Pam, on a mission to dig up dirt on the alleged Dwight/Angela affair, asks Phyllis about "secret office romances." But Phyllis thinks that by asking this, Pam's actually confessing about her relationship with Jim. Similarly, Jim is asked by the usually silent camera crew about these "secret office romances" ("Performance Review"). Yet Jim deftly fends off the question, asking them to grill Pam instead. After all, Pam is *technically* involved in an office romance with Roy, since he works downstairs in the warehouse. But Jim's real message seems to be: Ask *Pam*, she's just as involved in this mess as I am—at the very least, we've been embroiled in a full-on *emotional* affair.

But then there's Pam. She consistently rejects Jim, even after—as Jim puts it—he "lays it on the line, *twice*" ("The Convention").

Common sense tells us that there are two plausible explanations for Pam's behavior (read: what I'm about to suggest is *not* an opinion).

Possibility (1): She *does* know that she's in love with Jim, but from her perspective, love just isn't enough, despite comments like: "If you left, Jim, I'd blow my brains out" ("Halloween"). She could think this for lots of reasons. First (at least in seasons 1–2, and in the last part of season 3), her relationship with Roy might provide her with security and comfort, if not familiarity. Keep in mind that she's been with him since she was a teenager; "we have such a solid foundation," she dutifully remarks in "Business School." Second, Roy doesn't challenge Pam to follow her dream to be an illustrator, and this might be a good thing: dream-following is almost always harder than answering phones. Third, as we saw, Jim really gets Pam, he *knows* her. As a result, she can't hide from him. But, at times, this might be really disconcerting, maybe even invasive, possibly leading her to think things like: "What if he found out absolutely everything about me and turned out to be disappointed (or vice versa); then I would be left with no one!" Fourth, Pam might think that Jim's just not "cool," or "manly" enough. So any public relationship with him might do irreparable damage to her *reputation*; consider how obsessed she is with the "dorkyness" of his high school photo ("Email Surveillance," "Christmas Party"). Fifth, Pam might just be afraid of losing *control*. We all know that falling in love is a kind of surrendering, a kind of helplessness, and to lots of us, that's just downright terrifying. I mean, *yuck*, who wants to be a slave to an emotion—how *irrational*! What would Spock think? So it's no wonder that Pam says (after her lame season 3 reconciliation with Roy): "I'm really happy to be back with Roy—it shows maturity and dignity" ("Business School"). Sixth, it could be that despite the fact that she knows she's in love with Jim, she just can't bring herself to devastate Roy. Despite his lack of understanding and general disregard for her true nature, she may, nevertheless, *love* him—he might be a giant blockhead, but he's *her* blockhead. They *do* have a lengthy history together. So, in light of this love-inspired guilt, her affection for Jim might seem like some kind of fundamentally immoral habit—an unwanted *compulsion*. Choosing Jim over Roy would be the *immoral* choice, the selfish choice.[9]

Possibility (2): Although Pam *does* know that Jim's "onto" her—i.e., gets her in all her gory detail—at *some* level, she *doesn't* seem to know that (a) Jim's hopelessly *in love* with her and worse still (b) that she's *in love* with Jim.

Which possibility is right? It's number 2. The writers have been trying to convince us that at least on *some* level, Pam *doesn't* know that she's in love with Jim. Here's the evidence. First, Pam persistently insists that she and Jim are just good friends. "We're *friends*," she exclaims to Angela after being told about Pam Pong, to which Angela snidely replies, "Apparently" ("Office Olympics"). And after an awkward moment with Phyllis at Jim's party, Pam tells the camera crew that "Just because two people are hanging out, it doesn't mean that they're *together*, you know, like people can just be *friends*." In fact, she continues, "It was unfair of [Jim and me] to assume that something else could be going on [with Dwight and Angela]" ("Email Surveillance"). Similarly, in "Hot Girl," she insists that "Jim's a great guy, he's like a *brother* to me" (read: he's *not* like a lover to me). She goes on to say: "I really hope he finds someone" (read: I care about him, but I'm *not* in love with him, so that someone's never going to be me). Sure, it could be that Pam *does* know that she's in love with Jim and is just saying these things to throw *others* off the scent. But if we take a closer look at Pam's facial expressions and body language during these confessional moments, it becomes fairly obvious that she's trying to reassure *herself* that she's just "friends" with Jim, *not* the camera crew (which, since *The Office* is a mock-umentary, is actually the entire planet). Similarly, in season 3, she says to Karen— as if trying to reassure Karen *and* herself—that "I'm *not* into Jim" ("Ben Franklin"). Finally, why in the world would she force herself to get back together with Roy (late in season 3) if, at some level, she *didn't* know she was in love with Jim? Even *Roy* is blown away by Pam's lack of self-awareness. Late in season 3, after their second break-up, he says: "You're not even going to date the guy?!" ("The Negotiation").

Throughout seasons 1–3, whenever confronted with the evidence, whether it's in terms of acknowledging that Jim's in love with *her*, or vice versa, Pam gets really angry, which, experience tells me, is a classic sign of denial. Consider, for instance, when Jim playfully picks Pam up in "The Fight." Initially, she seems to be delighted by the whole ordeal, but as soon as Meredith spots what is going on, she angrily demands to be put down, as if Meredith's recognition of their affair triggers *Pam's* unwanted recognition of the affair—Pam does not want to be presented with *any* evidence that suggests that she *is* in love with Jim. Or, think of the moment where Jim coyly suggests that they had a "first date" in "The Client," which pisses Pam off, triggering Jim to reply: "At least I didn't leave you at a high school hockey game" (we learn earlier in this episode that Roy *did* accidentally ditch her at a hockey game on their first date). And in the Halloween episode, when things seem to be getting too close, too dangerous, too *obvious to deny*, Pam suggests that Jim should get a new job (far away from her), a remark that, of course, devastates Jim.

Finally, midway through season 1, Pam's anger and frustration starts to manifest itself in the form of what can only be described as cruel body language. In all cases, this sends the message of, at least, "LOOK, I'm *not* in love with you and am committed to making this (questionable) relationship with Roy work. No matter what. So buzz off Jim." We see the first case of this in "Basketball." Immediately after Jim and Pam blithely fight over whose team is going to win— Jim's or Roy's—Pam kisses Roy in front of Jim, as if to say, "*Roy* wins *my* game, my *heart*." And at the end of the episode, after Jim has given it everything he's got to impress Pam (and she *was* impressed; wildly clapping for all of Jim's on-court triumphs), she purrs to Roy, well within earshot of Jim, "Let's get you [Roy] into a tub." "What the hell does *that* mean?" Jim had to have thought, especially after all their kidding around and secret stolen looks into each other's eyes. In light of the evidence, it must mean something like: "Jim, maybe you've got all the appearances of 'winning,' yeah, you might seem to be more *appropriate* for me, but I'm in love with good old Roy here, not you. I'm not, I'm not, *I'm not*." Why the writers didn't have Jim vomit on the spot is beyond me.

How Very Much in Love They Still Are: Everyone Knows But Jim?

The writers of *The Office* are well aware that most normal people can only take so much, so in season 3, they have Jim transfer out of the Scranton branch. He has to get away from her. But this doesn't make for much of a show (even with Michael and Dwight carrying on as they do), so Jim comes back just a few episodes later. Yet rather than return unarmed, he comes back fully equipped with his new girlfriend, Karen.

However, Jim's efforts to make this relationship with Karen work are half-hearted at best. Although there are a couple of times where Jim returns the favor of Pam's cruelty—openly acknowledging his relationship with Karen in front of her—he ends up telling his benighted new lover that he's still got feelings for Pam ("The Return"). Meanwhile, he slides right back into his old habit of ganging up on the local-office-jerk with Pam (in this case, it's Andy, since Dwight has been temporarily fired ("The Return")). But as we all know, this is just an excuse for Jim and Pam to spend time together. Jim *knows* he is still in love; he feels it, and that's evidence enough.[10]

The Epistemology of Self-Deception

It's pretty obvious that Jim's an anthology of callow honesty, persistence, and maybe even stupidity. After all, he did come back to Scranton; you'd think that he'd just let it go. Pam, on the other hand, is a clear-cut example of self-deception (at least until the very end of season 3).[11] At *some* level, she *doesn't* seem to know that she's in love with Jim. But on another level, it's obvious that she *does* know. This is because like Jim, she *feels* it, and that's evidence enough. And *we* know that she has these feelings because of her behavior and body language. In fact, this is precisely why the rest of the office, including Jim, knows that Pam is in love. So, somehow, Pam has to be *ignoring* what she knows; she has to be *lying to herself* about what she knows, and then believing in those lies.

In her case then, and in others like it, we're dealing with *two* kinds of knowledge and a form of unjustified belief:

Knowledge (1): Knowledge of the facts (for example, Pam's knowing that she's in love with Jim).

Unjustified Belief: Telling yourself that you *don't* know the facts and then, somehow, *believing* in that lie (for example, Pam's lie "I'm not in love with Jim, *I'm not*"). However, it just doesn't make good sense to believe in something that you know is a mistake, is *false*. So this belief is *unjustified*, or in other words, it's *unreasonable*. It's *irrational*.

Knowledge (2): The knowledge that you're *ignoring* what's actually true. This knowledge, which is actually an unwanted realization, is usually accompanied with anger and outrage (for example, Pam thinking something like: "Oh my God, I *am* in love with him. Quick, before I accidentally tell him, do something cruel and chase him away").

So those are the two kinds of knowledge that are generally involved in self-deception, where the second emerges from the attempt to cover up the first. But you might wonder: How in the world could we get ourselves to *believe* in the lies that we tell ourselves? It's not that hard. In fact, ironically, when we're desperate to deceive ourselves, we often try to make our actions *seem* reasonable by appealing to— you guessed it—a set of reasons. In fact, those reasons might even be genuine knowledge claims! Remember, for example, the six reasons listed in possibility (1); some of them *were* knowledge claims. For instance, it's *true* that dream-chasing is usually pretty damn hard. And it's *true* that falling in love usually means losing some control, and that's disconcerting. And it's *true* that Roy would be hurt if Pam left him. So these all seem like good, pragmatic reasons why Pam *shouldn't* be in love with Jim: it's difficult, scary and hurtful to others. So when Pam tells herself, "I'm *not* in love with Jim," she could also be thinking "because, if I *were*, it'd be too difficult, scary and hurtful. So I'm not."

But "I *should* not" is not the same as "I *am* not."[12] So even if Pam's using these genuine knowledge claims (these *reasons*) to try to rationally justify her belief in the lies that she tells herself, her actions are still *irrational*. They are constructed out of a will to *ignore* the evidence, a will to lie. How "rational" is that?

Worse still, it's always possible that we don't try to rationalize our lies with genuine knowledge claims. Instead, we might make a somewhat frantic appeal to hypotheses, opinions, mistakes, or any combination of the three (recall the chart). For instance, as mentioned in possibility (1), Pam could be trying to rationalize her belief that she *isn't* in love with Jim by telling herself that he might damage her reputation. But at best, this is a hypothesis. Pam doesn't *know* this (besides, why should Pam be *so* concerned with her reputation?). Or, Pam might think, "Even though I'm mysteriously bewitched by Jim, he's really not that attractive." But this is an opinion; some think that Jim's attractive, some don't, and some just don't care. Or, Pam might think, "He doesn't love me *enough*, and so, could abandon me at the worst possible moment." Clearly, based on the evidence, this is a mistake; Jim seems willing to stick by Pam no matter what—even in the face of her cruelty (stupid Jim).

But regardless of *how* we vainly attempt to rationalize an irrational belief, there are moments where the evidence is substantial enough to make it obvious that we're actually *lying to ourselves*. Remember, this is where the *second* kind of knowledge kicks in; the knowledge that we're liars. It's no wonder, then, that this self-realization makes us really angry, and worse still, sinks us into despair (how happy does Pam look to you?). In fact, it's precisely this kind of anger and despair that makes it so difficult for many of us to watch *The Office*. By presenting case after case of exaggerated self-deception—so poignantly manifest in the Jim-Pam nightmare—the show reminds us of the lies that we, the audience, tell *ourselves* to make it through our largely uneventful, mundane, and disingenuous lives; an insight that most of us would just as soon avoid. But this is also what makes it such a great show—it's *honest* in way that we can't be.

NOTES

1   *Epistemology* is Greek for the "study of knowledge." So, in this chapter, I'm mostly interested in how we may approach the phenomenon of self-deception from the standpoint of a *theory of knowledge*.

2   Empirical evidence consists of what we *sense*, which may not only include the information that we get through our five senses (touch, taste, etc.), but may also include our *emotions* (anger, sadness, etc.). Meanwhile, rational evidence consists of, basically, logical thought. For example, when given the two claims "If A then B" and "if B then C," we can conclude "if A then C." When we combine rational thought with empirical evidence, we generally get what's called "common sense." For instance, jumping off the top of the Empire State Building (with no safety gear) *will kill you*; this is *common sense*, it isn't a matter of opinion. Disagree? Then I dare you to try.

3   For example, what if someone insists that "It's boiling outside," while the temperature read 10 degrees? This claim would clearly be *false*. In other words, it would be a mistake (of course, if someone had a raging fever, it might *seem* like it's boiling out. Nevertheless, we'd hustle her inside and cover her up because we know that thanks to her illness, she's *mistaken*).

4 Claims about the origins of the universe (e.g., the "big bang theory") are examples of hypotheses and/or theories—they are not confirmed as true, but one day, we hope that they will be.

5 Consider, for instance, the claim: "Angela thinks that Dwight is hot." It's true that Angela thinks this, but it's neither true nor false that Dwight is hot—some think he is, while others don't, I mean, they *really, really* don't. And some just don't care.

6 It's no surprise that late in Season 3, in what appears to be a transparent effort to get Pam back, Roy tells the camera: "What do I think is sexy? Pam's art" ("Ben Franklin"). In other words, Roy's trying to let Pam know (well after the engagement has been broken off) that he *does* get her, that *he's* onto her too.

7 Michael finds out only after Jim, in a moment of especially acute despair, foolishly tells him ("Booze Cruise").

8 And of course in Season 3, Roy *really* attacks Jim, after Pam tells him that they kissed ("The Negotiation").

9 If these possibilities were true, and Jim was aware of them, he would have to be absolutely devastated, regardless if he shows it or not. It would mean that his "lover" thinks that he is (1) disruptive, (2) too challenging, (3) invasive, (4) not popular enough, (5) scary, and (6) at best, a very bad temptation. So, although Pam might think that she's doing the "right thing" by protecting Roy, she has to be aware that she's simultaneously destroying Jim—making the "moral" choice here not so immediately obvious.

10 Remember that in my Crashed Crash-Course to Epistemology I pointed out that *feelings* can count as evidence.

11 Pam finally faces the truth in "Beach Day," spilling her guts to the whole office (including Jim). But don't worry, the writers will probably have her crawl back into her shell in Season 4. And even if they don't, sometimes people *can* wake up and face themselves. But to some (like Pam), this is as hard as walking across a pit of burning coals!

12 And so attempts to "rationalize" your way out of being in love never work. Rationalizing might prevent someone from *requiting* or otherwise *acting* on a relationship, but it will never stop the *feeling*. The only remedy is to discover something unbearable about your love object, to come to know something about him or her that you simply can't accept. Ironically, the obsessive desire to know your love object has the power to turn on itself; love is always capable—and, perhaps, is the *most* capable—of destroying itself.

What Dwight Doesn't Know Can't Hurt Him—Or Can It? Deception and Self-Deception in *The Office*

Randall M. Jensen

In the cubicled universe of Dunder-Mifflin's Scranton branch, Dwight Schrute secretly holds the seemingly important title of "Assistant Regional Manager," which is in fact an upgrade from his previous post of "Assistant *to the* Regional Manager." Of course, we viewers know that both of these titles are empty, for they're merely part of one of the many harebrained schemes Michael Scott has concocted to mollify Dwight and to avoid the actual work of managing an office. Since so many of Michael's plans end in total disaster, it's surprising that this deception is so effective. Why then is this particular ploy a success? In part, the explanation is quite simple: Dwight is astonishingly gullible. Jim Halpert, Dwight's comic nemesis, spends a fair amount of time pulling pranks on Dwight, whether it's by convincing him that today is Friday when it's really Thursday or by enlisting Pam's help to persuade Dwight that Jim has telekinetic powers. Dwight's an easy and absolutely irresistible target.[1]

But is that the whole story here? I don't think so. Dwight also believes in his false promotion because he so desperately wants to be elevated above his peers. In this respect, he cooperates in the deception. Deception and self-deception are at the heart of many of the most memorable and hilarious Dwight Schrute moments—the ones fans love to talk about around the water cooler at their own versions of Dunder-Mifflin. And since deception and self-deception are very important philosophical notions, too, it'll be well worth our while to spend some time exploring them in the context of *The Office*.

Dwight Meets Kant

Ethics (sometimes called moral philosophy) is the branch of philosophy that concerns right and wrong, good and bad, and how we should live our lives. Given how much we argue about such things, it goes without saying that this area is full of controversy. Yet if we can start anywhere in ethics, we can probably start with the claim that *there's something wrong with lying.* No doubt lying would make most people's top ten list of types of wrongdoing. But what *makes* lying wrong? And is it *always* wrong to lie?

The philosopher Immanuel Kant (1724–1804) is famous for arguing that it is always wrong to tell a lie. No exceptions. Suppose that Dwight has gone berserk because Jim has managed to put his personalized Schrute bobblehead in a green Jell-O mold. Now armed with his bo staff, Dwight is looking to give Jim a beating as an act of vengeance. He shows up at your house, with his mouth in that familiar grimace and his eyes bulging out of his head, and asks you if Jim is inside.[2] In fact, Jim *is* in your house, but he's begging you to tell Dwight otherwise. Not so much because he's afraid of Dwight, of course, but because he just doesn't want to deal with him until he calms down. Kant's view is that you've got to tell Dwight the truth, even under these circumstances. Even if you think Dwight really is going to kill Jim, Kant thinks you still have to tell the truth.[3] But why? What is so objectionable about a lie? How could it possibly be wrong to lie to save a life?

Kant believes that any kind of deception is morally off-limits because it violates the moral law. He explains this violation in two complementary ways.[4] Kant's first explanation is somewhat like the familiar moral objection, often expressed by your parents, that begins with "What if everyone did that?" If you're thinking of telling a lie, Kant asks you to identify the principle (or *maxim*, in Kantian lingo) on which your lie would be based and then consider what would happen to your attempt to tell a lie if *everyone* were to adopt that principle.

So imagine Michael is thinking about lying to Dwight. Why? Well, knowing Michael, the principle he's following might look like this: *I will tell a lie whenever it saves face.* What if we *universalize* that principle? That is, what if everyone lies whenever it saves face? Kant's claim is that if everyone were to adopt this principle, lying would be so pervasive and our trust in what others say would be so eroded that Michael's attempt to lie would be impossible. In a world where everyone lies, no one could get away with a lie. What this shows is that in trying to lie to Dwight, Michael is trying to play by rules that apply to him but not to everyone else. And this shows that his action would be immoral, for Kantian morality is *universalizable*: its rules apply to everyone. And one of those rules, according to Kant, absolutely prohibits any form of lying or deception.[5]

Kant's second explanation of the moral law prohibits deception because when you deceive someone, you treat that person as a mere means to an end rather than treating her as an end in herself. That is, you treat her as a thing—an instrument to be used to carry out your will—rather than as another person like yourself. When I deceive you I make you a part of my scheme without your knowledge instead of asking you to be involved in whatever I'm doing. Of course, often that's the very point of the deception, isn't it? Jim and Michael often lie to Dwight to get him to do something he wouldn't otherwise do. From Kant's point of view, by doing this they treat Dwight as an object and fail to treat him as a member of the moral community. And, according to Kant, lying is always wrong for this reason.[6]

Michael's Noble Lie?

Kant gives us some powerful reasons to think that there's something wrong with deception. But can it *always* be wrong to deceive someone? The long list of people who disagree with Kant begins with Plato (427–347 BCE). In the first book of one of Plato's most influential dialogues, the *Republic*, his character Socrates is considering the claim that justice can be defined as a matter of following a few simple rules, such as returning what you borrow and telling the truth.[7] Socrates refutes this claim by presenting a clever *counterexample* (which is just what it sounds like: an example that counters a claim someone has made). Would it be just (or morally right) to return Dwight's spud gun to him if he's out of his head when he asks for it back?[8] Obviously not. So it's not always right to return what you borrow. And it isn't always right to tell the truth, either, Socrates says, because you might lie to someone who's lost his mind, too. In general, it seems, life's just too complicated for a simple list of rules to suffice for living morally. No matter what list of rules we develop, we'll always be finding ourselves in situations where the rules don't seem to measure up.

In the *Republic* Plato goes so far as to identify a lie that is both useful and noble. The Socrates character distinguishes a true lie from a lie in words and claims that the latter is not nearly as significant as the former (Plato, 63–64). A true lie—hated by gods and human beings—is a lie that I hold in my soul, a lie I tell to myself about what's most important. Such a lie is always to be avoided. But merely lying with my lips isn't the same thing. Socrates says that a verbal lie can actually be quite useful as a political tool, even comparing such a lie to a drug prescribed for the health of society. Later on in the dialogue, Socrates gives a classic example of such a lie: the citizens of the ideal city he describes will come to accept their position in life because we tell them a "noble lie" about their having different metallic natures, some gold, some silver, and some iron or bronze (Plato, 99–100). This isn't a true story, of course, but it's good for the whole city that people believe this, because it promotes the city's order and harmony.

Is Michael's ongoing lie to Dwight about his position in the office a useful and noble lie of this sort? And if so, is it a morally acceptable lie? Let's think about this for a bit. Plato's useful and noble lie is meant to "medicate" the city by promoting its order, stability, and moral health. Does Michael's lie have that function in the Scranton office? It doesn't seem so. Because of his belief in his elevated position, Dwight often gets in people's way by questioning them, trying to order them around, carrying out unnecessary investigations, and so on. Think of Dwight's response to finding half of a joint in the parking lot in "Drug Test." Or just remember what happens when Dwight is entrusted with the responsibility of choosing a new health care package for the office employees in "Health Care." So this lie doesn't seem all that useful to Dwight's co-workers, although it is useful to Michael, since it solves some of his problems with Dwight. But if Michael deceives Dwight only because it's the path of least resistance, it's hard to see how that kind of lie is noble or morally justified. In fact, it seems like a pretty standard case of lying to someone for selfish motives.

On the other hand, mightn't Michael lie about the promotion at least in part for Dwight's sake? Michael does seem to care about Dwight, although he may not always realize this about himself and he may not express his concern in a normal or reasonable way. Think of Michael's awkward trip to bring Dwight back to Dunder-Mifflin from his self-imposed exile at Staples. Moreover, the moment when Michael tells Dwight that he is no longer merely the Assistant to the Regional Manager but will now serve as a full-fledged Assistant Regional Manager comes at the end of a very difficult day in their relationship ("The Fight"). Each has physically humiliated the other and Dwight has even requested that his emergency contact be changed from Michael Scott to "the hospital." So this particular deception is designed not just to save face or avoid work; it's meant to restore their friendship. No doubt there are morally preferable ways of doing this, such as apologizing and communicating honestly with one another, but this bit of deception may just be the best that Michael and Dwight can do. Remember that Plato thinks you might not tell the whole truth to someone who is insane. Dwight isn't (that) insane, of course, but maybe he's just strange enough that a bit of dishonesty is required in dealing with him. Perhaps Michael's lie has a bit of nobility in it after all.

It's Just a Prank!

At other times, however, it's all too clear that Michael lies to Dwight for reasons that have nothing at all to do with what's good for Dwight. And of course Jim's pranks often involve deceiving Dwight about something or other, often with Pam's assistance. In fact, sometimes all Jim has to do is offer Dwight a bit of carefully chosen misinformation and the show is on.

In "Phyllis' Wedding," Jim casually observes that there must be a lot of wedding crashers present. As a result, Dwight interrogates Phyllis' Uncle Al, who has dementia, and then kicks him out of the wedding because he can't answer Dwight's test questions about the makeup of the wedding party. In "Dwight's Speech," Jim casually mentions to Dwight that he majored in public speaking (which isn't true) and then gives Dwight some information that leads to the priceless spectacle of Dwight delivering a Mussolini speech at a sales convention. With his fists pumping the air and pounding the lectern, Dwight shouts, "Salesmen of Northeastern Pennsylvania, I ask you, once more, rise and be worthy of this historical hour!" Surprisingly, this goes over well, as the speech causes the cheering crowd to leap to their feet! In other episodes, Jim convinces Dwight that he's receiving faxes from his future self, that an unsuspecting Benihana waitress actually wants Dwight to give a graphic description of how to butcher a goose, that the CIA wants Dwight to go on a secret mission, that there really is a device called a "gaydar," and that there's an abandoned baby in the women's restroom (which leads to an awkward moment between Dwight and Meredith). None of these very funny pranks would have been possible without deceptions, some small and some large. But how should we think about all this from a moral point of view?

Perhaps Jim is simply cruel and selfish. He doesn't like Dwight. And he's bored with his job and is looking for anything to break the monotony. As much as we like Jim, there's more than a bit of truth in all this, I'm afraid. But things are more complicated as well. First, Dwight isn't a helpless and innocent victim. If he were, we'd think even less of Jim. But Dwight knows that he and Jim are in an ongoing conflict. And he's quite capable of taking care of himself. Dwight even gets the best of Jim sometimes, as when he steals Jim's big sale ("Diversity Day") or when he denies knowing anything about their so-called alliance when Jim is trying to explain it to an angry Roy ("The Alliance"). If we were to construct a "just prank theory" to govern office conflicts in the way that classical just war theory governs military conflicts, one of its principles would be that one shouldn't prank innocent bystanders. And Dwight doesn't fall into this category, so perhaps he's a legitimate target for pranking. In fact, Dwight annoys and frustrates a lot of people in the office. Even Angela was in the habit of filing complaints against Dwight before they started their secret relationship. So perhaps Jim is right when he observes that Dwight *deserves* all that happens to him ("Conflict Resolution"). Maybe Dwight's aggressive and obnoxious behavior should be seen as the opening hostilities, with Jim's deceptive pranks serving as a justified response.

Of course, as bitter as they may be, office conflicts aren't wars. So perhaps we should try to see such pranks in a more positive light. Perhaps pranking is a healthy part of the life of a community. Dwight and Jim are forced to spend a lot of time in fairly close quarters. If honest and meaningful conversation is out of the question, as it often seems to be for Dwight, this sort of rivalry and one-upmanship might just be the only kind of friendship Dwight is capable of. By playing pranks on Dwight, maybe Jim is relating to him and including him in the office in the only way that seems possible. In some perverse way, Dwight even seems to enjoy these pranks. And if this ongoing conflict between Jim and Dwight is mutually consensual, maybe Jim isn't treating Dwight as a mere means to his own ends after all. Maybe some office pranks—but not all—are morally acceptable.

What Dwight Doesn't Know . . .

"What you don't know can't hurt you," the expression goes. But is it true? The ancient Greek philosopher Epicurus (341–270 BCE) thought so. Epicurus was a hedonist, which means he thought that only pleasure is good and only pain is bad. Since pleasure and pain are essentially qualities that are *felt*, this means that something can be good or bad for you only if you experience it. Epicurus relied on this view of good and bad in developing his famous argument against the fear of death. Death cannot be a bad thing, he thought, because you never experience it. For whenever death arrives, you've already departed! The process of dying might be pretty awful, because you'll experience that. But death itself should be nothing to us. If we realize that, according to Epicurus, we'll be better able to live a life of happiness and tranquility.

And it isn't just death that should be nothing to us. *Anything* that we don't experience should be nothing to us and so not worth our time and worry. If Jim or Michael deceive Dwight, then, and he knows nothing of it, he hasn't been harmed. Nothing bad has happened to him. And this might be another reason to think that some deceptions might not be wrong, or might not be seriously wrong, anyway. If a deception goes undetected it cannot be regarded as a harm to the one who was deceived.

84

Is it right to say that deception doesn't harm you unless you find out about it? And that if there's no harm, there's no foul? Let's consider a significant deception rather than one that might be written off as harmless even if it were discovered. What if Angela were only pretending to care for Dwight as part of a long-term prank orchestrated by Jim? Surely that would be very wrong, wouldn't it? And it'd be wrong even if Dwight didn't have a clue and was very much enjoying her affections. So right away we can see that it has to be possible for a deception to be morally wrong even if it isn't experienced as harmful by the one being deceived. Such a deception would show a real moral fault in Angela and Jim. And if Dwight were to find out about this deception, he would be terribly hurt by it. Perhaps the wrongness of a deception can be tied not only to the harm it actually does, but also to the harm it would do if it were to be discovered.

Could we say something stronger here? Maybe Angela would in fact be harming Dwight simply by deceiving him, even if he didn't know a thing about it. It's a bit odd to say that something bad has happened to Dwight only when he finds out about the deception, because he seems to be finding out about something that happened to him some time in the past. Is Angela's deception so bad because it hurts Dwight so much when it's discovered, or does it hurt so much precisely because what he's discovering is that something horrible has (already) happened to him?[9] (Read that again!) Maybe deception is itself a species of harm, different in nature from the harms that consist in the physical and emotional pain we suffer. This would mean Epicurus is wrong to say that all harm must be experienced. And it opens the door to say that Angela's hypothetical betrayal is wrong not only because it reflects her own moral failings, not only because of how it would affect Dwight if he were to find out about it, but first and foremost because of what it is doing to Dwight right now! What we want to say to Angela, I think, is that we can't believe she's doing that to him! And that she's doing something horrible to him even if she's hidden it from him very effectively. And there are other harms that work this way, aren't there? If Dwight embezzles money from Dunder-Mifflin, the financial harm is done when he takes the money, not when he gets caught. Arguably, then, what Dwight doesn't know can hurt him after all. This means that we can't consider a prank harmless just because its victim is unaware of it.

Dwight Deceiving Dwight?

Dwight is deceived by all kinds of people for all kinds of reasons. When Jim deceives Dwight, Pam is often his partner in crime. But Jim may have another unwitting accomplice in Dwight himself. Dwight seems to buy the con about Jim's telekinetic powers ("Casino Night") because he wants to believe that he can have such special abilities, too, to add to his professed ability to raise and lower his cholesterol at will. And he is more than willing to believe in various conspiracies because he's so desperate to be an investigator and a crimefighter rather than a mere salesperson. It's also hard to avoid the conclusion that Dwight works pretty hard to convince himself to believe the very implausible claim that all of his conflicts with Michael during "The Fight" were really a test of his fitness to be Assistant Regional Manager. And it seems that he continues to fool himself into believing that he has an exalted position in the office in spite of the fact that sometimes Michael explicitly tells him that it means absolutely nothing. In such cases, Dwight seems to deceive himself. But how is that possible? And if it's possible, is it morally wrong for Dwight to deceive himself?

One obvious way to begin to think about self-deception is to look to "ordinary" deception, or "other-deception," as we might call it, as a model. Consider the following rough definition of other-deception: to say that Jim deceives Dwight is to say that Jim intentionally helps bring it about that Dwight believes something false. This definition has various elements, each of which seems necessary: an intent to deceive, a causal influence, and a false belief. If any one of these elements is missing, we don't have a genuine case of deception. Thus, for Jim to deceive Dwight, Jim must intend to deceive Dwight, Dwight must acquire a false belief, and Jim must influence Dwight's acquisition of that false belief. With this in mind, perhaps we can simply understand self-deception as a special case of other-deception: To say that Dwight is self-deceived is then to say that *Dwight intentionally plays a role in bringing it about that he himself believes something false.* But this seems paradoxical for a number of reasons.

Why on earth would Dwight intend to make himself believe something he knows to be false? After all, we have lots of good reasons for wanting to have true beliefs. Moreover, *how* could Dwight make himself believe something that he knows is false? Our belief formation processes seem to aim at forming true beliefs. When I find myself becoming convinced that something is true, I find myself believing it whether I want to or not. And if I'm not convinced that something is true, or if in fact I'm reasonably sure that it's false, I don't and I can't believe it. If you're not sure I'm right about this, please attempt the following task: with all your mental might, try to believe that Dwight Schrute is standing right behind you right now.

You can't, can you? Not even if someone offered you a starring role as the newest addition to the Dunder-Mifflin family. (If you *do* believe that Dwight is behind you now, please get help immediately.) We can't just make ourselves believe whatever we want through sheer effort. And we especially can't make ourselves believe that something that we think is false is in fact true via an extraordinary act of will. Whatever self-deception is, and however it works, it'll have to be more indirect, more subtle than this. Dwight does have to deceive himself, not force himself, right?

A Divided Dwight?

Part of the problem here is that we're assuming that Dwight somehow manages to be both the deceiver and the deceived at the same time. How is that possible? To be the deceiver, Dwight has to believe that the belief in question is false. But to be deceived he must come to believe that it's true. Isn't this impossible? Maybe not. What if we were to "divide" Dwight into (at least) two parts, one to deceive and one to be deceived? One kind of division is temporal: we might say that an early Dwight brings it about that a later Dwight is deceived. In a simple case, an early Dwight might try hard not to think about certain unpleasant truths so that a later Dwight will have forgotten them and so be free to believe a falsehood. We might also divide Dwight's psychological self in various ways, yielding Rational-Dwight and Irrational-Dwight; Conscious-Dwight and Sub-Conscious Dwight; Ego-Dwight, Superego-Dwight, and Id-Dwight; and so on. You get the idea. Perhaps Irrational-Dwight, a collection of appetites, urges, and longings, wants very much to be the big man in the office. So he tells Rational-Dwight not to pay any attention to the things that Michael and others say that suggest that his status as

Assistant Regional Manager is a mere facade, and his repeated whispers to Rational-Dwight serve to inflate any possible evidence of his importance to Michael.

What should we make of this idea of a divided self? Plato would be happy enough with it, since he argues in Book IV of the *Republic* that the human soul is made up of three parts: a rational part, a spirited/emotional part, and the appetites (Plato, 121–129), which he later in Book IX compares to a human being, a lion, and a many-headed beast, respectively (Plato, 292–293). So, for Plato, every individual human soul is made up of three different agents, each of which seems to have its own beliefs, desires, and volitions. While we're familiar with such pictures of the self, can we really take them seriously? Imagine a cartoon version of *The Office* with Dwight listening to an angelic mini-Dwight sitting on one shoulder, all garbed in white, wings and all, and then turning to talk to the demonic mini-Dwight on the other shoulder, decked out in devilish red with a pitchfork and tail. Perhaps both are trying to convince big Dwight of what he ought to believe. We use such images as metaphors to express conflict or indecision, but are there actually different agents inside each of us as this picture seems to intimate?

Aren't we awfully tempted to think there just cannot be different agents inside our heads? I seem to experience my conscious self as unified. I'm one person, after all, not a community of two or three people. Wouldn't I know if my self were divided, if I were not a self but rather selves instead? Actually, philosophers don't agree about this. René Descartes (1596–1650) famously argues in Meditation VI that we can perceive through introspection that the human mind (or soul or self) is *simple*, which in this context means that it is not divided into parts in the way that the body is.[10] In fact this is part of his case for *dualism*: the position stating that the mind and the body are two different things. Descartes trusts this perception of the simplicity of the mind because he thinks that the self is transparent and that in introspection we apprehend the nature and contents of our minds directly and immediately and therefore without error. If Descartes is right about these matters, then it seems we cannot try to understand self-deception by thinking of the self as divided.

Unlike Descartes, you and I are likely to think of the mind as the brain. And while we do *experience* a unified consciousness, why should we think that this experience accurately reflects the reality of what's happening in the brain? For one thing, as we all know, the brain is divided into left and right hemispheres. And interesting experiments have shown that these two hemispheres operate more autonomously than we ever would have thought.[11] Furthermore, it turns out that introspection only skims the surface of the brain's activities; much of what the brain is doing is beneath our notice. And whatever introspective capabilities we have seem to exist because they proved useful to the survival of hunter-gatherers rather than because they give us a true picture of our mental processes. Maybe perfectly accurate introspection no more exists in the wild than health care does ("Health Care").

For these reasons, it may make good sense to try to understand the phenomenon of self-deception by figuring out how some system in Dwight's brain works to cause a false belief in him in spite of the work of some other system that provides ample evidence of the truth of this belief. Perhaps what we'll divide is not so much the psychological self that we experience but rather the neurological "self" that is the ground of our experience. And perhaps we won't divide Dwight into component agents, but rather into systems (or modules or processes or subsystems or whatever notion fits best) that can only metaphorically be conceived as agents. If we take this route, self-deception becomes a subject for cognitive science to investigate.

Defending Self-Deception

Let's now think about self-deception from a moral point of view. When Michael deceives Dwight, at least some of the time we blame Michael for it and regard Dwight as the victim of wrongdoing, even if he's an unwitting victim. A self-deceived Dwight seems to be both victim and wrongdoer. Do we therefore blame one part of Dwight and empathize with another? We regard other-deception as morally objectionable. Is self-deception objectionable in the very same way? One of the things at stake here is the extent to which we ought to try to enlighten those who are self-deceived.

Does it even make sense to suggest that Dwight *wrongs* himself when he deceives himself? Dwight cannot steal from himself. It isn't that he can't take something that belongs to himself and make off with it. He could jump into his 1978 Nissan 280Z and drive off with tires squealing. But it can't be wrong to do that, for it's his car. Even if he were to take a sledgehammer to it and break all the windows, it wouldn't be wrong. It might be a really bad idea, of course, but it's not wrong. Can Dwight assault himself? He can hit himself on the head with his nunchuks, which is all too easy to do, but no matter how stupidly he hurts himself, morally speaking, it won't be an assault in the way it would be if Creed were to kick him where it counts. In all seriousness, we don't want people to hurt themselves, and we should try to convince them not to do so, but if someone does injure herself we certainly shouldn't place her in the same moral category as a violent offender.

Maybe morality only governs how we treat *other* people. Maybe we can't wrong ourselves. At the very least, it seems that an action that would be wrong if it were done to someone else isn't going to be as morally serious when done to oneself. If that's right, then even if Dwight somehow succeeds in getting himself to believe something that just ain't true, it won't be wrong in the way lying to someone else would be. This suggests at the very least that self-deception might be much more easily justified than other-deception. While it may not be right to lie to someone else just to keep her happy, it may be both reasonable and morally acceptable for Dwight to deceive himself if that is what's best for him. And if that's so, then perhaps it'd be better for his co-workers to play along with him, pranks and all, rather than cruelly confronting him with the truth about himself. The famous inscription at the Oracle at Delphi reads: "Know Thyself!" And *sometimes* that's really good advice, because seeing ourselves as we really are may be a very good thing for us. But maybe it's *not always* the best advice.

NOTES

1 In "Conflict Resolution," Dwight is infuriated because his many formal complaints against Jim have merely been stored in a box in Toby's office rather than being officially submitted. "Four years of malfeasance unreported!" Dwight exclaims. We're then treated to a nice selection of Halpert's pranks: Jim replaced all of Dwight's pens and pencils with crayons. Jim paid everyone in the office to call Dwight "Dwayne" for a day. Jim tried to convince Dwight he was a murderer by planting a

bloody glove in his desk. Jim tricked Dwight into going into the women's restroom by telling him there was an abandoned baby in there. Jim rigged Dwight's phone so that he knocked himself in the head. Jim fixed Dwight's computer so that it substituted "Diapers" for "Dwight" when he tried to type his name. Jim moved Dwight's desk a little bit every time he went to the bathroom . . . and this is only a small selection!

2   No doubt Dwight appearing at your front door for any reason is a bit frightening. Even when not enraged he's rather intense. As he says in "Conflict Resolution," "I never smile if I can help it. Showing one's teeth is a submission signal in primates. When someone smiles at me, all I see is a chimpanzee begging for its life."

3   This is an *Office*-style version of an example Kant discusses in his essay "On a Supposed Right to Lie because of Philanthropic Concerns," found in Immanuel Kant, *Grounding for the Metaphysics of Morals, with On a Supposed Right to Life because of Philanthropic Concerns*, translated by James W. Ellington (Indianapolis: Hackett, 1993).

4   The following two paragraphs are a simplified rendition of the first two versions of Kant's Categorical Imperative, which can be found in the second section of the *Grounding for the Metaphysics of Morals*.

5   However, we might wonder whether he's right about this. Maybe there's some universalizable principle that allows deception under certain carefully characterized conditions, for example, *I will tell a lie if it's the only way to save an innocent person's life.*

6   Again, some might wonder if Kant is right here. Even if lying is typically wrong because it involves using a person as a means to an end, is this inevitably the case? Mightn't it just be possible to lie to someone and yet to see her as an end in herself? Or mightn't there be some compelling moral reason to lie—to save a life, for example—that would outweigh this Kantian reason against lying?

7   Plato, *Republic*, translated by C. D. C. Reeve (Indianapolis: Hackett, 2004), p. 5. Any further references to the *Republic* will be to this text. Alfred North Whitehead famously said that all of Western philosophy was a series of footnotes to Plato, which is the sort of remark that's not really true but that will be repeated over and over nonetheless.

8   In "Conflict Resolution," as evidence that higher office security measures are called for, Dwight reveals that the duffel bag he brought to work one day contained a "spud gun" that fires potatoes at 60 pounds per square inch.

9   This follows a line of thought developed by Thomas Nagel in "Death," in his *Mortal Questions* (Cambridge: Cambridge University Press, 1979), pp. 4–5.

10 René Descartes, *Discourse on Method and Meditations on First Philosophy*, translated by Donald Cress (Indianapolis: Hackett, 1999).

11 One place to begin to look at the literature on the philosophical implications of commissurotomy (the procedure that severs the connections between left and right cerebral hemispheres) is Thomas Nagel's "Brain Bisection and the Unity of Consciousness" in his *Mortal Questions*, pp. 147–164.

8

Authenticity or Happiness? Michael Scott and the Ethics of Self-Deception

Jonathan Evans and Peter Murphy

Michael Scott has a problem. Actually he has lots of problems. Among them, though, is this one. He is not what he thinks he is. He sees himself as a ladies man; the hip, funny, dashing, popular guy who, when he is not off-the-clock, is "The World's Best Boss." But he is none of these things. Rather, he is self-deceived. This is a feat (of sorts): to preserve his self-image, Michael has to ignore the over-whelming evidence that he is none of the grand things that he thinks he is. Michael is not alone in this. Plenty of other people in *The Office* struggle with the same problem, though maybe not to the same extent. Pam thought she was in love with Roy, but she wasn't. Kelly believes Ryan is marriage material and will be the happy father of many of her children, but he's not, and he won't be. Dwight some-times envisions a thriving Dunder-Mifflin Scranton branch under his rightful, efficient leadership. Not going to happen.

Pam, Kelly, and perhaps even Dwight would probably be better off knowing that what they believe isn't true—but Michael's case is different. Michael probably *wouldn't* be better off knowing the truth about himself. On those occasions when the veil goes up and Michael realizes that he is none of the things he thinks he is, he falls into a depression that he can't get himself out of.

Everyone has this problem to some extent. We think that if we could just be honest with ourselves about our relationships and who we are, then we (and others) would be better off—but sometimes this just isn't so. Michael provides us with a case study: he appears to be one of those people whose happiness requires self-deception. So with Michael in mind let's explore the relation between happiness and authenticity in more detail—and think about what's better, being happy or being ourselves.

Authenticity and Happiness

We might begin to understand an authentic life as a life of self-discovery in which one truly understands who one is and what one's place in the world is. On some accounts self-discovery is indeed a discovery process; the person tries to uncover their inner nature so they can find their unique way of living. The other, more existentialist account, sees self-discovery as a process of self-definition and self-creation; where the individual creates who they are by choosing things for themselves. Regardless of which account is chosen, there is a common recommendation: authentic persons should not define themselves primarily in terms of the goals or expectations of others. This would be to "go along with the herd" or become one of the faceless masses. Philosophers often describe a person as *authentic* when they travel their own route in the process of self-discovery and succeed.

One of the difficulties in understanding authenticity is coming up with appropriate candidates for authentic living to help us focus our understanding. This is particularly difficult when we take a look at the employees of Dunder-Mifflin. Given our preliminary claim about authenticity we would probably have to admit that the person who best fits the idea is Creed! After all, he has no difficulty admitting who he is (often a free-loading thief) and what he does, and appears completely at home with himself. After all, anyone who would regularly own up to smelling bad, being cheap, and cheating at cards can't suffer from too much self-deception. Nor is this a life that others have chosen for Creed: he seems to choose and embrace the life he leads.

If Creed is living the authentic life, many of us might reasonably ask, why bother? Thankfully, we don't yet have a complete picture of what authenticity really is. In fact, many philosophers—if they watched *The Office*—would be horrified by the association of authentic living with Creed. For what makes life authentic isn't just coming to terms with who you are and living with it. Nor is it making a series of odd self-defining choices. There has to be more.

To save themselves from a Creed-like authenticity, philosophers have wanted to connect true self-discovery and awareness (authenticity) with having meaningful relationships and dialogue. Think about this, these philosophers would say: How is it that you really understand who you are as opposed to who you *think* you are? For many of us, this question brings back awkward school experiences where our egos were deflated by a recognition that our self-image was distorted. Hopefully, most of us have been able to make adjustments in our perceptions about ourselves from kind (and unkind!) suggestions and conversations with others. We might discover from a coach or teacher, for example, that though we are good, valuable people maybe we're not cut out to be a star athlete, musician, or actress. These sorts of experiences are widely shared, showing that one of the most powerful tools for learning about oneself is through healthy relationships with others—and especially ones that allow for meaningful conversation. In fact, we can go further—since humans are social animals, to live a life that is an authentically *human* life, social relations are not just an effective means to authenticity, they are part of the very nature of authenticity. So while Creed seems to have gotten to know himself very well without meaningful relationships with others, his is not an authentic human life, since he doesn't appear to have any friends and he doesn't seem to engage in the meaningful conversations that arise among friends.

But let's be careful here. The understanding of authenticity that we seem to be favoring in talking about Creed is the kind that assumes that authenticity is a kind of self-discovery, where one tries to focus on uncovering one's inner nature. On this understanding, it makes plenty of sense to require meaningful relationships with other human beings, since those relationships seem to be the most reliable way of giving us the feedback we need to defeat distorted conceptions of our true selves. But as we pointed out at the beginning, this is not the only way of understanding authenticity, and perhaps not even the most influential way.

This other understanding of authenticity—the "existential" authenticity—is the kind favored by philosophers who view self-creation as the goal. As expressed by the twentieth-century European philosophers Jean-Paul Sartre and Martin Heidegger, at least part of one's quest for the authentic life is a refusal to be defined or co-opted by the norms of others. In fact, the uncritical acceptance of a life constructed by others is the fastest route to inauthentic living. Re-examining Creed's life in light of this existentialist standard may seem to give us reason to fear that perhaps Creed's life is authentic after all.

But actually, regardless of which conception of authenticity one chooses (self-discovery or the existentialist's self-creation), we have no reason to worry. Sure, Creed could say he's his own man, and not one of those mindless morons who follow the herd. But the bottom line is that his type of life is not an authentic *human* life. As much as we might try to avoid falling into uncritical modes of living, we can't completely isolate ourselves from other people and their expectations. To do so would undercut one of the defining characteristics of human life: social relationships.

So on to authenticity-challenged Michael. Like Creed, Michael has no deep relationships that give him the love and respect that we human creatures, by nature, desire. Nor does he receive the feedback that can be so valuable in helping people know themselves better. Instead, Michael uncritically accepts certain "social standards" for success: a keen sense for interjecting locker-room humor into any social situation, the continuing quest to ensure that power relationships between the genders always favor males (except when someone else is being sexist), and developing activities that aspire to the goal of equal opportunity humiliation of all persons regardless of gender, race, or sexual orientation. When we examine these standards later we will refer to them as Packer norms (a name honoring the standards developed by Todd Packer—not Green Bay football fans.)

Let's look at Michael's life more carefully, so that we are clear about the sources of his inauthenticity. The first stop is Michael's lack of meaningful social relationships. If you're skeptical that Michael doesn't have any meaningful social relationships, think about who Michael would consider his closest friends: Dwight, Jan, and Todd Packer. All of these relationships are relationships of convenience. Dwight is a "friend" only insofar as he is a yes-man and a faithful subordinate—and it's clear Dwight isn't the most reliable of subordinates. We get a pretty good read on the nature of Dwight and Michael's friendship when Dwight arranges a clandestine meeting with Jan at a roadside diner:

> *Dwight*:   I can save the branch.
> *Jan*:   Really?

Dwight: If you let me run it.
Jan: Ok.
Dwight: "Ok" I can run it?
Jan: What would you do differently?
Dwight: Mostly get rid of waste. Which is half the people there. And clean house . . .
Jan: Dwight, you must feel strongly, to speak with me this way, behind Michael's back, and turn on so many of your co-workers.
Dwight: The decision to turn on Michael was difficult. But once I did it, I didn't look back. And mostly I feel that Michael would approve. It's really what's best for the branch. And I could care less about my co-workers. So, here we are. It's all, on the table. I want . . . the branch. And I await your decision. [Dwight then begins shoving pancakes into his mouth]
("The Coup")

So one "friend" is exposed for what he is: someone who sees his friendship with Michael as something that can be put aside for personal gain. But what about the others? Packer makes the list, probably because Packer considers Michael a friend and Michael is too scared to ever dissolve the "friendship"—think particularly of Packer's gift deposit on Michael's carpet ("The Carpet"). And with Jan there would be no relationship at all except for Jan's admitted self-destructive tendencies. This isn't a pretty picture. In fact, it's a train-wreck.

How did Michael end up with such dismal relationships? One immediate cause is his erroneous views about the nature of his relationships. He believes his relationships are better than they really are. For example, after discovering via email surveillance that Jim is inviting everyone in the office to a party (even Angela and Creed) except him, Michael offers this explanation:

There is always a distance between a boss and the employees. It's just nature's rule. It's intimidation mostly. It's the awareness that they are not me. I do think that I am very approachable as one of the guys; but maybe I need to be even more approachabler. ("Email Surveillance")

Could Michael be any further from the truth?

There are less immediate, more distant causes for Michael's dysfunctional relationships. Michael's probably developed these relationships because he's never taken a good look at himself and never had the feedback he needed growing up to feel confident in undertaking this endeavor. (Think of poor Michael's dream as a child: he just wanted to have lots of children so he would always have lots of friends.) Nevertheless, if authenticity is as good as some philosophers believe it is, even a Michael Scott childhood shouldn't prevent him from becoming an authentic person. Coming to terms with who we really are instead of engaging in evasion or self-deception allows us to develop stronger relationships and discard weak ones. So the real examination shouldn't be focused on Michael's current relationships or his childhood, but rather what would happen if he took seriously the project of determining (through choice or discovery) who he really is. This would at least involve reevaluating his standards for living—Michael's "Packer norms"—and determining whether those standards are consistent with a life expressing his own unique individuality.

We've just looked at the three main ingredients of authenticity: self-knowledge, self-determination, and meaningful social relationships. Let's now look at happiness. We need to pin down what we mean by *happy*, a word that in contemporary English is all too amorphous. Here, we're interested in the kind of happiness that has been the recent focus in academic psychology.[1] Roughly, this kind of happiness consists in *subjective well-being*, or roughly *feeling good*. Its opposite consists in *feeling bad*. Both are features of our conscious experience. In this sense, they're subjective. They encompass the gamut of pleasures and pains. These felt qualities of our conscious experience are sometimes very noticeable and short lived, as with the pleasures of getting the gold in the office Olympics, and the pain of finding one's stapler in Jell-O. But such feelings are fairly infrequent and easily overemphasized, particularly in comparison to what we might call our moods: the more frequent, though less obvious episodes of feeling good and feeling bad that form a kind of background for our experiences. These moods include melancholy (when Jim sees Roy and Pam together), the feeling of contentment (Kevin getting as many double-chocolate brownies as he can carry), the feelings that go along with being engaged in a worthwhile project (Dwight's martial arts activities), or even agitation. All, or virtually all, of our conscious moments include some mood; or, more often, a complicated mix of such moods. Though we often do not pay attention to these feelings, they nevertheless make up much—probably the majority—of the pleasure and pain of life. Though we may notice them less, these feelings are no less real.

Consider Michael's characteristic moods, and the tones of pleasure and pain in these moods. Of course, we can't feel exactly what Michael feels; but that's ok—in fact we should be glad that we can't. But we get plenty of the usual clues: how often he smiles, his facial expressions, his tone of voice, his demeanor toward others, what seems to be preoccupying him, his explicit reports about what he feels, and so on. In fact, when you think about it, we are quite good at detecting one another's moods, especially the moods of people we know well. In probably less than a minute of conversation with a friend, you can tell the kind of mood that she is in. Similarly, when Michael enters the office in the morning, it usually doesn't take long to discern his mood.

Michael's experience seems largely dominated by two moods. One is agitation. When things don't go his way, Michael often gets excited and does something even more foolish than the things he typically does. The other is a sort of precarious elation. Often, Michael seems to be feeling good—he has a smile on his face and he is joking with people. But Michael's moods never include contentment and, in general, there is no stability to his agitation and elation.

Michael is also a detriment to other people's moods. Here's Jim's take on why he didn't invite Michael to his party:

> It's true—I am having a party. I've got three cases of imported beer, a karaoke machine, and I didn't invite Michael. So three ingredients for a great party. And it's nothing personal. I just think that if he were there, people wouldn't be able to relax [and] have fun. ("Email Surveillance")

Aiming for Authenticity *or* Being Happy

So what is the connection between realizing one's unique individuality through meaningful relationships and being in mostly good (rather than bad) moods? Maybe the more a person really knows herself, the more she engages in critical evaluation of her own standards for living, and the more she enters into meaningful relationships with others, the better her moods will be.

99

But if authenticity leads to happiness, we can predict that if Michael were to begin really examining himself and his standards, while taking the time to really listen to the critical comments of others, he would eventually develop some good relationships with others. And in turn, this would improve Michael's moods. For example, were Michael to realize what he is and what he is not, one result would be greater modesty, something that fosters feelings of contentment. And by realizing that he is not the world's greatest boss, the world's gift to women, and so on, he would no longer have flashes of realizing that he is none of these things, episodes that result in sour childish frustration and bad moods (like when he plays the tape of his appearance on the children's show). Instead, through dialogue and critical reflection Michael would take on more realistic, yet satisfying roles and commitments that would lead him to happiness.

Things aren't so easy though. For one, even if Michael were to examine himself, confront his Packer norms, and listen to others, he is so obnoxious, needy, insecure, and deluded that it's unlikely he would develop good, meaningful relationships with others, let alone achieve any self-knowledge. Even if this remote possibility were to materialize, the meaningful relationships he achieves may not be enough for Michael to discover truly satisfying roles and commitments that will lead him to happiness—he's just too shallow for that! So while Michael might find himself in better moods if he were authentic, the problem is with *becoming* authentic. Michael is authenticity-challenged. Even if he tried he couldn't easily give up the Packer norms. Even if he knew that these norms were not consistent with who he is, he is too poorly equipped to get from where he is to living an authentic life. He wouldn't make it. Any attempt would probably be futile.[2] Those who doubt this should recall Michael's attempt to ensure he does not resume his dysfunctional relationship with Jan. While he surrounds himself with a core group of fairly reasonable people (the "office ladies") to ensure his will stands firm, he is overwhelmed by Jan's breast enhancement surgery and in the end rationalizes the decision to resume the relationship. Michael's inauthenticity and inability to renounce the Packer norms is highlighted when he says: "Jan is in a different place right now, and it is a sign of maturity to give people second chances. So I am going to hear her out" ("The Job").

But Michael's admission here shows even more: he seems to have his own route to affecting his moods. Or at least he seems to have found the best route that is available to him: deceiving himself, following the herd, and not listening to others—in short, being inauthentic! This is something we can easily overlook. While being oblivious to others and self-deceived sometimes lead to Michael's bad moods, just as often they facilitate his good moods.

Think, for example, of when Dunder-Mifflin Scranton receives a visit from a diversity officer ("Diversity Day"). On this occasion, Michael makes great efforts to demonstrate his progressive outlook on race relations. When Michael's insensitive imitation of a Chris Rock routine is revealed as corporate's motivation for instituting diversity day, Michael dismisses the real diversity trainer as a phony. He then goes on to make a dramatic attempt to enlighten the office— through a homemade video, an open discussion session, and a diversity exercise where participants are invited to play up racial stereotypes to be "real, raw, and honest." It's a disaster. Michael himself has some sense of this. When he asks Oscar, "Is there a term other than Mexican that your prefer? Something less offensive?," Oscar quickly points out Michael's mistake. Even more striking is the slap in the face Michael receives from Kelly when he begins an impersonation of a salesman with a bad Indian accent.

In spite of the continuing feedback that he is racially insensitive and unsophisticated, Michael is able to hang on to the illusory self-image of being progressive. And at the end of the day he seems quite satisfied with himself (though we know this won't last long). In later episodes, Michael perpetuates his false image and takes pride in it (think of his interactions with Darryl in the warehouse). By project-ing and sustaining this false self-image, Michael seems happy—or at least happier than he would be without it. So the life of Michael Scott may challenge Socrates' dictum that "the unexamined life is not worth living." Perhaps some people are better off deceiving them-selves! Let's call this the beneficial illusion problem.

But is the beneficial illusion problem really a problem?

Michael's Illusions and Their Benefits

In her book *Positive Illusions*, psychologist Shelley Taylor discusses three beneficial kinds of self-deception: overrating one's attributes and past behaviors, overrating one's control over things, and over-optimism about the future. Each is beneficial. Take overrating one's attributes and behaviors first. If I think I am really good at something, I am more likely to give it a try; and in many contexts it is in my best interest to give it a try. Similarly, if I overrate my control, then I may take more care, thinking that the outcome crucially depends on what *I* do. Lastly, if I overrate how good the future will be, I will not feel defeated and complacent about the future; again, this helps me to be more engaged.

All of the benefits just mentioned are motivational in nature. These illusions make a person more likely to act and to perform better. Michael, however, is an oddball—he doesn't seem to get these benefits. He is very lazy. Recall his epic struggle to complete the annual reviews. So though Michael does overrate himself and is often optimistic about the future, these attitudes are, at least in him, motivationally inert.

Still, Michael does derive some benefits from his self-deception. One is illustrated by his buoyant feelings about being well-versed in multiculturalism. So his optimism, even if it doesn't motivate him to *do* anything, does positively influence his mood. Michael often gets in trouble, though, when he is too expressive. He loudly tells people he is a good boss, a great ladies' man, good basketball player, and so on. And he goads them and challenges them. So when it becomes clear that he's not what he says he is, other people sometimes point this out to him (quite justifiably too).

The Dundies award ceremony at Chili's provides a case in point. Michael is painfully exposed as a poor master of ceremonies.

> *Michael*: [Michael is singing to the tune of "Tiny Dancer" by Elton John] You have won a tiny Dundie.
> *Guy at bar*: Sing it Elton.
> *Michael*: Hey, thanks guys. Hey, where you guys from?
> *Other Guy at Bar*: We just came from yo' mama's house.
> *Michael*: Oh, alright, yeah.
> *Guy at Bar*: Sing 'em a song dude.
> *Michael*: Uh, you know what guys, we're just having a little office party, so if you want, uh . . .
> *Michael*: [Something flies by Michael] Hey, you know, cool it guys, really— [The guy at the bar throws another object, looks like a wad of wet napkins, this time it hits Michael on the shoulder]
> *Guy at Bar*: You suck man!
> *Michael*: Let's cut it. [Dwight turns the music off]

Michael: [clears throat] [with a lot less enthusiasm] I had a few more
      Dundies to, uh, give out tonight, but, I'm just going to cut it short.
      And wrap it up so everybody can enjoy their food. Um . . . thanks
      for listening, those who listened.
("The Dundies")

But it's not just strangers who are willing to point out Michael's weaknesses. After reading aloud unflattering comments about himself from the office comments box and offending Jan, Michael pursues Jan to the elevator and asks about their status, this after having spent their first night together:

Michael: I just want to know, from the horse's mouth, what is the
      dealio?
Jan: Michael, it has nothing to do with your looks, ok. It is your
      personality. I mean you're obnoxious, rude, and stupid; and you
      do have coffee breath by the way; and I don't agree about the b.o.,
      but you are very, very inconsiderate.
("Performance Review")

Besides reminding us of how Michael constantly fails to learn from other people's observations about him, these scenes also help us see one cause of Michael's unhappiness. The real culprit here is not the illusions. It is the fact that Michael so frequently expresses his illusions and does so in a way that provokes others to point out his shortcomings.

So where does that leave us? Is Michael, overall, better off for all his self-deception? On the motivational score, it looks like a wash. Michael, as self-deceived as he is, is a lazy man. But he would probably be just as lazy were he to examine his life—his laziness seems to stem from some other part of his psychology. When it comes to his moods, his self-deception seems to be of some help. Moreover, were he to engage in the self-examination, self-cultivation, and meaningful dialogue advocated by proponents of authenticity, he would just get upset and fall into some pretty foul moods. If he were to make the attempt, it would probably be futile—he would probably not emerge an authentic person. Michael, it seems, is better off as he is. He has no good reason to change.

If our findings are correct, it appears that Michael cannot achieve happiness by trying to become authentic. However, it would be a mistake to conclude from Michael's case that becoming authentic does not guarantee happiness; for what we have learned is that Michael is just psychologically incapable of becoming authentic. His personal history and his fervent commitment to the Packer norms seem to defeat any real attempt at being authentic. So it still may be true that an authentic life is a happy life.

It would also be a mistake to conclude from our findings that because Michael has no good reason to change that Michael is happy. It seems clear that if our account of happiness allows Michael to be happy it is a seriously defective account of happiness. Michael is *not* happy. He is *happier*, happier for not engaging in a project (being authentic) that he will never remotely achieve. Being happier could just mean not being completely miserable as opposed to being completely miserable. And no one would confuse not being completely miserable with being happy.

So perhaps philosophers are correct after all: inauthentic lives are not happy lives. Nevertheless, Michael's case does yield an important and surprising conclusion: if a person is incapable of achieving an authentic life then perhaps it's better not to try at all.

NOTES

1 The account of happiness described here is not necessarily an account the authors endorse. Nevertheless, it is an account that is not only one long-standing understanding of happiness, but one which at least identifies a component of happiness. So regardless of what the final correct theory of happiness is, we should at least admit that one important criterion for determining whether someone is happy is their subjective conscious states.

2 John Stuart Mill claimed that it is better to be Socrates dissatisfied than a pig satisfied. Even if Mill is right, this bit of wisdom won't be any use to Michael since, if we are right, Michael doesn't have the means to achieving Socrates' degree of authenticity.

9

Humiliation in *The Office* (and at Home)

John Elia

Laughter and Humiliation

Television viewers often participate in the feelings and experiences of onscreen characters. For this we have to thank our capacities for empathy and compassion. But rather than feeling *with* Michael Scott, we often feel *in his place*, a kind of "feeling by proxy." The particular feeling we are most likely to have by proxy for Michael is not loss, depression, fear, love, or joy, but humiliation. You see, Michael Scott is largely immune to humiliation. He rarely notices when he has transgressed moral norms. The problem is his epic lack of self-awareness: Michael Scott's moral blindspot obscures his vision, first and foremost, of Michael Scott! Viewers, of course, rarely miss his transgressions, and since we are *not* immune to humiliation, we look away from the television, laugh nervously, and wish we could bury his head for him. Oddly enough, we enjoy it too. We come to expect and even desire these experiences in each new episode of *The Office*, settling down in front of the television wondering what totally awkward thing Michael will do next.

Why do we enjoy these experiences? One answer is pretty obvious. We enjoy laughter. Perhaps the joy of laughter outweighs the pains of humiliation by proxy. But other answers are available, too. As someone interested in ethics and moral education, I want to explore one of these alternatives—namely, that the humiliation we feel for Michael Scott reinforces our sense of goodness and character. Like humiliation proper, humiliation by proxy calls attention to our judgments of self and to our values. It informs us of our capacities for experiencing

105

a variety of humanizing moral emotions such as shame, embarrassment, and regret. Unlike humiliation proper, however, humiliation by proxy is not a response to our wrongdoing: humiliation by proxy does not so much transform character as reaffirm it. So long as we can reliably perceive others' moral errors, our experiences of humiliation by proxy show that we possess a degree of genuine goodness and moral sensitivity that they lack.

This might seem a lot of seriousness to impose on a little comedy such as *The Office*. Yet theorists of comedy have often talked about comedy in terms of its morally relevant functions. The British philosopher Thomas Hobbes (1588–1679), for instance, held that laughter was an expression of moral superiority.[1] Henri Bergson (1859–1941), a French philosopher, contended that comedy promoted moral values by humiliating people guilty of socially disruptive behavior.[2] But we should disagree with Hobbes and Bergson that laughter always or necessarily serves to humiliate others. After all, we often laugh at Michael *because* we are humiliated, not *in order to* humiliate. Laughter and humiliation have often been thought connected, and this resonates deeply with our responses to *The Office*. Of course, Michael Scott would like nothing more than to make people laugh, but, if I am right, he is good for more than this.

Beyond High School Humiliation

We use the concept of humiliation in at least two ways. One way we speak of humiliation is as a practice or process of being humiliated, whether it involves public denouncements and other public displays of power or private reflections on one's place in the cosmos. The other use treats humiliation as an emotion. Here we mean what it feels like to be humiliated and what makes an emotional response humiliation rather than something else like anxiety or fear or indigestion.[3] We all know from the inside what humiliation feels like because we have experienced it—we know, for instance, that to feel humiliation is to feel the pain of regret, shame, and embarrassment. But feeling is only one dimension of the emotion of humiliation. Humiliation involves additionally the judgment that we have transgressed important social or moral norms, neglected important values, or mistaken ourselves for something we are not.

Our capacity for humiliation, I think, says a lot about us. Minimally, it says that we see ourselves as possibly doing wrong or possibly overestimating our own merit. It also says that wrongdoing and overestimation are so important to us that we can be pained by them: if we didn't have these beliefs or couldn't feel this pain, we couldn't experience humiliation. Humiliation is a characteristically human emotion, for it connects our reflective capacities to our abilities to be moved to put those reflections into action.

The capacity for humiliation is very significant morally—and we know it can be abused. One such abuse has become a common part of our cultural narratives regarding humiliation: High School Humiliation. Its script runs something like this: mean, controlling, superiority-complex bearing alpha males and queen bees demean others so that they continue to enjoy their social status; betas and wannabes mimic these behaviors as they demoralize those below them on the food chain. The result is public confirmation of the power-disparity between the social haves and have-nots.[4]

Films and television shows about adolescence and high school often follow this script. As we well know, however, High School Humiliation does not end with the 12th grade. It is practiced, for instance, by both Jim and Michael in *The Office*. Jim displays smugness and class-security, especially in his knowing glances at Pam, as he plays junior high pranks on Dwight and, later, on Stamford-transfer Andy. Michael uses High School Humiliation frequently. For instance, Michael publicizes that Martin is an ex-con and then treats him as if he knows nothing about prison ("The Convict"). Michael uses High School Humiliation again to reaffirm his managerial authority after misleading Dwight into thinking he'd been named Michael's replacement ("The Coup"). Michael probably learned to use High School Humiliation from his BFF, Todd Packer, who parades around as if he's still captain of the high school football team. Surprising Michael from behind by pulling Michael's sport coat over his head, Packer bellows: "What has two thumbs and likes to bone your mom? [Packer points to himself] This guy!" Jim gets an equally thoughtful greeting: "What's up Halpert? Still queer?" ("Sexual Harassment"). But while High School Humiliation pricks egos, its targets are not typically false or inflated egos. It prefers instead to seek out easy prey, often persons whose status is perceived to be inferior. Furthermore, High School Humiliation is not aimed at promoting self-awareness or recognition of genuine wrongdoing; it vies merely to elevate the social status of its wielder. Victims of High School Humiliation rarely deserve such rough treatment!

Not all humiliation is High School Humiliation, obviously. Other forms of humiliation aim at social control too, but not primarily by elevating the status of their practitioners or by suppressing potential competitors in the social arena. Instead, they commonly aim to bind communities around shared values and norms. Think of Hester Prynne's treatment in Hawthorne's novel *The Scarlet Letter*. Think of public canings, whippings, or hangings. Think of local papers that publish the names and offenses of community members: drug possession, petty larceny, driving while intoxicated, even divorce. Michael Scott uses humiliation in this form as well. His "Name That Stereotype" game ("Diversity Day") was evidently intended to promote social values, on the assumption that everyone (else) would be humiliated by the stereotypes they secretly harbored. After Kevin gets pulled in to one of Todd Packer's sex jokes (this one about a guy at a convention of nymphomaniacs), Michael tries to humiliate Kevin for creating a hostile work environment ("Sexual Harassment"):

> *Todd*:   He is psyched because all these women are smokin' hot perfect tens, except for this one chick who looks a lot like, um . . . [pointing to Phyllis]
> *Kevin*:   Phyllis.
> *Michael*:   No, no, no, no, that crosses the line.
> *Todd*:   Exsqueeze me?
> *Michael*:   [to Todd] Not you. Kevin. . . .
> *Michael*:   [to Kevin] . . . There's a line and you went over it, so you must be punished. Go to your corner.
> *Kevin*:   You mean where my desk is?
> *Michael*:   Yes, your corner. Go.
> *Kevin*:   Ok, I have a lot of work to do anyway.

So not all humiliation is High School Humiliation. Some public humiliation is aimed at social control, but not the superiority of its practitioners. Other forms of humiliation may not even be public. But all forms of humiliation have the same necessary conditions: recognition of at least the possibility of wrongdoing or false self-appraisal, and the ability to be pained by such a recognition. There is no reason to believe that Michael Scott lacks a capacity for pain, of course, but he clearly has difficulty looking closely enough at himself to realize his own imperfection.

Michael Scott: Dishing Out What He Cannot Take

Everyone knows someone who is blind to his own foibles. We criticize such blindness because we tend to hold that persons should see themselves for what they are. If a person is prone to mistakes, or has significant faults or vices, we often praise him for recognizing it. If a person is skilled, if he excels in certain capacities, we praise that recognition as well (understanding, of course, that recognition of excellence is not the same as boasting of it, and that recognition of flaws is not identical with beating oneself up over it). Honesty with ourselves matters, and not simply because we care about truth for its own sake. Immense practical and moral value hangs on it: it's hard to achieve much if we're duping ourselves constantly about who we are, what we are able to do, and what others believe about us.

The problem is that we are about as good at self-appraisal as Dwight is at interrogation ("Drug Testing"). The errors to which we are generally liable come in two kinds. One involves overestimation and typically indicates a person's excessive pride, egomania, or narcissism; the other involves underestimation and indicates a person's servility, slavishness, or obsequiousness. Michael Scott does not characteristically underestimate himself. He is a narcissist who chronically exaggerates his status, believing himself to have the loyalty, trust, and friendship of his employees when he has actually alienated them; taking himself to be a creative leader when he is in fact an object of contempt; thinking himself a brilliant comedian when he is virtually without wit or comedic timing.

Good varieties of humiliation transform wrongdoers and correct their self-appraisals. For humiliation to transform us, we must believe that we have transgressed moral norms, neglected moral values, or mistaken ourselves for something we are not. This is because the emotion of humiliation is partially constituted by these beliefs: if we do not or cannot see that we have done wrong, we will not feel the sting of humiliation. This is precisely Michael's issue.

For instance, Michael Scott has the vague sense that racism, sexism, and homophobia are unacceptable. Perhaps he even cares in some fashion not to do what is unacceptable. But his behavior consistently defies his knowledge and care. Michael apparently cannot translate his notion of what is morally required of him into action. He seems not to perceive when and how his moral values apply. Perhaps this is because he does not recognize his situation as calling for those values. Think of the exception Michael makes for himself on "Diversity Day" (his name tag reads "Martin Luther King, Jr."), not seeing that he too harbors racial stereotypes (any doubt about this is smashed as he assaults Kelly with an impression of an Indian convenience store manager). Or consider the way Michael puts together a basketball team to challenge the warehouse crew ("Basketball"): he chooses Stanley first (evidently because he's black), rejects Phyllis (she's female), ignores Kevin (probably because he's overweight), and tells Oscar that he'll call on him if it comes to baseball or boxing (presumably because he's Hispanic).

As I see it, though, Michael's inability to perceive the morally salient details of his situation is rooted in something deeper: his lack of self-awareness. Michael Scott's moral blind-spot is defined by his narcissism. He thinks his jokes are funny; he thinks his grandstanding is deserved; he thinks those who disagree with him are out of their heads. Recall once more Michael's treatment of ex-convict Martin. Contrary to Martin's assessment, Michael attempts to convince everyone in the office that prison isn't really better than working at the Scranton branch. Michael can't imagine not being the expert, even though his only acquaintance with prison is from TV, the Internet, and gangsta rap ("The Convict"):

> *Michael*: [donning a blue bandana] I'm Prison Mike. You know why they call me Prison Mike?
> *Angela*: Do you really expect us to believe you're someone else?
> *Michael*: Do you really expect me to not push you up against the wall, beotch? . . . [In response to grumblings] . . . Hey, hey, hey, hey, that's just the way we talk in the clink . . . A lot of fun talk about prison today, but I'm here to scare you straight. I'm here to scare you straight!

Michael cannot conceive of the possibility that his own behavior could violate the demands of morality. He counts himself an exception to the rules, but only because, as far as he can tell, he is morally faultless, a paragon of virtue and moral fiber. A telling example comes when Michael tries to renege on his (unwitting) offer to give Oscar's nephew 25 dollars per mile for his charity walk ("The Alliance"):

> *Oscar:* I just think it's kind of cheap to undonate money to a charity.
> *Michael:* No, no, no, no, no, no . . . I wasn't, I wasn't, what I was . . . no, it's not about the money, it's just the ethics of the thing, Oscar . . . How's your nephew? Is he in good shape?
> *Oscar:* Yeah.
> *Michael:* How many miles did he do last year?
> *Oscar:* Last year he walked 18 miles.
> *Michael:* Son of a bitch! . . . That is impressive, good for him.

While Michael ultimately writes out a large check, he does so not because he thinks he'd otherwise do wrong, but because he wants to preserve his self-image—earlier that day he'd confided to the camera that he'd like to be *known* someday as the *anonymous* donor of a new hospital wing.

Michael's exaggerated self-appraisal is not dented by even glaring evidence to the contrary: Phyllis' new husband, Bob Vance of Vance Refrigeration, wrenches him up and drags him off stage as he tries to showboat at their wedding reception ("Phyllis' Wedding"); Oscar takes a leave of absence after having been outed by Michael and then forced to endure a make-up kiss as Michael tries to display his gay-friendliness ("Gay Witch Hunt"); Carol rejects Michael's unexpected marriage proposal at the Diwali celebration, causing him, later that evening, to try desperately to kiss Pam—his advances are rebuffed yet again and, though Pam takes him home, she makes him sit in the backseat ("Diwali"). One might expect Michael's beliefs about himself not to hold up under these conditions, raising the question how rich a fantasy life Michael must have in order to insulate these beliefs from falsification. But whatever the defense mechanisms, the result is unequivocal: Michael is blind to his moral transgressions because he has, at best, only the slightest inkling that he is morally impure. He can dish out humiliation, but he cannot take it, for he fails to meet the minimal condition of experiencing humiliation, the awareness that he could possibly do wrong.

Humiliation (not in *The Office*, but) at Home

Michael Scott is rarely humiliated by his actions. Because of his narcissism, he has difficulty conceptualizing the possibility of his doing wrong. Yet viewers of *The Office* know that no episode will go by without Michael doing something inconsiderate, awkward, indecent, offensive, boneheaded, or ridiculous—indeed, for many of us, it is precisely these moments of unabashed insensitivity that keep us tuning in. While Michael is apparently incapable of experiencing humiliation, however, we, his viewers, are not. We are betrayed by our emotional and behavioral reactions to Michael's behavior. As we laugh, we occasionally experience his shame and embarrassment. We regret his actions for him. We get a rush of anxiety. We blush. We avert our gaze from the television screen. We participate in Michael's humiliation by proxy, not so much feeling with him, since he is not humiliated, but feeling in his place.[5]

Our capacity for feeling by proxy is a sign of our empathy and compassion. These are fundamental moral traits that make possible our concern for others by enabling us to understand what others are going through, the only plausible form of mind-reading available to us.[6] They motivate us to do well by others and to help relieve their pain because we share it. Generally, compassion is understood to be a kind of feeling for or with others, as I have said previously. The case of feeling by proxy is rather different: indeed, it might be regarded, and not implausibly so, as a perversion of our compassion, leading us to feel even for those who cannot feel themselves, humanizing the emotionally inhuman. One might even worry that emotion by proxy is dangerous.

But I doubt this. Emotion by proxy could be troublesome if we tended to feel what others should feel while failing to recognize that they are not feeling that way themselves. Perhaps it would lead us then to sympathize with persons who are cold-blooded, ruthless, or unfeeling when we should not (the Todd Packers of the world). The experience of emotion by proxy does not entail such failures of recognition though. Nor is there any reason to believe that emotion by proxy is likely to occur in circumstances in which we are vulnerable to cold-blooded victimizers. More probable is the kind of case we have before us now, experiencing emotions right in the comfort of our own homes. Let's be honest, actors can be like Michael Scott on so many levels—though especially in leading us to feel emotion without truly feeling it themselves!

Still, humiliation by proxy differs from standard cases of humiliation. The most salient difference is that humiliation by proxy is less likely than humiliation proper to require that we reconsider the accuracy of our self-image—we have not *really* been humiliated after all, we have transgressed no moral norms—and, as a result, humiliation by proxy is less likely to cause personal transformation. The pain of humiliation is a powerful motivator of change, but only if something in one's character is calling for it.

Humiliation by proxy is not for this reason insignificant, however. Watching Michael Scott, taking on the humiliation that he deserves, we realize that we know better. Only a moral blunderer would make the mistakes that he makes without feeling any remorse, regret, embarrassment, or shame. And yet we feel tinges of each of these in Michael's place—we feel the relevant pains—and so we learn about ourselves that we are decent, caring people, with emotional repertoires fitting for our humanity. This is, after all, why we can experience Michael's humiliation.

Furthermore, we come to reaffirm commitments to our moral values as a result of by-proxy humiliation. True, this is not moral transformation, but it is important nonetheless. We measure our decency in part by the worth of the moral standards and the degree of self-knowledge that we possess (and, by contrast, that Michael does not). Were we to discover Michael flouting unacceptably stringent, hypocritical, or perverse moral standards, we would have no reason to feel humiliation on his behalf. This does raise a hard question about why Michael's behavior *should be* humiliating though. Isn't it often his racism, sexism, homophobia, and lack of sensitivity above all else that humiliates us, his viewers? Aren't we therefore endorsing a characteristically Hollywood (or Western or modern) set of values? Indeed, mightn't a non-Hollywood type actually praise Michael for challenging the doctrinaire norms of Hollywood political correctness?

First, labeling a set of values "Hollywood" ought not to belie its claim to justifiability. Many sets of moral standards might be said to be justifiable; Hollywood sets of values are not automatically excluded from their number.[7] Second, the moral standards Michael transgresses are not simply expressions of Hollywood values,

113

Western values, or even modern values, though we see them in these times and places perhaps more often than we do elsewhere. Different conceptions of ultimate value humiliate with remarkably similar results: a rethinking of self, a reworking of one's relationship to the world, and so on. This is possible because distinctive conceptions of value agree on certain fundamental matters such as the need for self-awareness, moral sight, integrity, and honesty with oneself. These values have to do with how we think about morality, the merit we attach to certain ways of moral reasoning, or with the relationships between values rather than the substance of those values themselves. Michael characteristically misapprehends the meaning and significance of his actions. He breaks moral norms haphazardly. He hurts people's feelings unknowingly. He thinks the rest of the world is more troubled and in error than he. This is Michael's staggering blindness at work: blindness that Hollywood and non-Hollywood types can agree is a moral fault. So even if one thinks that off-color jokes should not offend, that Hollywood mores are wimpy and too sensitive, or that the world should just suck it up, one should still be humiliated for Michael Scott.

A Plea to Corporate

Dunder-Mifflin's Scranton manager, Michael Scott, exhibits such pervasive moral blindness that he is rarely humiliated by his actions. We take on Michael's humiliation, even knowing that he will never begin to approximate full moral vision. By-proxy humiliation benefits us differently than humiliation proper, offering us a reaffirmation of our compassion and decency rather than a call to moral transformation. And while we should not overly congratulate ourselves for our decency, shifting too quickly into a mode of easy self-approval, basic forms of goodness, compassion, and character are nothing to scoff at. We discover in our humiliation for Michael something profoundly human—a fundamental moral conception of ourselves as possibly doing wrong. Michael seems not to possess such a self-conception. He is at once ripe for humiliation and yet, by the same measure, incapable of it. This guarantees that the laughs and self-affirmations will continue—at least as long as corporate doesn't succeed in humanizing Michael through its diversity seminars.

NOTES

1 Thomas Hobbes, *Leviathan: With Selected Variants from the Latin Edition of 1668*, ed. Edwin Curley (Indianapolis: Hackett, 1994).
2 Henri Bergson, "Laughter," in *Comedy*, ed. Wylie Sypher (Garden City, NY: Anchor Doubleday, 1956).
3 On the relationship between digestion and emotion, see Friedrich Nietzsche, *Twilight of the Idols and The Anti-Christ*, trans. R. J. Hollingdale (London: Penguin, 1984).
4 Rosalind Wiseman, *Queen Bees and Wannabes* (New York: Three Rivers Press, 2002).
5 I have no hard evidence of the regularity of experiences of by-proxy humiliation among viewers of *The Office*. My data is, shall we say, anecdotal. However, if there is value in by-proxy humiliation for anyone individually, that value will not simply dissipate upon remarking that others did not receive it, or that not many others did. And to those who've never had this experience, I am sorry to be the bearer of bad news. If I am right, you may well lack a certain degree of moral sensitivity, compassion, or empathy.
6 Karsten Stueber, *Rediscovering Empathy* (Cambridge, MA: MIT Press, 2006).
7 Justifiability is not identical to truth. Thus, any number of ethical systems could be simultaneously justifiable, while only one or none were true.

MEMO 3
FUNNY AND NOT-SO-FUNNY BUSINESS

10

Laughter Between Distraction and Awakening: Marxist Themes in *The Office*

Michael Bray

The Class That Dare Not Speak Its Name

America doesn't seem to care about class. Why care, when there no longer appear to be classes? And, if a recent article in *The New Yorker* is to be believed, the "American *Office* doesn't care about class" either. The British *Office*, on the other hand, "was a pitiless meditation on rules and class,"[1] but the American version focuses instead on the quirks of individual personalities and their efforts to escape the tedium of an unrewarding workplace. "The reason that bosses become blustery martinets is that any sensible employee at a place like Dunder-Mifflin would rather play video games or gossip than tutor clients in the manifold varieties of copy paper" (Friend, 98). In place of bitterness and anger boiling forever just under the surface, Americans have more genuine work-effort and more genuine camaraderie, if also no less genuine despair—albeit the kind born from boredom, not class position.

As a sketch of the difference in tone between the two series, American and British, this is certainly a decent start. No doubt, the British *Office* has an edgier tone, precisely because David Brent has so much anger and resentment boiling just beneath his management-speak, an anger not only against those whose economic position is above his but also against women. Brent, for example, attempts to manage his own insecurity relative to the college-educated temp by a series of put-downs, insults, and dismissals, as well as desperate efforts to prove his knowledge. On the other hand, when Michael Scott, the boss in the American series, finds out that Ryan, his temp, is planning to go to business school, instead of resenting him, he falls a little in love. But such differences in tone don't mean that the American series "doesn't care about class," at least not if that is meant to imply that the American version fails to register, or underplays, the significance of economic structures. The tedium and despair that haunt the American version, along with the quirky hopes and discomforts that animate its characters, are themselves the marked features of a peculiar class (once called "the salaried masses")[2] in a peculiar situation (that of twenty-first-century America, where class, while no less objectively present, has become largely unnamable, unthinkable).

The American *Office* presents a class that is ironically characterized by its disbelief in classes—a class whose self-image is grounded in the denial of a difference between them and the classes above. The middle is everywhere.

Reading Marx at Work

The daily world of most Americans doesn't look much like the one that philosopher and economist Karl Marx (1818–1883) prophesied: a world in which an ever-more impoverished class of manufacturing laborers would be driven, ultimately, by their own radical needs, to social revolution. Over the course of the twentieth century, the old-style "proletariat" has become a much smaller percentage of the American workforce, surpassed by seemingly endless waves of office and service industry workers. Thus, the clear dualism that underlay Marx's reading of modern society—the antagonism between the capitalists, who own the means of production, and the working class, which owns nothing but its own labor—seems to vanish into a mass of workers of different grades, positions, and powers. There are Pams, Jims, Dwights, Michaels, Jans, and Roys, whose identities seem to be grounded, not in the form of their labor, but in what they like, what they wear, and how they look; in other words, what they consume.

In place of the revolution of the world's working class, then, we got an apparently ever-expanding consumer society. But, despite what seems like Marx's fundamental error here, his theory actually provides tools for understanding this trajectory. On Marx's own analysis, after all, the accumulation of capital is a process that drives towards ever-greater expansion. Indeed, capital *only is capital* insofar as the process of its production and exchange yields a surplus beyond what was initially invested.[3] Capital is money invested in the production of commodities in order to yield *more* money. When it comes down to it, before everything else, the economy must grow—money must be made into more money (in the form of profits that fall mostly into the hands of a small elite)—or the economy will collapse. Of course, in order to continue to grow, the economy needs people to buy things. So, you might say, *since there was not a revolution*, then an expanding consumer society became necessary. But, Marx insists, it is the endless pursuit of money, surplus, and profit, rather than a rational grasp of the needs of individuals and of society as a whole, that defines capitalism as an economic form.

One of the defining elements of Michael Scott's character lies in his failure to properly implement his functions as manager in pursuing this logic. In David Brent's mouth, the constant invocations of how, in business, "it's the people that matter," is empty management-speak. In Michael's mouth, such proclamations appear as distorted but genuinely meant. Michael doesn't know what "people" are exactly, what they might want, how they should be treated, or how they should live. (Like David, Michael doesn't know any form of life other than the pursuit of success and ease that he can't himself embody.) But when Michael says it's the people that matter, he means it. Thus, as Jim observes when the manager of the Stamford branch leverages his promotion into a new job with Staples: "You can say what you want about Michael Scott, but he would *never* do that" ("Branch Closing").

And what is the proper function of the manager in a capitalist system? To generate profit—or, as Marx calls it, "surplus value." But the manager doesn't do this (at least, not most of the time) by tricking customers or overcharging other corporations. Managers, rather, spend most of their time overseeing, shaping, and controlling the work time and work processes of employees. At the very core of surplus value, then, is control and exploitation of those workers. This is why Michael constantly finds himself unable to do what corporate asks of him.

The key to the production of surplus value is labor. A commodity, in capitalism, gains value from the *amount* of labor-time it takes an average laborer to produce the commodity (thus, the value of paper produced in a paper mill is *less* than that produced by hand, since it takes less time to produce). The value of a laborer's day—her wage—is determined in the same manner, Marx argues. The value of a day's labor is equivalent to the value of goods required to *reproduce* that day's labor (so it is equivalent to the value of food, shelter, clothing, and everything else needed to have a life and family in present society). But the value of the wage is *less* than the value that a worker's labor power can produce through a full day of employment. The worker *adds* value to the goods he works on, and he is not compensated for this addition (only for what it will take to reproduce the labor he expends). Thus, the capitalist, or corporation, generates surplus value by paying laborers less value than they produce. The capitalist, and capitalism, lives off the worker.

Running Out the Clock

To make labor more productive *and* easier to replace, it's useful to make machines do more and more, eliminating human skills required to do a particular job. Anyone can work on an assembly line or enter data into a computer—and if anyone can do it, *you* can be replaced very quickly. As the autonomy, independence, and responsibility of work decreases, the *images* of autonomy, independence, and fun offered up to the worker by the world of advertising and consumption increase. Various modes of distraction must be introduced to keep people from reflecting on their real conditions. Thus, Jan, the representative of corporate, during her "Women in the Workplace" seminar, tells the women of the office to "dress for the job you want, not the job you have" ("Boys and Girls"). The women are disappointed, however, not to be able to talk about the clothes they like. "They devote themselves to an individualism that would be justified only if they could shape their fate as individuals" (Kracauer, 81). The joke is that neither dressing like Jan, nor as they like, will give most of them the real power to shape that fate.

Indeed, the irony of capitalism, for Marx, is that its own logic drives it to produce ever-more commodities but *never* to alter for the better the character of the labor, the work, in which most people spend most of their lives. There is a direct line from the famous pin factory in Adam Smith's *Wealth of Nations*, where one man spends his entire time doing nothing but making the heads of pins, through Henry Ford's Model T assembly line, to the advanced robotics employed in many factories today. Each such advance raises the productivity of labor and, thereby, increases the amount of surplus value generated. But each such advance also tends to render more repetitive, empty, and meaningless the actions done, all day long, by the individual workers. And *no* such advance liberates human beings from the need to work all day long, precisely because the production of value, as the measure of capital, is grounded in human labor-time. "The machine does not free the worker from work, but rather deprives the work itself of all content" (Marx, 548). Instead, new positions, new spheres of production are constantly opened up by capital and by corporations that constantly shift production, expand into new markets, and so on. In place of free time, workers gain, if anything, new things to purchase. That the accumulated knowledge, science, and technology does not free human beings from labor—that it, in fact, tends to reduce the majority of laborers to a kind of empty, repetitive labor that neither sustains nor develops their abilities—is, for Marx, one of the cruelest paradoxes of the capitalist world. On *The Office*, whatever meaning there is for the workers lies almost solely in interpersonal relationships, if it even lies there. "I wouldn't want to work here if Pam left," Roy observes. "Then it would just be unloading trucks without meaning" ("Branch Closing"). Pam's interest in art is sometimes seen as a possible source of greater meaning but, the show makes clear, even her art suffers from the deadening, empty routine of her career.[4] For her school art show she paints the objects around her—a coffee cup, the office-building, a stapler—in tepid watercolors ("Business School"). Despite themselves, workers become little more than "appendages" of the machines they serve and their drive to develop their capacities, to become "full" human beings is often thwarted.

Jim routinely notes the emptiness of his work, which is sometimes played off as a consequence of selling *paper*, but is often a more general statement on the very character of such sales work in general. Indeed, the ever-greater organization, or "rationalization," of labor didn't only transform and degrade the work-process of the manual laborer. As corporations grow, they have more and more data to process, more and more sales to oversee, and more and more services to provide. And so office labor becomes just as divided and planned as manual labor.[5] The worker cannot resist by working differently but only by not working, or working as little as possible. As when, visiting the warehouse (Michael's idea, of course) to get a taste of manual labor, Ryan—the business school student—proposes setting up an assembly line process for unloading a truck. Stanley rebuffs him: "This is a run-out-the-clock type of situation. Just like upstairs" ("Boys and Girls"). They keep taking the boxes one by one.

Downsizing Dreams

For every Dunder-Mifflin, there is a Staples, Office Max, or Office Depot looking to buy and liquidate it. This is the economic world that forms the backdrop for the series—which appears, most commonly, in the form of concerns about downsizing. "The existential insecurity of salaried staff has increased . . . and their prospect of independence has almost entirely disappeared" (Kracauer, 30). But although most forms of "mental" or "white collar" labor have ceased to involve initiative, autonomy, or control, the self-image of the workers involved *depends* on them not recognizing that this is so. Belief is sustained not by belief in what one is but by belief that, at least, one is *not* something else. The self-image of these salaried masses, these office workers, lies in their insisting, more or less unconsciously, on a fundamental difference between themselves and those workers who still carry on more traditional forms of proletarian labor, as well as anyone else who can be marked out as unprofessional. Such differences are found in everything from receiving a salary instead of a wage, to wearing a tie or jacket instead of a shirt with your first name on it, to working in the office rather than the basement, to holding on to certain ideals and beliefs that grow farther and farther away from the reality of your life.

Much of the comedy of *The Office* revolves around just such short-circuits between characters' self-images and their realities, as well as the subtle terror at play in professions in which one's image is, quite literally, one's worth. Michael is less "the boss from hell" than he is a man trapped in the space between decaying ideals and the reality of his own work and life, where little is left to him but to pass down corporate directives, to implement cost-cutting schemes, and to make more or less desperate bids at self-determination. Sometimes the show is at its best just when it is at its least funny, when it makes you feel quite strikingly the pain and anxiety of occupying that gap, when it makes you wonder if you aren't just a little like Michael Scott yourself. The show is at its best when it awakens us to the *experience* of class, in a way that most of our lives (and most of our entertainment) are designed to deny and to distract us from.

Take a few instances from the show, not quite at random: first, in the moment alluded to previously, Michael talks to Ryan about his plans for business school. What do you want to do that for, Michael asks. Do you want to be a manager? Not really, Ryan answers, I want to own my business. "That's ridiculous," Michael explodes, ending the conversation ("The Fire"). The gap between his own position and Ryan's aspirations is too stark to be reflected on. That Ryan's own aspirations will likely fall short (he later becomes a permanent employee in the office) is merely another element of the show's recurring theme: the characters want out. They secretly long for downsizing, precisely because it would force them to try to *do* something—something that might be better. When it looks like the Scranton branch will be closed, Pam, Stanley, and Toby are all secretly thrilled. "It's a blessing in disguise," Pam says. "In fact, not even in disguise" ("Branch Closing"). Without downsizing, though, they know all too well the slim chances their lives hold of being different and so they stay. So, when the branch stays open, Pam sees things differently: "Maybe this is for the best. Finding another job is a pain. There's another annoying boss, another desk. I'd have to learn everything over again" ("Branch Closing"). Everything would be different, yet be exactly the same. Or, as Pam observes in another episode, "Dreams are just dreams. They help get you through the day" ("Boys and Girls").

In another episode, Michael leaves work, with Dwight in tow, to finalize his purchase of a condo, the first housing purchase he's ever made. Outside, on a street of closely built condos, Michael rhapsodizes about his "sanctuary and party-pad" and the swing he'll build out front for his grandchildren. Projecting himself into this traditional vision of middle-class life, he suddenly realizes that he's looking at the wrong condo. The salaried man's home is not his personalized sanctuary but a blank consumer item, indistinguishable from any other. There isn't really room for a tree-swing anyway. And even this grasp at the dreamed ideal comes at a stiff price. Inside, Michael insists that although the condo's mortgage is more expensive than the rent of his current, larger apartment, nevertheless it's better, because he'll own it. "Diversifying," he says, in the language of the financial class he doesn't even understand. But, Dwight points out, with a 30-year mortgage, Michael won't be done paying off his purchase until he's in his 70s. "So much for retiring at 65," he tells Michael, who panics and tries to back out, until it becomes clear that he'll lose $7,000 if he does. "At Michael's age," Dwight observes in one of the show's talking heads shots, "buying is like buying a coffin" ("Office Olympics").

Finally, in an American episode written by the British creators, Ricky Gervais and Stephen Merchant, Michael finds out that a new worker, transferred from the closing Stamford branch, is an ex-convict. Martin, it turns out, has been in jail for insider trading. Prodded to describe what prison was like, he notes that, mostly, it was "doing the same thing every day" ("The Convict"), a comment that quickly draws comparison with the world of the office. Only, in prison, Martin admits, the convicts got two hours of "rec time" outside, water-color painting and business classes (taught by Harvard graduates), and a bigger TV than the lunch room has. Indignant, Michael defends the world of Dunder-Mifflin and, implicitly, himself: "People don't realize how lucky they are. This office is the American Dream and they would rather be in the Hole." The joke, of course, is that the distance between office and prison (white-collar prison, that is) genuinely seems a small one, no matter how much Toby reassures Michael that people really love the office.

What the American *Office* observes at moments like this is not so much the way in which class *doesn't matter* but the way in which it is both *denied* and *lived* by the people who occupy a strange, and ever-growing, place in the contemporary class system. The way that they try and fail to make their work meaningful; the way they try and fail to live lives outside of work that would express their freedom, independence, and individuality. These failures are not so much their fault as individuals as they are consequences of their social position. Michael *does* love the office, in his way, but as the show makes clear, only because his own identity is uncertain and unclear away from it.

This is, of course, the joke on Michael, but it is also uncertain how much he really differs in this respect from any other members of the office, who remain superior to him (if they do) only through their skeptical distance from their situation. The secret the show keeps, openly enough, is that most office workers are probably more like Michael (or Dwight) than they are like Jim or Pam, who often seem to have wandered in from another setting, another milieu.[6]

So why is a show that exposes us to ourselves, and so unpleasantly, such a hit? How can it be that the salaried masses—so badly in need of distraction and glamour to mask the boredom of their work-lives (a boredom that, if not relieved, could lead to the critical thinking about capitalist society)—would come to find humor in a stark presentation of the meaninglessness of their own social position? And how could it be that a media corporation would present such an image in place of its usual fare of distraction and glamour? Let me suggest the makings of an answer:

1 The routines of "rationalized" office labor have themselves become so common and durable that they can be presented, as laws of capitalism generally are, as a kind of fate to which individuals can only submit, such that comedy, here, borders on despair.
2 There are numerous aspects of *The Office* that work against its occasional starkness and, by doing so, suggest that individual autonomy and personality are still possible in "the office" (not only artistic ambitions but also the relationship story of Jim and Pam is key here, as well as the implication that Jim is more human, that is, more "cultured," than his manual-labor counterpart, Roy).[7]
3 At times, like in the examples given above, the tension between the show's despair and its gestures towards an actual humanity and happiness presents its most productive moments: demanding of and for its audience precisely the thing the real office cannot deliver. At such moments, the comedy, implicitly, demands a better mode of life for people, precisely by not denying their present conditions.

Of course, *The Office* is also damn funny—and in more ways than those just noted. Perhaps that is why *The Office* is itself an object of consumption. It plays similar roles to most such objects, offering hints of both distraction and an apparently meaningful identity. Yet, precisely by raising such aspects of contemporary life (almost) into focus, the show also seems to produce a certain tension with its setting and form. It exists in the same kind of gap between image and reality, between business and personhood, that it mines for comedy. The Marxist cultural critic Walter Benjamin once suggested that "authentic humanity" in modern society is located precisely in the tension between the two poles of professional and private life. If this is so, then Michael Scott, with all his gaffes, distortions, pretensions, and failures, may present an image of what is left today of "authentic humanity,"[8] the point from which any effort to alter conditions and people for the better would have to start thinking. "*People* will never go out of business," Michael asserts ("Business School"), and he means it, even if he doesn't know what it means. In failing to act in a professional manner at work, while failing, also, to find any other system of meaning or value to live by in his private life; in failing to use management-speak for its proper ends or to live by any code other than management-speak. In his almost childlike failure to come to terms with the world he lives in (as well as himself), Michael acts as a *critique* of that world. That his character is presented as almost childlike, infantilized, suggests the lengths one has to go to in order to still believe in the present system.[9] Recognizing the possibility of a more genuine critique would require the naming of the class and the economic structures that neither the show nor its characters ever quite name. The strangeness of the show, the "edginess" that people often observe in it, is precisely that it often stands on the very edge of such naming.

NOTES

1 Tad Friend, "The Paper Chase: Office Life in Two Worlds," *The New Yorker* (December 11, 2006), p. 96. Quoted subsequently as (Friend, page number).
2 See Siegfried Kracauer, *The Salaried Masses: Duty and Distraction in Weimar Germany*, trans. Quintin Hoare (New York: Verso, 1998). Quoted subsequently as (Kracauer, page number). This book was written in 1930s Germany as an effort to understand the rise of the new class of office workers, salespeople, etc., the character of their labor, and the illusions they foster.

3 This point, and the synopsis of Marx's views that follows, draws primarily on Marx, *Capital*, Vol. 1, trans. Ben Fowkes (New York: Penguin, 1976). Quoted subsequently as (Marx, page number).

4 The idea that art could provide a richer, fuller model for individual life amid the deadening fragmentation of mechanized divisions of labor goes back at least to 1790 and Friedrich Schiller's *On the Aesthetic Education of Man*, trans. Elizabeth M. Wilkinson and L. A. Willoughby (Oxford: Oxford University Press, 1967).

5 For a full account of the changed character of manual and office work in the twentieth century, see Harry Braverman, *Labor and Monopoly Capital: The Degradation of Work in the Twentieth Century* (New York: Monthly Review Press, 1976).

6 They may well be the stand-ins for the creators, writers, and producers, as well as elements of the audience, all of who may once have had a summer office job (or even one that went on for a year or two) while working on their screenplays or acting classes. Pam's passion for drawing is the most direct sign of this: the artist stands apart (in the creators' own dreams at least) from the emptying out of meaningful work. They are the onscreen stand-ins for the mock-documentary filmmakers who likewise stand apart from the office workers, "not trying to protect the characters," as Greg Daniels, the American producer puts it, during a commentary track, but "trying to expose them" ("Pilot").

7 Indeed, the fact that the show, at least in its American version, draws one of the most highly educated and wealthiest audiences in television suggests that it has another meaning: the opportunity to laugh at the pretensions of those beneath us.

8 For a compelling recent argument that such "humanity" is at the core of Marx's critique of capitalism, see Michael Lebowitz, *Beyond Capital: Marx's Political Economy of the Working Class* (New York: Palgrave MacMillan, 2003).

9 Though this maintenance of belief more often takes an extremely negative form, as the British show suggests: after all, Michael's character, from another perspective, also presents a kind of "glamorization" of the class resentment that David Brent embodies. As David's character expresses, the more common (more realistic) response to the impotence and lack of autonomy that the working world represents is a kind of free-floating rage and resentment that has shown itself, at times, all too willing to side with authoritarian powers to deny its own suffering. Kracauer's concern, for example, writing in 1930s Germany was that the "salaried masses" would prove fertile ground for National Socialism. This was, in fact, the case.

11

Being-in-*The Office*: Sartre, the Look, and the Viewer

Matthew P. Meyer and Gregory J. Schneider

Imagine this: you're fixing your hair, trying to impress someone you are secretly interested in, and someone who knows about your crush catches you in the act. Knowing that you've been caught, a feeling of shame washes over you, and you look away. This is exactly what happens to Pam in an episode titled "Hot Girl" in season 1 of *The Office*, only Pam doesn't get caught by just anybody. She gets caught by the camera—and by us.

We've all been caught doing something we were ashamed of. Curiously, we may not have known that we were doing it, or were ashamed of doing it, until we got caught. But there are also those moments in which we almost get caught—where we hear the wind slam the door shut and quickly extinguish a cigarette, and where we realize it's not someone else catching us that brings the uneasiness and the shame, but us catching ourselves—from the outside, so to speak.

The famous French existentialist Jean-Paul Sartre (1905–1980) makes much of this "getting caught." Calling it "the Look," he tells a story of a man walking down an empty hall who decides to stop and look through a keyhole. The man clearly is not thinking of what he is doing, and is consumed for the moment by curiosity. For the moment that he is looking through the peephole, he ceases to exist, consumed by what he sees . . . until he hears a noise down the hall, and glances up to see that there is someone else down the hall, looking at him looking through the keyhole. All at once the peeping tom is brought back to himself, away from the keyhole, realizes he's been caught, and blushes.[1]

In the routine of everyday life, it's easy to get so caught up in ourselves that we forget that the proverbial cameras are rolling—that we could be seen at any moment. It's this phenomenon that Sartre analyzes, and which we can see in virtually every moment of *The Office*.

Bad Faith and the Look

One key idea of Sartre's existentialism is that "existence precedes essence" (Sartre, 438). This statement is a response to the age-old question, "What's the meaning of life?" Sartre claims that the meaning of life isn't something we discover in the world or within ourselves. It's something we create through the lives we live: it is through our actions and choices that our lives acquire meaning. There is no model of how to live or who to be, and there's no single, prescribed meaning to discover. This is the core of a profound freedom: the freedom to be whatever we have the courage to be.

But sometimes we shirk this freedom and pretend that we have to be this, that, or the other thing. When we pretend we cannot change who we are or our situation, we are acting (or not acting) in *bad faith*. Consider Pam's attitude toward her relationship with Jim. By the end of the second season, the viewer is well aware that Pam is interested in Jim. And yet while Jim at some point voiced his feelings to Pam, Pam does not voice her crush either to Jim or the camera until the end of season 3. (You will see that Pam becomes more truthful and comfortable with herself as she becomes more truthful with others. This is why at the end of season 3 she actively confesses her care for Jim in "The Job.") But up until that point, her view of their relationship is quite the opposite: there are several times she refers to them as "friends" (Yeah right!). This is partly due to the fact that she was engaged to Roy. Pam didn't want to deal with making a choice between Jim and Roy, so she pretended that there was no choice to be made and stayed with Roy. This is an instance of what Sartre calls bad faith, a kind of self-deception. In bad faith we fool ourselves into believing we have no control over a situation, when actually we do. Pam pretends she has to remain engaged to Roy, even though she's into Jim. Pam pretends that once engaged, there is nothing she can do to end her relationship with Roy and begin one with Jim. She pretends that she has no choice—which amounts to choosing not to choose between the two men.

Even at the beginning of season 3, when Pam has broken off her engagement to Roy (conveniently after Jim left Scranton), she still cannot face the idea of Jim as anything but a friend, saying, "That's always a thing that makes people happy: to have an old friend back" ("The Merger"). In order to so successfully pull the wool over her own eyes, Pam must teeter-totter between pretending she is capable of choosing and pretending that she cannot choose. Consider how awkwardly Pam acts when trying to avoid the issue of being into Jim in a conversation with Karen ("Ben Franklin"):

Karen: Hey, um, I want to talk to you. I know this is weird or whatever, but Jim told me about you guys.
Pam: Whad'ya mean?
Karen: Well, that you kissed . . . I mean we talked it through and it's totally fine. It's not a big deal; it's just a kiss. [Pause] Wait, you're not still interested in him?
Pam: Oh, yeah.
Karen: Really?
Pam: Oh, no. I was confused by your phrasing. You should definitely go out with Jim. I mean, you are going out with Jim. You're dating him, which is awesome 'cause you guys are great together.
Karen: Ok . . .
Pam: And I'm not into Jim . . . Yeah.
Karen: So, um, we're good?
Pam: Yeah . . . sorry.
Karen: What are you sorry about?
Pam: Um, what?
Karen: What are you sorry about?
Pam: Nothing, I was just thinking of something else.

Pam is clearly avoiding responsibility for her feelings. Her inability to choose her own feelings so befuddles her that she can barely get out a complete sentence. While Karen chooses to play it straight and attempts to clear the air, Pam continues avoiding the decision to face, or once and for all forget, her attraction to Jim. Sartre calls something that can choose a "being-for-itself" and something which cannot choose a "being-in-itself." Thus, when we are in bad faith, we're pretending to be what Sartre calls the *in-itself*—some object that cannot change—instead of being a person who can. So by acting in bad faith we attempt to bridge the opposition between a for-itself (a person) and an in-itself (an object). But pretending we are unable to change ourselves can also be seen (no pun intended) as a matter of changing perspective. Sartre says about bad faith that: "We can equally well use another kind of duplicity derived from human reality which we will express roughly by saying that its being-for-itself implies complimentarily a being-for-Others. Upon any one of my conducts it's always possible to converge two looks, mine and that of the Other" (Sartre, 57). What Sartre means by "the Other" is really just understanding ourselves from the perspective of another person. We recognize that other people exist, and yet we cannot get into their heads. All we have of them is the way they look at us and the interpretation we give that look. In being looked at, we become the object (in-itself) of the Other's gaze. If someone catches me staring inappropriately at a woman, in that person's eyes I am a pervert. I become a pervert through *their looking* at me. But we can also take this external view ourselves, seeing ourselves as though from the outside. In other words (and here is the key connection between bad faith, "fooling ourselves," and the look, "being seen"), to be in bad faith is to imagine ourselves being seen from the outside, from the standpoint of the Other. It's to be under the intense pressure of the Look.

For Sartre, the Look is an everyday event that informs how we understand other people and how we understand those other people understanding us. In fact, analyzing someone else looking at me can give me some key insights into what it means to be a person surrounded by other people. It can also help us see how we are able or unable to connect with others. One thing we can say about being looked at by someone (the Other) is that it's not in our control.

I cannot control what the Other is doing or thinking in looking at me. If we could control the thoughts of the Other, we could save ourselves explaining a lot of embarrassing situations! Imagine the reaction of his co-workers when Michael burns his foot on the grill ("The Injury"), or when Michael attempts to stop the spread of a private photo (of Michael and Jan) that he accidentally sent to the entire packing email list ("Back from Vacation"). In each of these situations, if it were possible for Michael to control what his co-workers think he could save himself a lot of trouble and embarrassment. When the Other looks at us, Sartre tells us, "The Other's freedom is revealed to me across the uneasy indetermination of the being which I am for him" (Sartre, 262).

Of course, all of this embarrassment could also be avoided if the employees of Dunder-Mifflin were constantly aware of the presence of the camera, but this is nearly impossible. Were we to see such awareness, the camera would show its true nature as that view which controls what it views without being controlled in return. A few decades after Sartre, the French historian and philosopher Michel Foucault (1926–1984) appropriated the perfect scenario for such an uncontrolled-controller from the earlier English philosopher Jeremy Bentham (1748–1832). The scenario was the panopticon. In its original form it was a plan for a highly efficient prison. In the panopticon there is a center tower with obscured glass surrounded by stories of cells that only have an opening toward the center tower. The result is that the guard in the center tower *could* be looking at you at anytime, but as a prisoner you are unable to see him. As a result, the prisoners learn to police themselves. The power, as Foucault puts it, is *visible*, but *unverifiable*. Power is always looking.² Sometimes such an awareness of power can be seen by certain Dunder-Mifflin employees. Consider how Dwight and Angela act around each other when they anticipate the camera's presence ("Phyllis' Wedding"):

> *Dwight*: Hello Angela.
> *Angela*: Hello Dwight.
> *Dwight*: You look as beautiful as the Queen of England.
> *Angela*: Thank you.
> [Then a pause and for no apparent reason]
> *Angela*: Don't linger. Break left.
> [Pause, Dwight walks to the right.]
> *Angela*: LEFT!
> [Frustrated, Angela goes left.]

Or consider the conversation between Michael and Jan on Michael's cell phone while he is driving Dwight to a company cocktail party ("Cocktails"):

> *Michael*: Hewo you.
> *Jan*: Michael?
> *Michael*: I'm on my way right now. I should be there in about fifteen . . .
> *Jan*: Let's just blow this party off.

Michael: That's what she said.
Jan: [Laugh] Am I on speaker phone?
Michael: Ummm, yes you are.
Jan: Is anybody else . . .
Dwight: Hello Jan.
Jan: Hi Dwight. Ok Michael, take me off speaker phone.
Michael: No le probleme. [Michael can't seem to take the phone off
    of speaker mode]
Jan: Ok, let's just go to a motel and get into each other like we did on
    the black sand beach in Jamaica.
Michael: Ok, Jan. Jan, this party is actually a big step for us so, I . . .
Jan: Am I still on speaker?
Michael: Uuum, I th . . . Uh, I don't know. [Michael knows they are
    still on speaker]
Jan: Are the cameras there?
Michael: Maybe. [They are and Michael knows this]
Jan: Alright. See you soon.
Dwight: Talk to you later Jan.
Michael: Alright. Bye.

In these two conversations it's abundantly clear how people would
act if the cameras were not rolling. Thus, in the very possibility that
a camera could be watching Dwight and Angela, or listening to Jan,
they shut down. This is the effect of the panopticon: even though no
one may be watching, people act as though they are being watched.
They essentially internalize the possibility that the Other is always
watching, and act accordingly. (There is a convenient and hilarious
contrast to the "awareness" of Jan and Michael later in "Cocktails."
On the way home from the party Michael and Jan are sharing an
intimate "make-up" conversation, when to the viewer's surprise
Dwight has been in the back seat all along!)

We are intimately and unknowingly affected by the possibility of
being seen. When people are around we must adjust ourselves to the
"permanent possibility that a subject who sees me may be substituted
for an object seen by me. 'Being-seen-by-the-Other' is *the truth* of
'seeing-the-Other'" (Sartre, 257). When we see someone like ourselves, we realize that they can see and think just as freely as we can
see and think. This leads us to why we react the way we do to getting
caught. In the Look, I have my freedom to be what I want taken away
by the way that the Other sees me. Angela, who is notorious for being
judgmental, demonstrates this well, and her judgmental glance can be

seen in the following two conversations. First, from "A Benihana Christmas":

> *Angela*: Phyllis, I need you to pick up green streamers at lunch.
> *Phyllis*: I thought you said green was whorish.
> [Angela quickly looks up and down Phyllis' orange blouse]
> *Angela*: No. Orange is whorish.
> [Pam has a look of disbelief on her face]

And we can see the same judgmental look in this scene from later in the same episode:

> [Angela looks at Kevin collecting another plate of food at her poorly
>   attended Christmas party]
> *Angela*: Uh-uh. No one has seconds until everyone's had some.
> *Kevin*: You've *got* to be kidding!
> [Angela stares directly at Kevin's gut]
> *Angela*: You've got to be kidding.

In each of these cases the Other's look removes Phyllis' and then Kevin's ability to determine how they are to be seen. In implying with her glance that Phyllis dresses like a whore, and that Kevin is a pig, the look says more than her words and determines who Kevin and Phyllis are at that moment, much to their dismay.

In bad faith, on the other hand, I take away *my own* freedom by pretending that I do not have a choice and by determining myself as the Other *might* see me. Both the Look and bad faith concern our relationship to our freedom, whether we accept it and whether we have to give it up for the moment.

Let's now turn to how bad faith and the Look play out in Pam Beesley's visible shame, and David Brent's obvious pride.

Pam Beesley's Shame and the Camera's Unwelcomed Look

Even though the camera does not have eyes, it serves to grant us that outside position of the Other from which we can imagine ourselves. In the third season, Jim returns from Stamford. It's in the next few episodes that our suspicions about Pam's feelings for Jim are confirmed. And they are confirmed by the way Pam looks at Jim and Karen. Keep in mind that all of this is shown through Pam's looks— at Jim and Karen, at the camera, and at the ground.

In the episode "The Merger," Michael, for the sake of solidarity between the newly united offices, stages a prank by letting out the air in the employees' tires. When he calls them out to see what "someone" has done, people are awkwardly milling about in the parking lot. The camera focuses in on Jim and Karen walking back inside when suddenly Karen affectionately scratches Jim's back. The camera then pans back to find Pam looking at the exchange between Jim and Karen—she looks right at the camera, devastated, and then looks down. Here we see Pam ashamed at getting caught looking at Jim. It's painful moments like these when we want to be seen the least. This is precisely it—all of a sudden, Pam cannot rise out of that situation. "Shame reveals to me that I am this being, not in the mode of 'was' or of 'having-to-be' but in-itself" (Sartre, 262). In other words, one of the most disturbing aspects of being ashamed, though we may not often realize it, is that in shame we are ultimately turned, by way of the Other looking at us, into an object *not* of our own making. Surely, Pam's crush on Jim is innocent enough. However, in getting caught pining over Jim being with another co-worker, it becomes real and serious. Pam all of a sudden becomes responsible for her feelings—which she had never really felt before, precisely because she is not willing to face up to them. She takes up the burden of her feelings on someone else's ground—at someone else's choosing. Being ashamed is being imprisoned in the position opposite the Look that the Other throws at us. We can feel this lack of freedom when we respond indignantly: "How dare you look at me that way!" Shame, on the other hand, is almost a silent acceptance of being how the Other sees us.

This means that shame—when we take it up as our own and listen to what it says about us—can be a good thing. We can learn from understanding what the Other, as a subject, sees us as and the feeling we get as a result of that representation. In getting caught pining over Jim, Pam can understand that she does actually like Jim. (Getting caught in the act is no fun, so we might as well get something out of it!) We can, at least in theory, own up to the person we see ourselves as through the Other's Look. As we will see with pride, this ability to make the best of the Other's look is foreclosed by the prideful person's turning the Other into an object first.

David Brent's Pride and the
Welcomed Look of the Camera

But what if we could control the effect that the look of the Other has on us? The arrogant person attempts just this. Like shame, pride and arrogance are common responses to the Look. But these differ from shame in that the one looked at actively tries to take control of the situation. In other words, arrogance is the move to use the Other's look to eliminate shame and replace it with affection, camaraderie, or respect. The epitome of this reaction is found in David Brent. One of the hallmarks of David 's managerial style is his over-the-top striving for self-promotion. He's constantly selling himself to his employees, the camera, and, ultimately, to himself. In the language of Sartre, by recognizing himself as an *in-itself* (an object), David attempts to use the Look of the Other to rewrite the situation as well as the way that he is viewed by himself and Others. But because the Other is *for-itself*, that is, a free subject, this attempt to control the look necessarily fails, leaving David to face his own bad faith.

In the first episode of the second series[3] of the British version of *The Office*, an employee stands at a fax machine next to David's office. As he types in the fax number, David appears in the open doorway of his office, glancing quickly at the employee and then at camera. He then retreats into his office, returning a moment later with a trade magazine in hand to brag to his employee and the camera about his picture on the cover:

> Oh no . . . going through some old stuff . . . found that, look at that: *Inside Paper*. [Looks at camera, displaying magazine, giggling] It's the trade magazine for the paper industry [employee looks at camera confused] . . . my ugly mug on the front [points to head shot] . . . Oh no [giggles] . . . Embarrassing . . . Alright [shoos the unimpressed employee away] . . . Ohhhh . . . he's put me off what I was doing . . . what was I? . . . oh yeah . . . phone calls [David returns to office].

What is critical in this scene is that the employee hasn't done anything. David has put himself off by trying to use the looks of both the camera and the employee to create an image of himself that would cultivate a feeling of respect in the employee, in the audience (via the camera), and thus in himself. But we know David, we know what he is up to, and as he slinks back to his office, it's clear that for a moment he knows all of this as well.

David Brent clearly realizes that he is determined by the way others see him. With this realization, he makes the next logical step: once we understand that the Other's look can force us into a state of being (into shame, for example), we can attempt to control the effect of the Other's look. After all, if my feelings of shame are a result of this look, then it seems reasonable that if I can do things like show off my picture on *Inside Paper*, then I might successfully create another, more pleasant reaction. Hence, through pride we can play offense, though alas it is mired in bad faith.

Sartre argues that "vanity impels me to get hold of the Other and to constitute him as an object in order to burrow into the heart of this object to discover there my own object-state. But this is to kill the hen that lays the golden eggs" (Sartre, 291). David's attempt to control the outcome of his employee's look requires that he constitute the employee as an object (an in-itself) rather than as a subject. This is to deny the employee his freedom. Unfortunately for David, this results in a paradox: at the same time that he "kills" the employee's freedom (in Sartre's explanation, "the hen that lays the golden eggs"), he requires it in order to feel truly proud (Sartre, 291). After all, if he hasn't been given respect freely, it isn't worth much.

The effect of this paradox is to throw David's own freedom, literally, back in his face. In his pride, David has not only denied the very thing he requires. He has also, in effect, attempted to circumvent his own freedom and responsibility by treating himself as an object for the Other. But David cannot control the situation. The Other, after all, is free. He will see David as he wants. David's attempt to control the Other must fail. We see this as the scene comes to a close and David tries to act as if the entire encounter was his employee's fault. In this failure, David's own freedom is made palpable, for it was only as a free subject that he could attempt to objectify both himself and the Other.

The Viewer and the Look

Our experience watching Pam's shame-filled reactions and David's awkward attempts at shameless self-promotion make *The Office*, at times, difficult to watch. In fact, some people have been so affected by the show that they have stopped watching it altogether (the silly fools). But this difficulty in watching the show is also what makes it such a brilliant success. Pam's shame and David's pride exist because the camera (and the viewer) exists. Through the look at the camera, the audience is made complicit in the events and experiences that transpire on the screen. We become fellow employees and co-workers. Hence, the power of *The Office*: via the look of the camera, we are allowed to be in the office without "being-in-*The Office*."

NOTES

1 Jean-Paul Sartre, *Being and Nothingness*, trans. by Hazel E. Barnes (New York: Gramercy Books, 1956), 260.
2 Michel Foucault, *Discipline and Punish*, trans. by Alan Sheridan (New York: Vintage, 1995), p. 201.
3 What Americans would call the second "season."

12

A Boy Who Swims Faster than a Shark: Jean Baudrillard Visits *The Office*

Russell Manning

Like a Xerox machine monotonously spitting out copies, the everyday office produces goods and services of remarkable uniformity and shapes employees to be as predictable as Finch's sexual escapades. So we laugh at David Brent (not with him) because he is the antithesis of what the *real* office demands. Brent produces chaos. By laughing at Brent we are covertly and inadvertently supporting the system that produces Neil Godwin, a "real" manager and entertainer. In laughing at Brent, we are tacitly *endorsing* another system—one that we ought to be wary of. The Godwin system produces homogeneity in behavior, actions, and beliefs—as if we were all being spat out of the "social-cultural photocopier." To get a sense of this let's employ the service of French philosopher Jean Baudrillard (1929–2007)[1] and his concepts of "the hyperreal" and "fatal strategy." The Brentmeister and his protégé Gareth Keenan will bring the French theory back to British reality.

Jean Baudrillard and Simulacra

Who says famine has to be depressing? (2:5)

French cultural theorist and philosopher Jean Baudrillard achieved cult status in the 1980s for his writings on *simulacra*. For Baudrillard,

141

this term translates as an "unreal appearance" drawing from Plato's idea that common reality is in fact a shadow of a higher, more perfect reality. The simulacrum, for Baudrillard, is the illusion of "social reality." We understand that in a television situation comedy like *The Office* the cast are not real people (nor real office workers). They are a constructed appearance for the purpose of entertainment. This simulacrum becomes philosophically interesting, however, when we, as viewers, lose our ability to tell the difference between the appearance and the reality. Some people aspire to live the lives they see on TV, considering these to be the best (or only) ways available. To be as successful with women as Finchy or as suave as Neil Godwin—this is the stuff simulated dreams are made of! Television in this instance has won the duel between reality and appearance, creating a whole new substitute reality.[2]

Simulacra are highly effective in the construction of social reality. The rapid development of technology has promoted things "more real than the real world itself"—it has promoted appearance, consuming reality itself. We are becoming more interested in imitating the cast of television shows (such as *The Sopranos*, or *Desperate Housewives*, or *The Simpsons*) than being ourselves. While we have always looked to fashion to help shape our outer selves, we have never been as dependent on technological media for this as we are now.

Social reality is being replaced by *hyperreality*—what appears to be reality but which is merely a simulacrum of it. Consider Hollywood's penchant for digitally altering and constructing images in blockbuster films. A battle in Steven Spielberg's *Saving Private Ryan*, for example, becomes more real to the viewer than the battle itself in two ways. First, the cinema patron "lives the experience" of the battle by the sheer visceral power of the presentation. Second, the viewer comes to the (impossible) conclusion that they now know what it's like to be in a battle. This, in Baudrillard's terms, is taking cinematic experience as a replacement for real experience. Of course, the cinematic experience is designed principally to sell tickets. So the corresponding advertising will tell you that you are "so close that you will actually feel like you are there." You can experience the world of dinosaurs, "Death Stars," or the sinking of the Titanic—all of which are designed to relieve you of the price of the ticket while getting you to think you've had a *real* experience. This is hyperreality. You'll recognize it because you've been there.

Problems emerge, according to Baudrillard, when simulated experience deadens our ability to tell the difference between the simulacrum and its origin. With hyperreality, appearance is *all* you experience. This is the "reality" in which David Brent is irretrievably lost. Brent never knows if his philosophical wisdom constructs or destroys a social reality. His "motivational techniques" performance is a supreme example (2:4). As Brent dances to Tina Turner's "Simply the Best" he is lost in his own clichéd world of banal jargon and deplorable witticisms. And this is the paradoxical genius embedded in the series. While we cringe at his performance, we have to judge him against another completely illusory ideal boss.

Baudrillard's work is controversial and obscure, making many deliberately preposterous and inflammatory claims.[3] He writes this way to get readers to respond to the system they live in, examine the "codes" that produce their social reality in order to duel with them through challenge. Baudrillard's project was to examine the broadening gulf between reality and appearance, forcing us to try and grasp the "disappearance of the world" into hyperreality. *The Office* offers a similar intellectual challenge. It forces us to evaluate the hapless Brent and the pathetic Gareth. But it also forces us to evaluate the systems that we offer up in their place.[4]

Brentian Hyperreality: The Simulated Boss/Philosopher

It's like bloody Dead Poets Society out there. (2:4)

Let's examine the man who "talks the talk," the Brentmeister General. In our very first meeting with David Brent we see him fabricate a CV (that's a resume, for you Yanks), commit a *faux pas* ("How is Elaine? Has she left you yet?"), and lie as he boasts of a potential employee that "he gives the forklift tests." Brent is the master of the politically incorrect gaffe, suggesting "I will not have her tunnel bandied around this office willy-nilly" or "Some women like it the wrong way" (1:1). He is also a gross (mis)reader of the workplace situation, claiming "You don't need luck when you've got 71.4 percent of the population behind you" (1:6). His command of Wernham-Hogg is tenuous and employees' looks (to the camera) of exasperation are plenty, with even the scurrilous Chris Finch declaring that Brent is "a waste of space." The Brentian management system sketches a neat encapsulation of what Baudrillard saw as the hyperreal. Hyperreality exists in three stages, which Baudrillard sees as the *three orders of the simulacra.*

First, in an ideal world a boss should have a set of admirable and obligatory virtues. We could include with these empathy and, borrowing from Aristotle (384–322 BCE), wisdom, prudence, understanding, and judgment.[5] In classical terms these would seem to indicate an effective and productive manager of the workplace. In Baudrillard's terms they would equate to the "first order of simulacra" where the actions of the boss (his signs or codes) correspond to or reflect an underlying "profound" reality[6] (Neil Godwin, perhaps).

In the second order of simulacra, Baudrillard says, the signs start to *mask* this profound reality. At this level Baudrillard says the hyperreal or simulation begins to occur where the virtues are tampered with. What was originally considered virtue is now masked by the misapplication of it, in this case at the expense of the defenseless worker. This is captured in the fiasco that is Gareth Keenan. When he is assigned to offer health and safety training to Donna, he uses his role as a strategy to seduce Donna:

> *Gareth*: Basically there's a correct way and an incorrect way to lift stuff. All right. This is the incorrect way [bends over 90 degrees and lifts box, knees straight the entire time]. Ok? Incorrect. The correct way, two things to remember. First of all, keep your back nice and straight. Straight back. And then . . .
> *Donna*: Bend your knees
> *Gareth*: Shhhh . . . Back straight and bend your knees. All right? Very important. That's the correct way. Do you wanna try that with me?
> *Donna*: I'm fine.
> *Gareth*: Well, I'm supposed to witness you do it so I can tick the box . . . so just do it with me a couple of times. All right? So . . . [they begin to lift boxes] nice straight back, bend your knees, up . . . [Donna and Gareth pick up their respective boxes] that's it, same on the way down as on the way up . . .

After a cutaway to Tim and Dawn, we're treated to the rest of the health and safety training:

Gareth: . . . down again. Good. One more time [they bend down again]. Nice straight back! Nice straight back! That's it. That's it. Good. One more time [and they bend down again]. Great. So have you got that?

Donna: [looking annoyed] I'll practice it at home.

Gareth: Excellent. Good. Well done. If there's any questions you want to ask, or, you know, if you want to talk about anything at all just . . . I know you've um . . . slept with Jeff.

Donna: [annoyed, walking away] All right, are we done then?

Gareth: You made a mistake . . .

Donna: No I haven't made a mistake . . .

Gareth: I'm just checking whether you're going to be sleeping with him again or spreading it around a bit.

Donna: Right. Bye. [Walks out]

Gareth: Good. Yeah. Excellent pupil. Fast learner. She won't be spilling any fluids or lifting things incorrectly. "A" I'm going to give her . . . [shows clipboard to camera]. "A."

What was once a legitimate (and even virtuous) workplace event (giving workers all the information they need to stay healthy and safe) degenerates into a painful case of sexual harassment. The signs of health and safety merely mask Gareth's sexual desires. Lifting boxes indeed.

In the third order of simulacra the sign masks the absence of any profound reality. Baudrillard says that now the sign has its own reality. Now the workplace is run by hyperreal strategies that have little connection to tradition or virtue. They are driven by the mesmeric, vertiginous chase for profit combined with the untrammeled flexing of personal ego. When the hyperreal experience tries to "produce" its own reality, we're in big trouble.

And in this world we find Brent. His management technique is purely hyperreal. When we examine his actions and his pithy expressions we can see that they do not refer to any original virtues but in actuality mask the fact that he is saying nothing—a crucial part of his strategy to hide the fact that he is not a boss. There is no greater example of his hyperreal ineptitude than in the "training" episode (1:4). Brent destroys the initial role-playing exercise:

Rowan (director of the training session):   Now it's time for the dreaded role play. We'll kick off with your leader, David Brent. David, if you'd like to come up here . . . Big round of applause for David. [Staff claps unenthusiastically]

David:　No, no, no. Cheating really. I've done this before.

Rowan:　Good. That should make it a lot easier for us.

David:　Yeah, yeah.

Rowan:　Ok. Nice and simple to start with.

David:　Hard as you like . . .

Rowan:　Well, let's kick off with something easy. I want us to play out a scenario that highlights customer care. All of you have to deal with people . . .

David:　All the time . . .

Rowan:　It's always possible to improve people skills. In this scenario . . . we'll start with something nice and easy . . . I'm going to play a . . . and this will be the wrong way to do it . . . I'm going to play a very bad hotel manager who just doesn't care.

David:　[interrupting] If it's a Basil Fawlty type character, maybe I should do it for the comedy.

Rowan:　Let me just play it now to kick things off, Ok?

David:　I'll probably bring some of that to this role anyway . . .

Rowan:　Right. You've got a complaint. Come and complain and I'll show you the wrong way to handle it. This will be the *wrong* way . . . Ok. So off we go.

David:　[looks confused] Sorry. What's the complaint?

Rowan:　Just make it up.

David:　Anything [turns to address staff]. There's no right or wrong thing in this scenario. We'll tell you the right thing afterward.

Rowan:　You complain.

David:　Get on with it, yeah? Ok, I'd like to make a complaint, please.

Rowan:　I don't care

David:　[a little flummoxed] Well, I am staying in the hotel . . .

Rowan:　I don't care. It's not my shift.

David:　Well, you're an ambassador for the hotel.

Rowan:　I don't care. I don't care.

David:　Well I think you will when I tell you what the complaint is . . .

Rowan:　[more loudly] I don't care!

David:　[shouting] I think there's been a rape up there!

[Everyone is silent, bewildered.]

David:　[addressing the staff] I've got his attention. Get their attention.

(1:4)

David clearly doesn't understand role-playing. But what does he understand? Contemplate this list of Brentian ineptitudes: the Internet, women, Dutch girls' boobs, dwarves, the disabled, music, fundraising, and comedy. Brent masks his ignorance and insecurity through a particular brand of managerial doublespeak that is hyperreal *par excellence*. Hyperreal management has arrived. Simply put, this management style has the capacity to "interfere" with what should be considered effective management traditions. The genius of Gervais is to let Brent get too close to reality in his portrayal of management technique. We all witness Brentisms every day. The jargon of management-speak distorts any attempt for clarity.

What is interesting here is not the lack of credibility in David Brent but *our* attitude towards him. We laugh at his ineptitude, his *faux pas*, and his grand rhetorical hashes: "Trust received, responsibility given and taken" (1:5) sounds sensible until it is investigated. Likewise, consider these two gems: "mutual likewise reciprocated" (1:2) and "I call it team individuality" (2:3). By seeing these pearls as swine we are elevating that "ideal" form of boss that is meant to be in place of David Brent. Hence, we are in effect consolidating the system itself and are using the hyperreal Brent to posit another Boss, an ideal effective virtuous model.

But this means we're conceding that the boss is a necessary facet of the system. Strangely, then, by laughing at Brent we are reinforcing the status quo of the consumerist system that produces offices and bosses (and therefore the high potential for exploitation and corruption in all its forms). When recognizing Brent as an ineffective manager, what are we positing about our own view of the world? Unfortunately, we seem to be endorsing the view that it is good to be managed, even though good management by necessity implies (albeit soft) exploitation to squeeze work out of us.

The Fatal Strategy of Gareth Keenan

Two Lesbians, probably sisters—I'm just watching. (1:4)

Gareth Keenan, the Brentian mini-me, is a consummate example of Baudrillard's "fatal strategy." A fatal strategy is a system that cannot sustain itself—that is doomed to destruction. For Baudrillard, social systems always contain the seeds of their own destruction. The rise of terrorism is the fatal strategy of desire for freedom; obesity is the fatal strategy of the desire for consumption.

Idolizing Brent, Gareth models his language and lifestyle on him: "Just the eight pints for me last night then." He sees himself as a womanizer with deadly pick-up lines like "Are you going to be sleeping with him again or spreading it around" (1:5) and as both sensitive and strong, suggesting "I'll do you from behind if it's just a quick in and out" (2:3). In his desire to become Brent, Gareth produces violent reactions. He has occasional victories (the menage-a-trois with the bikies at Chasers (1:3), the dreadlocked blonde at the end-of-year financial party (1:6), the "sex toys"). But these victories are overshadowed by the failures. Gareth, utilizing the systems and codes of Brent, takes them to a higher, more hyperrealized level and they cave in on him. His sexism intensifies when he opines "Women who work in factories are slappers" (2:3). His homophobia heightens, leading him to facetiously conclude "And that's one of the main arguments against letting gay men into the army," all the while insisting that he is not homophobic. "Come around and look at my CD collection. I've got Queen, George Michael, Pet Shop Boys. They're all bummers" (1:2). Gareth's inability to sustain and develop interpersonal relationships sees him finally dissolve into a bumbling mess in Brent's office, begging to be "assistant national manger" at the end of series one (1:6).

Gareth uses his insensitivity to claim that he is sensitive; he uses his homophobia as evidence that he is not homophobic. In his attempt to ingratiate himself into a conversation (the Brentian desire for universal acceptance) Gareth pushes the boundaries of the conversation to the extreme through either being offensive, as in explaining the negativity of sexually transmitted diseases in the army ("Paxton sir he's got knob rot off some tart" (1:5)), or banal, as in challenging the competency of technology:

> *Gareth*:   [on the phone] I just got a complaint from a very important client, claiming that the figures I gave him were wrong, and . . .
> [Pauses to hear person on the other end of the line]
> *Gareth*:   Yeah, well basically I've checked all other possibilities and it's come down to the calculator [pauses again]. Well, I don't know. Circuitry? Sorry, who is this I'm talking to?

The absurd is another thing that interrupts the flow of normal conversation, and pushes the boundaries of intelligibility. Consider

Gareth's conversation with Tim about Tim's plans to go back to university:

> *Gareth*: What do you want to be a psychiatrist for? They're all mad themselves, aren't they?
>
> *Tim*: I want to be a psychologist.
>
> *Gareth*: Same difference. All right then Einstein, what am I thinking about now?
>
> *Tim*: You're thinking, "How could I kill a tiger armed only with a biro?"
>
> *Gareth*: No.
>
> *Tim*: No? You're thinking, "If I crash land in the jungle, will I be able to eat my own shoes?"
>
> *Gareth*: No, and you can't.
>
> *Tim*: What are you thinking, Gareth?
>
> *Gareth*: I was just wondering, will there ever be a boy born who can swim faster than a shark?
>
> (1:5)

For Jean Baudrillard, "fatal" announcements such as Gareth's create their own world—effectively "doubling the world," albeit momentarily. If Gareth were a powerful and seductive orator his doubled world would remain and we would find ourselves contemplating the rapidly swimming boy, the position of snipers on roofs, or the use of frog venom to take out an enemy. Gareth's fatality is that he cannot effectively double the world with his speech because the content is encoded with its own destruction. His extreme, antagonistic social patter, such as "Condoms come in all different flavors, don't they?" (1:5), reverses itself on its audience and Gareth is marginalized and ignored.

Jean Baudrillard Did Not Visit *The Office*

But he might have. Indeed, he might have lived there, under a desk, or behind a vending machine. And while we laugh at David Brent and Gareth Keenan, Baudrillard would surely laugh at us. We think that their banter is absurd, that their actions are contradictory and buffoonish. But we are no better, you and I. For the system that we think is *real*—the system of Neil Godwin, redundancies, and diminishing expectations—is no less absurd than "team individuality" and boys who swim faster than sharks.

NOTES

1 Jean Baudrillard passed away during the writing of this chapter. His obituaries were stunning testimony to his enigmatic thought and theory.
2 We can now see this at a more sinister level with petty criminals "learning" to behave through watching *The Sopranos* (And some of the members of *The Sopranos* learned to behave from watching *The Godfather*).
3 Perhaps most controversially, he claimed in 1991 (in French, though) that "the Gulf War did not take place." For the same claim in English, see *The Gulf War Did Not Take Place* (Bloomington: Indiana University Press, 1995). On the surface this is preposterous. When read carefully, Baudrillard was actually asserting that because it was so mediated and controlled by television, for many people it was *as if* it was a hyperreal experience, not a real one, which is the typical collision between his inflammatory statements and their being misread.
4 Therefore, if Brent is not "Simply the Best" what do we think is? From where do we draw the examples to juxtapose against Brent's pathetic motivational performance?
5 Aristotle, in the *Nichomachean Ethics*, prescribes a set of personal characteristics which could be achieved through the combination of rational thinking and excellence of practice. They have been deeply influential in the construction of ethical systems and the measurement of personal behavior since.
6 Jean Baudrillard, *Simulacra and Simulation* (Ann Arbor: University of Michigan Press, 1994). See chapter 1, "The Precession of Simulacra," in particular.

MEMO 4
MIND YOUR BUSINESS!

13

Stakeholders vs. Stockholders in *The Office*

Rory E. Kraft, Jr.

In break rooms around the country there is a common complaint: "They only care about the bottom line; they don't care about us at all."[1] "They" is synonymous with management, the ones who appear to decide the fate of the world—including whether the water cooler is going to remain in the break room, given the new budget cutbacks. From workers to suppliers, from customers to the larger community, a wide range of people and organizations are impacted by the decisions and actions of the corporate elite. The study of business ethics has given a name to this collection of interested parties. They are the *stakeholders*—and *The Office* is full of them.

Stakeholder Theory[2]

Stakeholder analysis is the consideration of which groups will be impacted by a business practice and what that impact is.[3] Igor Ansoff's version of stakeholder theory sums things up in this way:

> This theory maintains that the objectives of the firm should be derived balancing the conflicting claims of various "stakeholders" in the firm: managers, workers, stockholders, suppliers, vendors. The firm has a responsibility to all of these and must configure its objectives so as to give each a measure of satisfaction. Profit which is a return on investment to the stockholders is one of such satisfactions, but

does not necessarily receive special predominance in the objective structure.[4]

While there are different versions of stakeholder theory, the basic idea is the same: the more stakeholders that are satisfied by an action, the better the action is for the company.[5] A real issue in utilizing stakeholder theory is determining who out of a potentially infinite set of people are *salient* stakeholders, or the stakeholders that matter in determining a course of action. One potential solution is to identify the stakeholders "to whom management *should* pay attention" by examining:

1 the stakeholder's *power* to influence the firm;
2 the *legitimacy* of the stakeholder's relationship with the firm; and
3 the *urgency* of the stakeholder's claim on the firm.[6]

Using the Mitchell model, management is able to both consider the impact of a decision on a broad group of those impacted by it and focus on the satisfaction of those who will be most impacted by that decision. Using a smaller set of salient stakeholders is an attempt to address the fact that given the global nature of business, "it is bewilderingly complex for managers to apply" stakeholder theory in decision making (Mitchell et al. 1997: 857).

While much of stakeholder literature assumes (as I do here) that doing good by the stakeholders will result in financial benefits for corporations, "there is as yet no compelling empirical evidence that the optimal strategy for maximizing a firm's conventional financial and market performance is stakeholder management" (Donaldson and Preston 1995: 78). Donaldson and Preston also note that using corporate reputation surveys shows that increased satisfaction of stakeholders does not come at the expense of other stakeholders. If we consider stockholders to be stakeholders, then this implies that the happiness (probably measured in dividends) of stockholders is not necessarily diminished by increasing the happiness of others (i.e., employees, customers). Further, there is "no notable evidence of [stakeholder theory's] *in*consistency" with profit (p. 81). But strong motivations for using stakeholder theory come from moral, not financial, pressures.

Looking at Dunder-Mifflin, a midsize paper and office supply distributor in the American Northeast with an emphasis on servicing small-business clients, we can see how these concerns play out. The immediate stakeholders are obvious: the stockholders (Dunder-Mifflin is "traded on the New York Stock Exchange, ever heard of it?"—as Andy Bernard informs us in "Traveling Salesmen"), the employees, and suppliers, and the customers. But in actuality the stakeholders go beyond these limited numbers. Focusing for a moment solely on the Scranton branch, we can see that Billy Merchant, the building supervisor for the Scranton Business Park, has an interest in the continued success of Dunder-Mifflin, as does Bob Vance (of Vance Refrigeration). Bob Vance, interestingly, is impacted by Dunder-Mifflin policies not only as a shared tenant of the office park, but (as of season 3) also as the spouse of Phyllis Vance (née Lapin). *The Office* has not yet explored how any tensions between these two roles will be reconciled. (In a similar manner, we did not know how Jan Levinson and Michael Scott would resolve any potential tensions between upper-management and mid-management priorities when Jan worked for Dunder-Mifflin.) Bob Vance did offer to take over the warehouse and hire all of the warehouse workers when it appeared that the Scranton branch of Dunder-Mifflin was being closed ("Branch Closing"). So it seems that Vance Refrigeration, though not directly impacted by the success or failure of Dunder-Mifflin, could indirectly benefit from the failure of the branch. This sort of impact on stakeholders is not always apparent—nor can businesses often consider it. Yet stakeholder theory calls for a business to realize "that the actions it takes have definite and often far-reaching effects—effects that go beyond stockholders, employees, and customer."[7]

If we turn from this basic stakeholder picture to the individuals who make up Dunder-Mifflin, we can understand conflicts more clearly in light of the stakeholder model.

Stakeholders and Individuals

On a small scale, we can see a divide between Michael Scott and the rest of the Scranton office on what appears to be an insignificant difference. Michael favors dining at large chains, while employees favor local restaurants and taverns. For example, Michael believes that Chili's is "the new golf course" (even going to the point of sending a letter to *Small Business Man Magazine*) ("The Client"). He offers Devon Chili's gift certificates as a bit of a consolation after firing him ("Halloween"), and even holds the annual branch awards event at Chili's ("The Dundies"). Michael also frequents Hooters ("The Secret"), goes to Sbarro Pizza when in New York ("Valentine's Day"), and appears to be sending Ryan Howard out to various Boston Markets for chicken ("The Injury"). Even in supposedly small matters, he favors national products; thus he subscribes to *USA Today* instead of the local paper, and drinks coffee from Starbucks ("Hot Girl"). In contrast to this, after his firing Devon invites everyone (except Michael, Creed Bratton, Dwight Schrute, and Angela Martin) to Poor Richard's, a local tavern in Scranton. In an odd coincidence, after it is determined that the branch is not closing (and having sold company property for $1,200), Creed offers to buy shots at Poor Richard's for everyone. In addition, while they cannot agree on where to eat, the office staff does briefly consider (at Phyllis Lapin's suggestion) going out for lunch together—all at local restaurants[8] ("Branch Closing").[9] Throughout the series we can see in the break room a menu for a local Scranton pizza shop, and when the staff goes out for coffee they do so to apparently locally owned stores ("Traveling Salesmen," "The Negotiation").

Aside from conforming to the idea that one ought to frequent smaller and local shops as opposed to larger national and multinational shops, this divide between what Michael does (or rather, where he shops) and what the others do invokes a bit of ethics that is often obscured in the more business oriented understandings of stakeholder theory. Much stakeholder theory is implicitly happiness-oriented. It assumes that the more stakeholders who are happy as a result of an action, the better that action is. For example, an action that resulted in the employees, the customers, and the near-neighbors of a branch being unhappy would be less desirable than one which brought about more happiness (or at least maintained the current level of happiness.) This approach relies on a view famously articulated in John Stuart Mill's *Utilitarianism*. Mill (1806–1873) claims that "actions are right in proportion as they tend to promote happiness; wrong as they tend to produce the reverse of happiness."[10] By continually preferring national chains, Michael is setting up a situation where the local community is potentially losing its distinctive flavor. His employees, on the other hand, are supporting local flavor.

Michael's dining habits could actually result in a lack of engagement in the community, distancing the Scranton branch of Dunder-Mifflin from the community (its customers, employees, and other stakeholders). If we think in terms of utility, we can see that by shopping locally the Scranton employees of Dunder-Mifflin are enabling their neighbors to continue to own, run, or work for local businesses, which ideally will be more understanding of local concerns than national megabusinesses. In contrast, Michael's almost exclusive patronage of chains sends money, decision-making powers, and supposedly happiness outside of his community. Stakeholder analysis would find that the better action is the one that makes the most stakeholders (perhaps weighed in some manner) happy. However, even if the difference in happiness between local and national buying impacts only a very few individuals, we need to remember that the "great majority of good actions are intended not for the benefit of the world, but for that of individuals, of which the good of the world is made up; and the thoughts of the most virtuous man need not on these occasions travel beyond the particular persons concerned" (Mill, 19). Given this guidance, consider again Michael's preference for Chili's over Poor Richard's. In both cases, it seems clear that the servers at the restaurants would be pleased for business (and tips), but in addition the profits from Poor Richard's would stay in Scranton, providing further financial impact to the city than a sale to a national chain can provide. By shopping locally, which is to consider stakeholders in economic decisions, businesses (and business managers) have the opportunity to exponentially spread happiness—something which, at least according to Mill, is morally correct to do.

We don't have to look far to see larger-scope instances of stockholder concerns trumping stakeholder concerns. Consider these: the Pittsfield, Massachusetts Dunder-Mifflin office was closed over rumors of a union being formed ("Boys and Girls"). Devon is fired purely for financial reasons, and his selection is particularly random (even more so after it switches to Devon from Creed) ("Halloween"). The company health plan is restructured without consideration of need ("Health Care"). Obviously, these actions prioritize financial (stockholder) concerns over more communitarian (stakeholder) concerns. In each situation a decision is made apparently only because of profit and without consideration of who would be impacted by that decision.

Less clear is an interesting (and rare) example of Jim Halpert acting purely for profit. In "Diversity Day," we see Jim attempting to increase his commission by "pushing" recycled paper on his biggest customer. When Dwight poaches the client from him, Jim's actions end up backfiring even more than he could have imagined. Dwight becomes 2005 Salesman of the Year ("literally the highest possible honor that a northeastern Pennsylvania-based midsize paper company regional salesman can attain") at least in part through taking Jim's client ("Dwight's Speech"). Jim's action is uncharacteristic of him. As we see in "Traveling Salesmen," Jim is aware that one of the best selling points that Dunder-Mifflin has is the service it can offer to customers that larger companies cannot.

On the other hand, Dwight's stealing Jim's customer is consistent with some of what we know about Dwight's character. When given the opportunity to pick a health care plan, Dwight opts for the one that will save Dunder-Mifflin the most money, regardless of the impact on himself or fellow employees. (This comes up again in "Michael's Birthday" when Toby Flenderson counsels Kevin to get alternate health insurance if possible given the possibility that Kevin has skin cancer.) When attempting to usurp Michael's role as manager Dwight emphasizes to Jan (and later to the whole office) that there is a lot of room for firing unnecessary people ("The Coup"). Perhaps most tellingly he is able to aptly role-play David Wallace (the chief financial officer of Dunder-Mifflin) when explaining to Michael that Scranton is being closed for business reasons ("Branch Closing"). (Michael dismisses Dwight's role-playing, believing that it is clear that the chief financial officer will understand that closing the branch will have a big impact on people.) On numerous occasions Dwight has made clear that he believes in a competitive business environment and that rules are necessary to separate us from the animals. It is less clear what we are to make of Dwight's apparent knowledge of all of the outlet stores (and their contents) in the area between Scranton and New York. Perhaps Dwight has attempted to sell paper and office products to them, or perhaps, like Michael, he has begun to favor larger national chains.

Dwight's "stockholder" concerns are somewhat balanced by what could be termed "stakeholder" concerns, or concerns about the larger community. Dwight was for some time a volunteer for a local sheriff's office (though as deleted scenes for "Drug Testing" make clear he probably overstepped his authority). He supports the local minor-league baseball team the Scranton/Wilkes-Barre Red Barons (as evidenced by the Bobble-heads on his desk), and listens to local country-music station Froggy-101. By emphasizing the customer service of both Dunder-Mifflin and his own extreme accessibility ("Here's my card. It's got my cell number, my pager number, my home number, and my other pager number. I never take vacations, I never get sick, and I don't celebrate any major holidays."), Dwight is (inadvertently?) showing that he does understand that in business, the customer is important. Dwight has accepted at least the SRI model of stakeholder theory (which had stockholders as separate from stakeholders.) The tension in Dwight between, on the one hand, understanding that concern for stakeholders makes good business sense and, on the other hand, desiring to maximize stockholder profits (and thus show his own worth) makes him a fascinating character. In his own flawed way, Dwight's attempts to excel by two different standards set him apart from Jim and the rest of the sales staff, who in Stanley Hudson's words are simply "in a run out the clock situation" for much of their workdays ("Boys and Girls").

No analysis of the stakeholder dynamics in Dunder-Mifflin would be complete without looking critically at Michael. Michael doesn't feel deeply connected to the community (as evidenced by his shopping and dining at large chains rather than local companies). He also doesn't feel totally connected to the people in his office. In "Take Your Daughter to Work Day" he introduces Creed as being "in charge of . . . something . . . right?" To which Creed only responds, "That is correct." (To date it still isn't clear what Creed's job is in the office, as he is not in sales, accounting, customer service, or a part of the corporate office.[11] He appears, like Melville's Bartleby, just to exist in the office.) Michael also minimizes the importance of customers when they are not, or cannot, do what he wants. For example, in "Health Care" Michael tries in vain to find an exciting surprise for the office, calling at one point the Lackawanna County Coal Mine Tour and hanging up in disgust after he finds out there is not a "free fall." In the deleted scenes we discover that the Tour is one of Michael's customers. Alternately, in "Business School" we see how Michael's need for acceptance causes him to waver back and forth between stakeholder and stockholder concerns. When a student asks

Michael how he responds when a customer says he is leaving for a large competitor, Michael answers with a stakeholder response, pointing out the customer will be losing service and local connections that the big chains cannot match. When asked what he says when the customer does come back, he explains, "We don't want them back. They're stupid."

This interchange is fascinating when compared to the moment in "Take Your Daughter to Work Day" when Michael explains what Dunder-Mifflin does:

> *Michael*: You need someone in the middle to facilitate—
> *Jake (Meredith's son)*: You're just a middleman.
> *Michael*: I'm not just a middleman.
> *Melissa (Stanley's daughter)*: Wait, why doesn't the manufacturer just sell the paper directly to people?
> *Michael*: You are describing Office Depot. And they are kind of running us out of business.

(Dwight has the next line, which emphasizes the stakeholder response to stockholder concerns: "We have better service than they do!") Office Depot may be running Dunder-Mifflin out of business (in the next five to ten years if Ryan's estimate in "Business School" is accurate), but Michael cannot or will not look beyond the betrayal of his trust to take back a previous customer. No moment better shows the conflict of stakeholder and stockholder concerns within Michael than his job in convincing Christian, a decision-maker for all of Lackawanna County, to go with Dunder-Mifflin instead of a larger chain. In the midst of explaining that he "is" Scranton, that he grew up in Scranton, went to school in Scranton, and knows everything about Scranton, he and Christian are drinking in Chili's, not in a local Scranton restaurant. Christian buys Michael's (true) story, but only on the condition that they get a price concession ("The Client"). This compromise between stakeholder and stockholder concerns seems to have been the right balance, and in other successful sales calls we see that all of Michael's staff utilizes their knowledge of Scranton and the customer to their advantage. This may be, quite inadvertently, a unique aspect of working for Michael. In a scene from Stamford we see Jim volunteering to contact new businesses as potential customers—and being labeled a suck-up for doing so ("Gay Witch Hunt").

160

Learning from Dunder-Mifflin

Despite, or perhaps because of, the tensions in Dunder-Mifflin regarding the relative importance of stakeholders and stockholders, we can see through *The Office* a real hope for better, and more ethical, business practices. It's far too easy to focus on the fun and games, like encasing office supplies in Jell-O, egging non-customer businesses, or Flonkerton. We can see real lessons about how acting ethically in the business place creates a better business environment. Stakeholder theory emphasizes that in order for a company to succeed, it needs to think about the impact of business decisions and practices on those who are stakeholders in that business, be they customers, suppliers, employees, or the larger community.

Frank Abrams wrote that part of selling a business and a product is "the exercise of conscientious care and restraint in our businesses and part is the simple matter of remeeting the 'folks'" (33). Michael and his staff understand this. They embody Scranton, and understand the importance of customer contact. Think about Phyllis and Karen Fillippeli's successful sale after getting a make-over to resemble the client's wife. In contrast to this, consider Andy's botched attempt to make Dunder-Mifflin out to be a big player, or Ryan's many failed attempts to make a sale. (Again, it's worth considering that the only sales failure we see Jim having comes when he forgets the customer's interests and tries to maximize his own commission.) Michael is successful when he connects with people, as when he woos Hammermill out of an exclusive deal with Staples ("The Convention").

By contrast, in a standard business model employees are considered mere assets. Employment "involve[s] an implicit agreement to the effect that, in return for wages, an employee [does] not expect his employer to be concerned with his personal goals and objectives. Hence he could be . . . treated as though he was a replaceable part of a machine."[12] Michael, probably subconsciously, sees upper management as operating on this model. Thus, his presentation to David Wallace emphasizes "The Faces of Scranton" ("Valentine's Day"). Consider also Michael's poignant concern about what will happen if the Scranton branch closes:

> It is an outrage, that's all. They're making a huge, huge mistake. Let's see Josh replace these people. Let's see Josh find another Stanley. You

think Stanleys grow on trees? Well they don't. There is no Stanley tree. Do you think the world is crawling with Phyllises? Show me that farm. With Phyllises and Kevins sprouting up all over the place. Ripe for the plucking [long pause]. Show me that farm. ("Branch Closing")

Workers, his workers, are not cogs in the business machine. They are people, and "people never go out of business" ("Business School").

Involvement with the larger community is one of the serious business lapses we see at Dunder-Mifflin in Scranton, though this can be explained partially because *The Office* has only recently ventured outside the workplace and work life of the employees. But the Diwali celebration ("Diwali") and the show at Pam's art school ("Business School") may be the beginning of *The Office* and its employees taking a greater interest in the community.

What can be learned from *The Office*? The concerns of stock-holders and stakeholders don't have to be at odds with one another. Good (ethical) business can be good (bottom line) business, or in the very least, ethical business practices need not be bad business practices.

NOTES

1 The wording of this complaint is remarkably consistent, and almost always evokes the mysterious "They." For the philosopher, this cannot help but raise specters of Martin Heidegger's concerns with "The They" (*das Man*) in *Being and Time*. As interesting as that analysis might be, the focus here is on business ethics. Go read Heidegger for yourself.

2 As Thomas Donaldson and Lee Preston note, "Unfortunately, much of what passes for stakeholder theory in the literature is implicit rather than explicit," which results in "diverse and somewhat confusing uses of the stakeholder concept." See "The Stakeholder Theory of the Corporation: Concepts, Evidence, and Implications." *Academy of Management Review*, 20, 1 (1995): 65–91. In the following a bit of the flavor of these "diverse and confusing uses" is provided.

3 The folks at Stanford Research Institute (now SRI International, Inc.) apparently first used the term *stakeholder* in an internal memo in 1963. From their understanding, stakeholders (as opposed to stockholders) were "groups without whose support the origination would cease to exist." The SRI memo is quoted on page 31 of R. Edward Freeman's *Strategic Management: A Stakeholder Approach* (Boston: Pittman, 1984).

Freeman's book did much to popularize stakeholder analysis; so much so that many business students mistakenly believe that he developed the concept himself (apparently never having read the book that he wrote about the method).

4   R. Igor Ansoff, *Corporate Strategy* (New York: McGraw-Hill, 1965), p. 34. While Ansoff uses the *stakeholder* term he references this passage's source as a Frank Abram's article referenced below, from 1951—twelve years before SRI's use of the concept. These bits of "history of ideas" are endlessly fascinating to academics, but most folks in the business world don't pay attention to footnotes and references so never notice this. Wait, are you still reading this? Go back to the main text. I don't want to see you down here again.

5   The differences between models show conflicting priority. In the Ansoff model (as well as Abram's model), stockholders are considered stakeholders. In the SRI model they are distinct classes. As such, the SRI model tends to lend itself to an adversarial understanding of stakeholder and stockholders while other models aim for a more communitarian understanding. These differences, as well as other models, result in some analyses weighting some stakeholders (most commonly stockholders and employees) more highly than others.

6   Ronald K. Mitchell, Bradley R. Agle and Danna J. Wood, "Toward a Theory of Stakeholder Identification and Salience Defining the Principle of Who and What Really Counts. *Academy of Management Review*, 22, 4 (1997): 853–856.

7   Frank W. Abrams, "Management's Responsibilities in a Complex World," *Harvard Business Review*, 29 (1951): 29–34.

8   Ok, Kevin Malone suggests Hooters. But what else would we expect from him?

9   In an odd turn of events, the local restaurants and taverns mentioned in *The Office* appear to all be actual places in Scranton, PA. However, Chili's, Hooters, and Benihana do not have locations in Scranton.

10   John Stuart Mill, *Utilitarianism* (Indianapolis: Hackett, 2001), p. 7. (Mill's essay was originally published in 1861 in *Fraser's Magazine*.)

11   We discover in "Product Recall" that *one* of his job responsibilities is to do weekly Quality Assurance checks at suppliers, but it seems implicit that his job entails more than just these spot checks.

12   Russell L. Ackoff, *Redesigning the Future* (New York: John Wiley, 1974), p. 34.

14

Attacking with the North: Affirmative Action and *The Office*

David Kyle Johnson

Abraham Lincoln once said that if you are a racist, I will attack you with The North. And those are the principles that I carry with me in the workplace.

Michael Scott ("Diversity Day")

Michael tries to hide it, but he is one of the most racially insensitive people on the planet. Michael suggests that we should all be "color blind,"[1] but clearly he isn't. Three people bear the brunt of his insensitivity at the Scranton branch of Dunder-Mifflin: Stanley (who is African-American), Kelly (who is Asian-Indian-American), and Oscar (who is Mexican-American). Michael has *"faux pas'd"* them all. He corrects Stanley by suggesting that "collard greens" are actually called "colored greens" (assuming that they are named after "colored people" because, according to Michael, they are the only people who eat them); he stereotyped convenience-store clerks as Asian-Indians in front of Kelly (demanding that she try some of his "googey-googey"); and he asked Oscar if there was a label he preferred besides "Mexican" since the word "Mexican" has certain—as Michael puts it —"negative connotations." In fact, each *faux pas* was committed on "diversity day," a day set aside by corporate for "diversity training" as a response to Michael's insensitivity.

One of the goals of affirmative action is to ensure *diversity in the workplace*. The enforcement of a racial quota can require a business to ensure that a certain percentage of its workforce is made up of minorities.[2] In addition to racial quotas, affirmative action may involve set-aside programs where a certain number of "open slots" are reserved for minority candidates only. (These are often used in the university/college setting.) Affirmative action can also take the form of minority preference in the decision-making process. (In such a system, an under-qualified minority applicant will not get preference over a well-qualified non-minority applicant—being able to do the job is required of anyone being offered that job; however, a qualified minority will get preference over a *very* qualified non-minority.) All in all, affirmative action gives minorities a better chance (than they had before) at employment. It not only increases the percentage of minorities in the workforce, but increases the number of minorities with well-paying jobs.[3]

Those who object to affirmative action point out that it does more than prohibit hiring practices that favor whites. Affirmative action demands (in many cases) hiring practices that favor minorities. They thus suggest that affirmative action is unjustified.

When it comes to affirmative action, sorting through all of the relevant arguments is as difficult as going through salesman-hazing with Dwight. But we're going to do just that! (We'll sort through the arguments, I mean. I would not be so vicious as to wish Dwight's salesman-hazing on anyone. I certainly don't want to go near Dwight's beet farm, and I definitely don't want anything to do with cousin Mose.) As we do, we will see that most of the common arguments against affirmative action fail. But in the end, we will see one very good reason to conclude that affirmative action is not justified and should be abandoned (in favor of alternate efforts with the same goal).

Affirmative Action and Racial Diversity: "What have you got for us Ryan?"

Some people object to affirmative action by focusing on its goal of racial diversity. Such objectors ask if there is something morally deficient about a labor force that is made up of one race. They grant that racially and ethnically diverse workforces are not bad things. But, they point out, those who defend affirmative action seem to assume that a racially and ethnically mixed workforce is something that is intrinsically good—something that is good to accomplish

165

in and of itself—without even offering up an argument! It seems, according to these objectors, that instead of favoring minorities to ensure diverse workforces, we should simply be encouraging non-discriminatory hiring practices (that favor no one).

These objectors do get one thing right: an ethnically mixed work-force, although not bad, is not intrinsically good; there is nothing wrong with non-mixed workforces. To help make this point, consider the episode "Traveling Salesmen" from season 3. The sales staff at Dunder-Mifflin breaks off in twos and ventures off in an "Amazing Race" like sales competition. On the way to one of Stanley's sale contacts, Ryan (who is paired with Stanley) asks Stanley to let him "take the lead" and make the sales pitch. But, when they arrive, Ryan discovers that the entire management staff he must pitch to is made up of large African-American males. The managers are super-friendly and absolutely love Stanley, but—when they ask "what have you got for us, Ryan?"—Ryan is so intimidated all he can manage to say is "hi" over and over again. Notice that, when we see that the manage-ment staff is all one race and one gender, we don't pass moral judg-ment on the group. We don't think any one of them is a bad person, and we don't think there is anything morally deficient about the group itself. Granted, if the company has a policy of only hiring African-American males, we would have cause to complain. But as long as that is not the case (perhaps the mangers are four college buddies who went into business together after graduation) everything is fine.

For the same reason that we shouldn't complain about an all-male African-American management team, we shouldn't complain about any labor force that is made up of any one gender or any one race.[4] Granted, if a particular large labor force is made up of only one race or gender, that is probably a good basis for suspicion and investiga-tion. But as long as our investigation doesn't uncover discriminatory hiring, we've got nothing to complain about.

This objection, however, fails to recognize that racially diverse labor forces are not the ultimate goal of, nor the prime justification for, affirmative action. Granted, diversity can be set as a goal—as it is with quotas or set-aside efforts—but setting such a goal is only one way of enforcing affirmative action, it's not the goal itself.[5] Having a diverse labor force, while certainly nothing to lament,[6] isn't something that's intrinsically good (good in and of itself). When diversity is enforced, it's only good in virtue of the fact that it eliminates majority-favoring hiring practices.[7] [8]

Affirmative Action as an Effort to Eliminate Racism: "What you want? A cookie?"

Consider a different objection to affirmative action. Racial insensitivity and racism, the objection runs, is the root cause of discriminatory hiring practices. Many objectors suggest that affirmative action should thus eliminate such things (or at least should make major progress in this area) if we're going to use it at all. But affirmative action does no such thing! Racial insensitivity and racism are still major problems, even within companies that enforce affirmative action. Thus, affirmative action isn't justified.

Michael is a clear example of non-discriminatory hiring practices not eliminating racial insensitivity and racism. Michael clearly is a proponent of affirmative action. The racial and ethnic make up of Dunder-Mifflin's Scranton branch meets every appropriate quota.[9] And yet Michael is still racially insensitive—perhaps even a racist. When Oscar skips work on spring cleaning day, Michael calls him and suggests that the office could use his "Mexican cleaning ethic." His assumption that Stanley must have an African-American wife is so entrenched that he can't bring himself to acknowledge that his wife is white, even after he sees Stanley and his wife holding hands at the Dundies. And on the bus to the beach in "Beach Day," Michael tells Stanley to sit in the back.[10] And, of course, Michael's Chris Rock routine reeks of racial insensitivity:

> Basically, there are two types of black people, and black people are actually more racist because they hate the other type of black people . . . Every time, [raising his voice to a yell] *every time* black people wanna have a good time, some mean-ass [bleep] [bleep] it up. I take care of my kids! [Bleep] always want credit for something they supposed to do! . . . What you want? A cookie? ("Diversity Day")

After Michael performed this routine in the office, corporate sent Mr. Brown, of *Diversity Today*, to lead a seminar on diversity in the workplace. Michael, of course, does not believe that this black gentleman's name is *actually* Mr. Brown and rather than be instructed by this outsider, Michael organizes his own diversity training where he forces his employees—as an exercise in understanding what it is to be a minority—to spout out, to each other, racial slurs based on stereotypes! Even if Michael isn't a racist, he's certainly racially insensitive—despite the fact that his office would meet any appropriate quota! If the goal of affirmative action is to eliminate racial insensitivity and racism, then clearly affirmative action is missing the mark.

Affirmative action, however, is not always defended as an attempt to eliminate racism. Indeed, its justification is often nothing of the kind. Rather, affirmative action is an effort to address past instances of racially discriminatory hiring practices. Those past practices caused injustice, and affirmative action is aimed at making up for that injustice—a goal that can be accomplished regardless of whether racism is eliminated or not.[11] So, pointing out that affirmative action does not eliminate racism doesn't show it to be unjustified.

Affirmative Action as Compensation: Injustice at the Ol' *Schrute* Beet Farm

Of course, if we defend affirmative action in terms of justice, we'll have to face a different objection: quite often affirmative action negatively affects individuals who have never discriminated against anyone. Affirmative action can cause a perfectly innocent non-minority applicant to be denied a position that he would have received had affirmative action not been enforced—and this seems wrong. In the same way that it is unfair to award a job to someone based on how many hot dogs they can eat in ten minutes (as Michael proposed in "Beach Games"), it is unfair to make a person "pay for" discrimination when that person has never discriminated against anyone (in neither case does the person deserve what they get). In fact, it seems that the only persons who should pay for past discrimination are those who carried it out: our ancestors themselves. But since they are long dead, the chance to make up for past instances of discrimination in this way is long past.

To make this point, let's imagine the following: suppose that, many years ago, there was a need for a work hand at the Schrute beet farm. (We'll pretend that the Schrute family had a shortage of newborns, since they usually "grew" their own workers.) Suppose that despite the fact that Stanley's grandfather was the most qualified applicant for the job, Dwight's grandfather wouldn't let Stanley's grandfather work on his beet farm. Dwight's grandfather simply didn't like African-Americans. Also suppose that, when Michael was choosing his "replacement" at the end of season 3,[12] Michael choose Stanley instead of Dwight despite the fact that Dwight is the more qualified of the two,[13] because Michael was enforcing affirmative action. Even though we like Stanley just fine and might even prefer to work under him, we might think that somehow justice had not been served. It wasn't Dwight who refused to hire Stanley's grandfather, it was his grandfather. Dwight didn't do anything to deserve to be "punished." He had no choice about what his grandfather did—how could we hold him responsible? In fact, it seems an injustice has been done in this case; Dwight was more qualified! It seems, since their grandfathers are long ago dead, the chance to make up for the past injustice of Stanley's grandfather is as gone as the Stamford branch. Punishing Dwight only accomplishes further injustice; it *makes up for* nothing. In general, it seems that punishing present-day white job applicants for the sins of their ancestors only accomplishes further injustice.

Objecting to affirmative action in this way, however, misses the mark. The goal of affirmative action is not to "punish present persons for the crimes of their ancestors." The goal is to correct *the present effects* of past discrimination.

Question: "What present effects could past actions of discrimination possibly have?" Thanks Dwight, I'm glad you asked

Past discriminatory hiring practices kept most minorities out of well-paying jobs. As a result, most minorities lived in poverty and, consequently, could not afford a good education for their children.[14] Thus, their children could not find well-paying jobs either and so they too were doomed to poverty and could not provide for their children's education. Their children too were thus doomed to poverty—and the pattern continues today. Because their ancestors were discriminated against, a large percentage of the minority population today is stuck in a "cycle of poverty." And this is the present effect of past discrimination—the thing that affirmative action is trying to counter: a very high level of poverty in the minority population.

We can learn four things from this revelation.

First, we can see why simply abolishing discriminatory hiring practices—simply assuring that *the most qualified person regardless of race* gets the job—doesn't solve the problem. Since members of an impoverished family don't have the financial resources to become the most qualified person for a well-paying job, they have no chance of getting a well-paying job. Ensuring that the well-paying jobs always go to the *most qualified* (regardless of race) only ensures that the well-paying jobs go to those who can already afford *to be* the most qualified: the members of the non-impoverished population.

Second, we can see the real goal and understand the strategies behind affirmative action. The goal is to reduce minority-impoverishment, thus breaking the cycle of poverty; the strategy is to funnel more money into the minority population, and thus funnel more economic opportunity (e.g., the opportunity to become better educated and qualified for well-paying jobs) into the minority population by giving minorities better paying jobs.

Third, we can better understand the logic of the minority preference strategy. The minority preference strategy does not suggest hiring unqualified people for jobs. (You obviously should never hire Michael Scott to teach a business class, the entire market would break down and condemn *everyone* to poverty.) But it does suggest that when two qualified people are competing for a job, if one of them is a minority, then the minority should be given the job—even if the non-minority is better qualified. The justification is that, even though we are missing the opportunity to do one justice—to give the *best qualified* applicant the job—we have the opportunity to do an even greater justice: help fight minority impoverishment by employing a minority and thus increase the economic opportunity of the minority population.

Lastly, we learn that affirmative action need not be permanent. The goal is to reduce poverty in the minority population—to move down the minority "poverty bar" (if you will). Once the bar is moved, the goal will have been accomplished, and affirmative action will not be justified (or needed, or desired) anymore.[15] [16]

Affirmative Action as Reverse Discrimination: The Tale of Hank Tate

It can't be denied that affirmative action does have negative effects. Affirmative action will inevitably lead to a reduction of efficiency in the workforce due to instances of well-qualified minorities being favored over better-qualified majorities.[17] And this can also have a negative affect on the economy, and perhaps even on the self-esteem of the very people affirmative action aims to help. (Although I can't imagine that Stanley would care one iota if he discovered that he was hired or promoted based on his race. As he said in "Beach Games" when Michael forced them to eat hot dogs for his job, "I would rather work for an upturned broom with a bucket for a head than work for somebody else in this office besides myself. Game on!") As the contemporary philosopher Thomas Nagel argues, these objections really can't be answered; but affirmative action is justified nevertheless—the cost is worth the benefit. And what is more, the negative effects are limited; eventually affirmative action will accomplish its goal and be no more. So, it seems, the social good of permanently *moving the poverty bar* accomplished by affirmative action outweighs the social evil of these temporary negative effects.[18]

But perhaps the "evil" of affirmative action does not lie in its consequences. A very common objection to affirmative action is that it promotes reverse discrimination. And that it does is undeniable. Discriminatory hiring practices eliminate certain candidates and give preference to others, based on their race (or other inappropriate factors such as age or gender). And this is exactly what affirmative action does in most instances—it just does it in "reverse." Affirmative action, many times, eliminates whites from consideration and favors minorities. Of course, the discrimination of affirmative action is motivated differently. Past discrimination was rooted in hatred of minorities and a part of a larger social system bent on repressing minorities. The reverse discrimination of affirmative action does not have the same basis; it is rooted in a desire for social justice. But it is racial discrimination nonetheless. And many argue that racial discrimination is an injustice and that we must always stop injustice.

That discrimination is an injustice is fairly uncontroversial, but the latter part of the previous statement is as hairy as Michael's David

171

Hasselhoff imitation. Some things are more important than others and it is unclear that all injustices must be stopped at all costs. Couldn't the positive consequences of discrimination ever justify it? It seems so. Consider this scenario.

Hank Tate is the Scranton branch's security guard. (You may remember him from the episode "Drug Testing," where he inducted Dwight as an honorary Security Guard. Unfortunately, he also had to tell Dwight that he wouldn't get a gun and he couldn't bring his bo staff to work.) Hank is African-American. But suppose that the security guard before Hank was a white racist, and every night at quitting time he insisted on searching Stanley, Darryl, and all other African-American workers to make sure they weren't stealing office supplies. (Of course, he should have been searching Creed.) This really pissed them off—and they were very vocal about it, and this caused a lot of unrest in the whole branch—and so, finally, Michael fired the racist security guard. Now suppose that when Michael was looking to hire a new security guard, he had a choice between Hank (an African-American) and a much more experienced white man. Michael established that the white man was not a racist and, based on his experience, was qualified for the job better than Hank. But imagine that with uncharacteristic insight, Michael realized that hiring an African-American security guard would completely "calm the unrest" within the branch—a white security guard might still make everyone uneasy—and so Michael hired Hank.

In this story, Hank is hired on the basis of his race and is less qualified for the job than the white man. Clearly, this is an instance of racial discrimination. But Michael justifies the discrimination based on the action's consequences. Yes, he is hiring an African-American because he is African-American, but doing so will calm the unrest in the branch. It seems that Michael's decision is morally justified because the happiness of everyone at the branch morally outweighs the discrimination.

In the same way it seems that alleviating minority impoverishment —a consequence of affirmative action—morally outweighs the reverse discrimination of affirmative action. If all things were equal, and minority impoverishment didn't exist, then the job should go to the most qualified candidate, regardless of race. But if a discriminatory action can have significant positive consequences (such as breaking the minority "cycle of poverty"), then those positive consequences can morally justify it.

But this last example opens the door for one last, very telling, objection to affirmative action. If Michael could have calmed the unrest at the branch while still hiring based on qualification (and not on race), he should have. And there are multiple ways that Michael could have done so. If he had simply proven, to everyone, that the new security guard wasn't a racist there would have been no problem. And it seems that he could have done so, most simply, by telling everyone what he discovered about the man in an email (and he could have attached vacation pictures of him and Jan to make sure that everyone would see it). So, since he could have calmed the unrest at the branch without discrimination, it seems to me his discriminatory hiring was unjustified.

In the same way, if we could eliminate minority impoverishment without racially discriminatory hiring practices, then racially discriminatory hiring practices cannot be justified in the name of eliminating minority impoverishment. And I can think of at least one way that we can. As we learned before, the reason that past discriminatory hiring practices have locked the minority population into a "poverty cycle" is because poverty prevents minorities from affording the education necessary to be "the best candidate" for well-paying jobs. Consequently, it seems that increasing education in the minority population would also eliminate minority impoverishment, and thus racially discriminatory hiring practices are not needed to accomplish this goal. And increasing education in the minority population would not only not require discrimination, but would seem to be more easily accomplished and would have other benefits as well (the benefits of a good education don't end with better paying jobs.) Thus, since the same goal can be accomplished in a better, easier and non-discriminatory way, it seems that affirmative action is, ultimately, unjustified.

Conclusion

Ultimately some may object to the *education option*. Perhaps some will argue that it is slower; others will argue that it will not be easier to implement. We will have to save that debate for another time. But what I have shown, using examples from *The Office*, is that many of the classic objections against affirmative action fail—mainly by misunderstanding the ultimate purpose of afterimage action: the

173

elimination of minority impoverishment. This goal would justify the reverse discrimination of affirmative action, if affirmative action were the only way to accomplish this goal; but since it is not the only way (it seems education could do just as well), I conclude that affirmative action is not justified.

NOTES

1 In "Diversity Day," Michael suggests that the Scranton branch is a "color-free zone" and that, for example, he doesn't see Stanley "as another race." As Mr. Brown (of *Diversity Today*) rightly pointed out, we don't have to pretend to be color blind and doing so is fighting "ignorance with more ignorance."

2 Usually the percentage required reflects the percentage of minorities in the population that constitutes the business's potential labor force.

3 Affirmative action here and throughout the chapter is discussed in terms of racial minorities. But it's also possible and common to have affirmative action on the basis of gender.

4 Of course, one could complain, but one shouldn't. If there is nothing morally objectionable about a group being made up of only African-Americans, there is nothing morally objectionable about a group being made up of only Asian-Indians or Caucasians.

5 Quite often, quotas are a kind of "last ditch" effort, imposed on companies who refuse to eliminate discriminatory hiring practices. In such situations it is obvious that meeting the quota itself is not the ultimate goal.

6 As Mr. Brown taught us in "Diversity Day," diversity is something to be celebrated.

7 But the question still remains: Shouldn't we simply be trying to establish hiring practices that favor no one, instead of instigating ones that favor minorities? We will address this question shortly, and it should then be clear why doing so is not sufficient to accomplish the real goal of affirmative action.

8 It is important to note however that affirmative action in college admissions is often justified—in part—in the name of diversity. However, a college campus is very different than a business workforce. Ethnic diversity on a campus can provide a student with the opportunity for enriching experiences and to learn different points of view—part of the reason a student goes to college. I imagine some employers would offer the same justification—certainly it's used as part of the justification for

hiring minority faculty members on campuses—but most businesses are not concerned with the cultural *education and enrichment* of their employees.

9   As is turns out, Scranton is only 3.02 percent African-American, 1.08 percent Asian, 2.62 percent Hispanic (source: www.scranton.area-connect.com/statistics.htm). Speaking strictly of the workforce on the second floor, the racial quota that could be enforced at the Scranton branch is clearly already met. With only 15 employees (pre-merger), one employee makes up 6 percent of the entire workforce; the presence of Stanley, Kelly, and Oscar entails that 6 percent of the upstairs workforce is African-American, 6 percent is Asian, and 6 percent is Hispanic—each percentage being well above what would be required under a quota. (And the merger in season 3 did not change this fact.)

10 Although, in this instance, I think Michael's mistake was innocent. He was responding to Stanley's smart-aleck remark and he immediately also gave him the option of sitting in the front or driving.

11 Of course, it goes without saying that the world would be better if racism was eliminated.

12 Recall, at the end of season 3, Michael thought he was going to get a job at corporate and considered Dwight and Stanley (among others) as his replacement. He appointed Dwight before he got the job—but then took it back once he "withdrew" himself from consideration.

13 We will suppose, for the sake of argument, that Dwight's higher sales and refusal to take off major holidays—and Stanley's "I-only-work-for-pretzel-day-run-out-the-clock" attitude towards work—make Dwight the more qualified candidate. I personally would rather work under Stanley.

14 Their poverty would have held back their children's education in numerous ways. Obviously, they couldn't afford to send their children to college, but in addition, their poverty would have also prevented them from receiving a good basic education. They would be forced to live in poorer communities with not-well-funded schools—schools that would obviously not provide well-funded educations.

15 Because of this, it is also important to note that, in this entire effort, a close eye needs to be kept on our progress towards the goal and we need to stop when we have reached it. If we move the minority's poverty bar down too much, we may move another population's bar up too far, and then we would have to start the whole process over again. We simply need to move the "poverty bars" so there is equal economic opportunity for all populations.

16 It is worth noting that a slightly different rationale would need to be offered for affirmative action in favor of women.

17   Again, this is not to say that minorities are never the best qualified candidate. But at times they are not (usually because of the present effects of past discrimination); and when they are not, affirmative action demands that the best-qualified applicant be passed over if giving an aptly but less-qualified minority the job is an option. And when a less-qualified person does get the job, it is undeniable that the work doesn't get done as well as it could have if the best-qualified person— i.e., the person who would do the job best—had been hired.

18   See Thomas Nagel, "A Defense of Affirmative Action." In Tom Beauchamp & Norman Bowie (eds.) *Ethical Theory and Business*, 7th edn. (Englewood Cliffs, NJ: Prentice-Hall, 2004).

15

Darkies, Dwarves, and Benders: Political (In)Correctness in *The Office*

Thomas Nys

In the very first episode of the second series[1] of *The Office*, Gareth Keenan tells this memorable joke:

> Gareth: Alright, it's Christmas dinner. Royal family, having their Christmas dinner. Camilla Parker-Bowles goes, "Ok, we'll play *20 Questions*. I'll think of something—you have to ask me questions and guess what it is." So what she's thinking is "a black man's cock."
>
> David: Ooh, trust Camilla! Not racist is it?
>
> Gareth: No. So, Prince Philip goes, "Is it bigger than the bread bin?" She goes, "Yes." Prince Charles goes, "Is it something I can put in my mouth?" She goes, "Yes." Queen goes, "Is it a black man's cock?"
>
> (2/1:26)[2]

Despite Gareth's confident reassurance, the Black Man's Cock (BMC) joke is obviously racist; it involves a degrading stereotype about black men.[3] Yet, it's also quite funny because it involves the Queen thinking of huge penises. When David Brent later tells the joke to some colleagues at the Welcome Swindon party, he suddenly stops when they are joined by Oliver, the black co-worker. The result is another awkward and mortifying *Office* moment. Clearly, he has realized that the joke is racist. Later on, however, when both David and Gareth are accused of telling racist jokes on the work floor, they do all they can to argue that the BMC joke is not racist at all. Gareth tries to convince Jennifer that the stereotype is actually true (by saying that he can provide the necessary photo material to

177

prove his point), and David, who agrees with Gareth on this empirical fact, adds that, if it is indeed true, then the joke is "a compliment if anything" (2/1:38). Besides, Oliver himself thought it was funny once Brent was talked into finishing the joke, so no harm was done.

Certainly, we can say that the BMC joke is *politically incorrect*. As Jennifer tries to point out, it is offensive to reduce black men to large genitalia—as if this myth were the only interesting thing about them. Political correctness is a central theme in the humor of Ricky Gervais and Stephen Merchant, and it is prominent in *The Office*.[4] In the course of 14 episodes, almost no group is spared from political incorrectness: black people, women, homosexuals, the handicapped, the disabled, the obese, the bald, and so on.

Although many comedians use offense and shock to make their audience laugh (think of Sacha Baron Cohen's *Borat*), Gervais and Merchant go further by showing us the genuine struggle people have with being politically correct. On *The Office*, the rude person isn't totally unaware of the damage he does, and so the comedy is enhanced by revealing the complexity of the issue. David Brent is totally inconsiderate and rude, yet he also openly professes that he is a "philanthropist" who would never do something to offend people. The ambivalence in Brent's character adds depth to the comedy.

And, of course, if you like depth, then you'll like philosophy. Despite the fact that it is a recent phenomenon, political correctness is a topic that interests moral philosophers. For indeed some important questions arise. Should we be politically correct? Should we, for example, refrain from telling the BMC joke? And can we take legal measures against people who do? Let's delve into the subject. Or, as Brent would say: "Into the fray!"

Political Correctness

The problem of political correctness (PC) arose in a very specific context. By the early 1990s, the term was used by conservatives to describe certain liberal reform movements that wanted to change the curriculum and teaching methods at various universities. These movements believed that the current curricula were unfairly biased. Literature, for example, was all about white men (thereby excluding important female and black authors), and history was nothing more than a one-sided story told from the perspective of the oppressors (those in power). Therefore, they wanted to restore the balance by giving due attention to the neglected authors and the untold histories.[5]

Moreover, the reformers believed that this biased view is so deeply engrained in our society that it has become part and parcel of our common language. We are used to saying "chairman," for example, but why should this be a chair-*man*, when obviously a woman can be a chairman too? Our use of "chairman" is an unjustified relic from a patriarchal history, and we should now say "chair." Come to think about it, why do we say wo-*man* if we know that a woman is not just some special kind of man? As if women have no essence of their own! Hence, some feminists believed that we should spell it as *womyn* instead of *women*. And, if we really look carefully (now that we have our magnifiers on), then it's obvious that the prevalence of male vocabulary is everywhere, and that by using it we are (tacitly) confirming, or at least condoning, the supposed inferiority of women. So, we no longer attend a business "seminar" (which, pardon my French, reeks of male semen), but we go to a business "ovular." Any language suggesting that people are not equal should be erased and replaced by a suitable alternative which does not suffer from this deficiency. Hence we say "differently abled" rather than "disabled" (and, as Brent notices, rather than Gareth's mention of the "crippled"; 2/5:183).

As these examples make clear, however, the enterprise of PC quickly becomes a laughing matter. And, of course, that's exactly the way the conservatives wanted to depict the project: as a pipedream of over-sensitive lunatics.[6] They obviously succeeded and today the term PC still has a pejorative ring to it. Very few people would want to be accused of PC. On the contrary, it seems bold and mature (and funny!) to reject or ignore the issue altogether. Just say whatever you want to say, because we prefer crude honesty over lame hypocrisy. Yet, if charges of political incorrectness were just silly, we wouldn't laugh as hard as we do with *The Office*. The shame we feel when Chris Finch, for example, tells a rude joke is real, and we are anxious to explain that we don't, in fact, believe that women are inferior to men. So, underneath the silliness of "womyn" and "ovulars," PC might still point to a genuine concern.

Sticks and Stones

To understand that PC is a real concern, we should first acknowledge that words can indeed do serious damage. In episode 4 of the second series, David calls Gareth into his office to rehearse the speech he is going to give at the community center. Gareth is asked to insult David so that he can show his audience that, as a good boss, "sticks and stones may break his bones, but names will never hurt him" (2/4:151). Unfortunately, the wisdom of this proverb proves to be rather worthless, for although these names do not damage David's bones, they sure cut deep. As soon as Gareth reveals that the Swindon crew calls him Bluto or Mr. Toad ("the ugliest of all the amphibians") behind his back, David is deeply offended and he storms out to settle the matter in his typically awkward way.

Words can wound because our self-esteem depends on the way other people perceive us. We are anxious to believe that we are loved for who we are, and we want to make sure that those we care about have a positive image of us. Hence, it comes as a shock if we find out that we are perceived in a different, less favorable, light. Even a narcissist like David Brent is not immune to the impact of this shock (although, precisely because he is a narcissist, he does not begin to question himself, but directs his anger outside). Our appearance, for example, makes us vulnerable because, to a certain extent, it exists independently of our wishes or intentions. Of course, we might change a lot (our haircut, our clothes, our boobs), but there are limits to that enterprise. Our physical look, whether we like it or not, will always taint the way people perceive us ("the jolly fatty," "the stupid blonde"). We're convinced that people should look past appearances and discover who we really are, but we all know how difficult that is.

Hence it is simply false that, by absence of physical damage, words are entirely harmless. By the use of a mere word, people can crumble our reality. Think of David. His world collapses when he is finally made redundant. Or think of Tim who is so deeply in love with Dawn, and who is convinced that the feeling is mutual, but who is rejected twice. We feel his pain, and anyone who has ever experienced how deep love's teeth can sink, knows that this pain is well worse than a bump on the head. To keep in line with the bone-breaking metaphor of the proverb: nothing breaks like a broken dream.

But the plea for PC is ill-founded on the criterion of (emotional) harm. Whether racist or sexist language is morally wrong doesn't merely depend on whether or not, and to what extent, someone *feels* offended. If this were true, *anyone* could claim to be offended by *anything*. Indeed, those opposed to PC think that this subjective element is what feeds the absurd wildfire of issues included in the PC project. Over-sensitive people want us to adapt to their personal and weak-hearted preferences. But the argument also goes the other way, because, if the feeling of offense is what matters, then it seems that if we could just teach those people *not* to feel offended, everything would be all right. But that's not the case either.

The BMC joke is offensive even if, in fact, it would not cause emotional upset for anybody. The point is that there is *reason* to say that it is disrespectful of black people, because it joyfully celebrates and affirms a degrading stereotype. When David finds out that, in fact, two white women and a white man found the joke offensive and informed Jennifer about it, he is, at first, very surprised. The joke doesn't have anything to say about them, does it? Eventually, how-ever, he's forced to agree that white people can be offended by racism as well, not because they are the direct object of the joke, but because they find racism deplorable. Princeton philosopher Harry Frankfurt has argued that our identity in an important way depends on "the things we care about."[7] These things might be people, or projects, or ideas, or whatever, and they are a very significant source of motiva-tion. Almost everything we do can be explained by reference to what we care about. If these things are threatened, our identity is threat-ened as well, and we are spurred into action. This explains why we can personally be offended even though we are not the direct object of the offense.[8]

Clearly, people who care about equality and human dignity might be offended by cases of political incorrectness. So, in sum, although words can indeed hurt, the prime argument for PC rests on offense, not as an emotion, but as a token of disrespect for human equality.

Contexts and Conventions

In one of Gareth's favorite movies, *The Dam Busters* (1954), the protagonist's dog is called Nigger, a fact that David tries to justify by saying this was in the 1940s, "before racism was bad" (1/6:254–255). Of course, racism has always been bad, even if it was not recognized as such. What the Nigger example makes clear, however, is that PC depends on a certain context. As the term suggests, it depends on the political context one is in, and this particular context might be deeply immoral or unjust (for example, the context in which the equality of men and women, or blacks and whites, was not yet realized). Perhaps, in the 1940s, one could still say "nigger" without being scorned and labeled as a racist because the contempt the word expresses was then part of the existing social arrangements. Sadly enough, one genuinely believed that blacks were inferior to whites. In Aristotle's day (384–322 BCE), one could call someone a "barbarian" or a "brute" to describe that he was in some way less sophisticated than the Athenians. Or, in the nineteenth century, one could still call a person with inferior mental capacities an "idiot." Such words expressed inequality and the common belief that some people were better than others.

Because context is so crucial, the use of words requires a certain sensitivity, and those who lack this sensitivity can be rude without knowing it (think of *Borat*). A person might use an offensive word without realizing its offensiveness, and this might exempt the person from moral blame. This, however, does not mean that ignorance is a valid excuse for being offensive. We can, after all, blame a person for being ignorant. For example, we would think that a prime minister who referred to black people as "niggers" *should* know better, and that ignorance or stupidity is a very poor excuse in this case.

Gareth, however, is right when he notices that in a complex society such as our own, it has become very difficult to maintain such a sensitivity:

> That's it, see. A lot of people can't keep up with what words are acceptable these days and what words aren't. It's like my dad, for example, he's not as cosmopolitan or as educated as me, and it can be embarrassing, you know? He doesn't understand all the new trendy words, like, he'll say "poofs' instead of "gays," "birds" instead of "women," "darkies" instead of "coloureds." (2/1:40)

Unfortunately, in using this last word Gareth perfectly illustrates that he himself has lost track quite a while ago.[9]

Liberal reform groups in the 1990s wanted to show how deeply certain prejudices were entrenched within our society. As they saw it, we are under the sway of a powerful *ideology* that not only fosters inequality but, at the same time, also prevents us from recognizing these inequalities. The term "ideology" is often linked with Karl Marx (1818–1883), who claimed indeed that it was a set of ideas that prevented the working class from seeing the capitalist chains they were caught in. Yet, of course, the presence of a comforting ideology does not justify these chains.

As an ideology, that is, as a set of concealing ideas, the "white male" bias has serious consequences of unfairness. So, to defend the status quo is to defend an unjust situation. Even if all legal obstacles for women or minority groups were cleared, the way in which they are generally perceived would still pertain.[10] A policy of equal opportunities cannot root out all inequalities. Even if, in principle, all doors are open to both men and women, they might still be more open to the former than to the latter.[11]

A Case in Point: Pornography

In episode 2 of the first series, David is shocked that a pornographic email is circulating among the employees of Wernham-Hogg. He declares this highly inappropriate and propels himself as the guardian angel of PC. To that purpose David hires Gareth to find the perpetrator and swiftly bring him to justice. Of course, the *real* reason why David is so keen to find the culprit is that the email showed his face on some female porn star's body (with, as Gareth so eloquently puts it, "two blokes jizzin' on him"). David likes a good joke, as long as it's not on him. However, to hide the fact that he is personally offended, he wraps his story into a general plea for PC.

Now, of course, the idea that pornography is degrading to women is by no means far fetched. In pornographic pictures and movies they are often portrayed as mere objects, rather than human beings, and one does not have to be a bra-burning feminist to recognize this fact. The women are just there to fulfill male desires, and that's probably why a genuine storyline in porn movies is rather redundant. The audience does not want to know "who they are" and what they care about, they just want them to be there to have (virtual) sex with.

Moreover, the element of subordination seems to add to the excitement. So, although the viewer does not want to know the personal history of these male actors either, the idea that the man is in charge (that he is "irresistible" in whatever possible way) seems to be a general turn-on.[12] No doubt, men tend to have different fantasies as well (consider Gareth on his ultimate fantasy: "Two lesbians probably. Sisters. I'm just watching"; 1/4:166). Nevertheless, it is the reduction to something less than fully human—a reduction to the merely physical—that is degrading. In porn we see "women whose agency has been erased or reduced to a slavish desire to please men sexually."[13] The female body is reduced to orifices. And indeed, David himself complains that this dirty picture with his head on it "objectifies" him.

This reduction is typical of degradation or offense (as Brent says of Dolly Parton: "And people say she is just a big pair of tits"; 2/6:253), and it doesn't matter whether the feature one is reduced to is positive or negative. David's defense that the stereotype about a black man's cock is "a compliment if anything" does not prevent it from being degrading. It is the *pars pro toto* (Latin for "taking a part for the whole") that is offensive.[14]

Still, while most of us can understand why some porn can be demeaning to women, it is not banned in our society. Those who like watching or reading it are perfectly free to do so. The only restriction—and this is a mild one—is that they shouldn't bother others with their hobby. No one should be forced to look at porn. The personal preferences of those who do not like it should be respected as well. The general idea is that as long as one is not forcibly exposed to it, there is no clear harm to others.[15]

Pornography, however, has also been defended on different grounds. In fact, a lot of instances of political incorrectness have been supported by emphasizing the importance of *freedom of speech*. On this account, the plea for PC is unconstitutional, flying directly in the face of the First Amendment. Nowadays, as soon as someone starts waving the First Amendment, we are inclined drop all accusations, but why is freedom of speech so important?

In the early nineteenth century, reformers such as John Stuart Mill (1806–1873)—"the zippy philosopher and libertarian," whom, in his undergraduate philosophy days, Ricky Gervais was quite fond of[16]— defended freedom of discussion out of a concern for social progress. If people weren't allowed to express their opinions, mankind (oops

... humankind?) would be trapped in a dull same-old-same-old. Nothing new would ever see the light of day, and we would just rehearse and repeat the same ideas over and over again. If Galileo Galilei (1564–1642) didn't have the opportunity to present his revolutionary ideas to the world—his discovery that the earth revolved around the sun and not vice versa—then the truth would be withheld from us. In fact, the Catholic church was not very keen on accepting Galileo's findings because they obviously undermined the idea that God had placed mankind in the center of the universe (according to Psalm 93:1 and 96:10). As a consequence, his book was banned by the Inquisition and Galileo was very literally "grounded for life." Of course, by that time it was already too late and his ideas were so convincing that the biblical picture seemed more symbolic than realistic. But, to return to our topic, if free discussion is prohibited and dissent is nipped in the bud, then this seriously jeopardizes our chances for arriving at truth.

This makes sense. Today, however, we do not share this nineteenth-century optimism about social progress and the gradual ascent to truth. We might still believe that this is possible in the realm of science, but we have come to understand that there are domains in which the question of truth has many answers, that is to say, in which there is no "better" or "worse," but only a "different." Religion seems to be such a domain in which one god is not necessarily better than another. This is not to suggest that religion is just hogwash and that it isn't important. Much to the contrary, it is extremely important, and this is exactly why we should be tolerant with regard to different conceptions of god and the good. When someone invokes the First Amendment and the importance of free speech it is generally on the grounds that everyone should be entitled to express his or her own conception of the good, and criticize those of others. It should be a *free* discussion in the sense that no one should be compelled to agree. If there is no single, absolute truth then we should, indeed, as Brent says, "agree to disagree" (2/4:159).

All in the Name of Fun

Porn, however, does not intend to be the expression of any serious opinion. Its purpose is "entirely and plausibly to induce sexual excitement in the reader or observer" (Feinberg, 127), not to persuade or convert them. Therefore, it should not be taken seriously, in the sense that it "asserts nothing at all" (Feinberg, 147). Therefore, it is the particular *context* in which these images are shown that somehow exempts pornographers and porn-lovers from moral blame; it is a piece of make-believe. Walt Disney cartoons do not tell the truth, and *Casper the Friendly Ghost* clearly belies the fundamental laws of physics. Yet, are these films corrupting the minds of our poor children? And should they therefore be prohibited? It seems not. Their purpose is to entertain, not to convey an opinion.

Still, the discussion about whether pornography should or should not be legally banned is a difficult one. Liberal philosophers like Joel Feinberg (1926–2004) and Ronald Dworkin (1931) argue that pornography causes no great amount of harm (e.g., that it does not propagate rape), that its offense is something that can reasonably be avoided, and that one has every liberty to voice one's disgust in a public debate. Most importantly, though it might be immoral, pornography does not infringe on the equal *rights* of women. Porn belongs to the realm of fantasy, and this is fine as long as, in the real world, women are respected in their rights. The opposition, however, will claim that the offense is deep (comparable to neo-Nazism's offense to Jews), or that the image of women that pornography conveys is not innocent at all. With porn becoming ever-more violent, it sets a very sad ideal for young males, and this will, in the end, cause significant harm to women.[17] Instead of being a mere fantasy, instead of being "just words," it creates a social reality.[18]

However, with regard to the dirty picture with David's head on it, we should bear in mind that the purpose of this email is not pornographic. It is meant to be funny, not erotic. So perhaps rudeness in the context of humor (for example, jokes involving political incorrectness) is not so bad.[19] The reason seems obvious: jokes should *never* be taken seriously. To take a joke seriously is to not understand that it's a joke. It is to show that one does not have a sense of humor. However, the term "sense" already makes clear that it requires a special sensitivity. A person with a sense of humor is not merely someone who likes a good laugh, but a person who also knows when and how to tell a joke. Such a person *knows* what's funny. The fact that something is meant to be a joke, does not mean that it can be told at any time and place.[20]

Neil seems to master this sensitivity very well when he shoots the bull with Chris Finch (Finch: "Tell [Lucy] that I'll take her up the 'dole office' "; Neil: "The 'dole orifice' " 2/3:126). Brent, however, says that porno laughs are never funny because of their offensive nature *vis-à-vis* women.[21] Of course, he doesn't mean that—he just wants to impress Jennifer by reprimanding Tim. In fact, what Brent lacks is this sense of humor, this social sensitivity. He frequently goes too far. For example, his smug assurance that there are clear limits to his comedy, and that he would never laugh at the handicapped (1/3:115), is quickly shattered by his infamous impression of the "wanking claw" (2/1:33).

Conclusion: Equally Filthy?

The Office brilliantly portrays the life of David Brent, a man of many moral shortcomings, whose main moral flaw is that he is too busy with *looking* good, instead of *being* good. When the cameras are rolling, Brent is very much aware of the demands of PC, because he does not want to seem intolerant, or judgmental, or narrow-minded, or illiberal. Instead, he wants to be remembered for his humanity, his charity, and his humor. Brent therefore tries to present himself as a person of moral excellence. Yet, as we all know, this attempt fails miserably because his commitment to the values he wants to uphold is only skin-deep. Even his charity work is just a means for personal glorification.

Moreover, Brent doesn't know how to behave appropriately. He very much wants to be loved by all, and, in doing so, he gets entangled in the various roles he has to play.[22] He lacks the social sensitivity of Neil—who is perfectly able to be a good, respectful, competent, and strong leader with a strong sense of humor. Brent's terrible ignorance (combined with a near pathological need-to-please) makes him so tragically funny. I say *tragic* because he does not want to be a bad person. He's a failure, not a delinquent. And indeed, after 14 episodes we have to agree with his newfound love that, underneath the clumsiness and the layers of bullshit, there is actually a very sweet man, yearning to be loved.

There's a bit of Brent in all of us. His struggle with political correctness is emblematic for our society. PC-language is often just rhetorical make-up, covering up the existing inequalities that persist.

Like Brent, we go through the motions and watch our language, but this verbal correctness stands pale against the obvious inequalities and differences that continue to exist beneath the surface. For instance, our society is obsessed with standards of beauty, wealth, and success. Yet at the same time we proudly proclaim that everybody's equal.

This is a recipe for mass hypocrisy. Instead of focusing on real social problems, even the most obvious differences are denied out of fear of political incorrectness. Saying that a man is physically stronger than a woman, for example, counts as a sexist remark. Saying that Bowie is better than the Spice Girls is a sign of cultural elitism. Ricky Gervais and Stephen Merchant clearly understand the absurdity of this situation and they show us how the project of PC quickly derails, especially in those who just "talk the talk" without knowing what they are talking *about*.

For example, in arguing that pornography at work is offensive to women, David is quick to realize that, in fact, women might be as guilty as men. So, his plea for equality also shows in his accusations:

> Well, I'm angry, and not because I'm in it, but because it degrades women, which I hate. And the culprit, whoever he is, is in this room. Or *she*, it could be a woman. Women are as filthy as men. Naming no names, I don't know any, but women . . . are . . . dirty. (1/2:73)

This absurd kind of verbal gymnastics—always looking over your shoulder trying to avoid any charges of political incorrectness so that you no longer see the enormous trap that's lying before you—is also apparent when he tries to defend himself against charges of positive discrimination:

> *Alex*: Now, I'm gonna ask you David, why, when there are three other forklift operators, do you decide to fire me and not Anton? You know, is this positive discrimination? Do you have disability quotas you have to fill?
> *Brent*: I don't know what you mean.
> *Alex*: Are you keeping Anton because he's disabled?
> *Brent*: Anton is not disabled.
> *Alex*: He's a midget, David.
> *Brent*: Yeah, but you're not disabled if you're a midget are you? That's not a disability. That's just small.
> (1/6:232–233)

There's no "better" or "worse," only "different." So rather than use the term "disabled," David starts a ridiculous discussion about the difference between midgets, dwarfs, elves, and pixies.

A genuine concern for equality should not be turned into a spasm for PC. Not that all speech is harmless, very far from it, but we should keep a clear head and fight inequality where it matters most. Morality is not about keeping up appearances, but about doing the right thing for the right reasons. The character of David Brent is, in Nietzsche's famous words, "human, all too human," and we recognize ourselves in his little ways. As such, he is an endearing warning sign for all of us not to get carried away by our selfish concerns even if they're wrapped in big words.

NOTES

1   This is what Americans would call the second "season" of the British show.

2   All references between brackets refer to the official *The Office* scripts: Ricky Gervais & Stephen Merchant, *The Office: The Scripts* (London: BBC Books, 2002, 2004). First, I refer to the series, then to the episode, and then to the page number.

3   On the official BBC website, Ricky Gervais and Stephen Merchant confess that this is the joke which received the most complaints from the audience: www.bbc.co.uk/comedy/theoffice/defguide/defguide15.shtml.

4   Perhaps it is still even more prominent in *Extras*, the follow-up to *The Office*. There it seems that each episode takes a piss at various minority groups in society (blacks in the episode with Samuel L. Jackson, the handicapped in the one with Kate Winslet, gays in the one with Ian McKellen, etc.).

5   Another controversial policy to restore this balance is *affirmative action*, a corrective measure whose stated goal is "to counteract past and present discrimination sufficiently that the power elite will reflect the demographics of society at large, at which point such a strategy will no longer be necessary." The idea is that a company (or a university, etc.) should hire women or blacks, because if they don't, then the existing inequalities will persist. However, the main argument against such positive discrimination is that it gets in the way of qualitative criteria so that, in the end, the lesser woman will be preferred over the better man. Brent himself seems to practice positive discrimination when he fires Alex—the person he hires in the very first episode—instead of

Anton, the midget. For more discussion of this issue, see chapter 14 of this volume.

6   The fact that some people have become very sensitive indeed when it comes to language is clear from the David Howard incident. In 1999, Mr Howard, an aide of the Washington mayor Anthony Williams, used the word "niggardly" when discussing budget issues. Although "niggardly" of course means "ungenerous" or "stingy," Marshall Brown, a black colleague of Howard, thought that this was an inappropriate racial slur, and filed a complaint, eventually resulting in Howard's resignation. In a similar vein—though perhaps slightly more comprehensible—some people have contested the use of the terms "black economy" and "black market."

7   Harry Frankfurt, *The Importance Of What We Care About* (Cambridge: Cambridge University Press, 1988).

8   Think of Brent, who takes offense at the poem "Slough" by Sir John Betjeman (1906–1984): "Come friendly bombs and fall on Slough/It isn't fit for humans now/There isn't grass to graze a cow/Swarm over, death!" (1/5:228). Interestingly, as Michael Heatley notices, Brent does not quote the fourth verse, which goes, "that man with double chin/who'll always cheat and always win." Michael Heatley, *Ricky Gervais: The Story So Far . . .* (London: Michael O'Mara Books, 2006), p. 106.

9   Not only is it difficult to keep track of neutral, politically correct terms, but the exact meaning of derogatory words often eludes us as well. We just use them because other people use them, without much reflection on their origin. For the US *Office* DVD, Gervais had to add a glossary of British words, and he recalls the following incident: "I had to explain the word 'bender'. I was at this serious meeting and I was like, 'Bender is a derogatory term for a gay man. It's derived . . . probably because gay men bend over.' And then a gay guy there said, 'No, actually it's from the eighties' *gender bender*.' I wanted to crawl in a hole and die." Michael Heatley, *Ricky Gervais: The Story So Far . . .* , p. 83.

10 "Some feminists have argued that women in patriarchal societies have been induced to adopt a depreciatory image of themselves. They have internalized a picture of their own inferiority, so that even when some of the objective obstacles to their advancement fall away, they may be incapable of taking advantage of the new opportunities. And beyond this, they are condemned to suffer the pain of low self-esteem." In: Charles Taylor, *Philosophical Papers* (Cambridge, MA: Harvard University Press, 1995), p. 225.

11 The so-called "glass ceiling" argument claims that women only rarely advance to top-level management positions. The fact that the barrier is transparent doesn't make it less real.

12 This theme of "low-grade sadism . . . and banal fantasies of phallic prowess and feminine responsiveness" are nearly always present. Therefore, George Steiner complains, "the stuff is predictable as a Scout manual." In: Joel Feinberg, *Offense to Others* (Oxford: Oxford University Press, 1985), p. 131.

13 Cynthia A. Stark, "Is Pornography an Action? The Causal vs. the Conceptual View of Pornography's Harm," *Social Theory and Practice*, 23 (1997): 294.

14 Again, the funny thing is that even in arguing that he is not a racist, David uses one of these (positive) stereotypes, which undermines his entire argument: "No, I don't have a great many ethnic employees, that's true. But it's not a company policy. I've haven't got a sign on the door that says, 'White people only', you know. I don't care if you're black, brown, yellow—Orientals make very good workers, for example" (1/1:56).

15 Clearly, pornography can be valuable. As Kenneth Tynan mockingly writes, four classes in particular are likely to benefit from pornography: (1) those with "minority tastes who cannot find like-minded mates," (2) the "villainously ugly, unable to pay for the services of call girls," (3) "men on long journeys, geographically cut off from wives and mistresses," and (4) "uncommitted bachelors, arriving alone and short of cash in foreign cities where they don't speak the language." Kenneth Tynan, "Dirty Books Can Stay," in *Perspectives on Pornography*, ed. by Douglas A. Hughes (New York: St. Martin's Press, 1970), p. 112. There is a certain social utility to porn. Some believe that without porn (or without prostitutes), the number of criminal offenses, like rape, would dramatically increase (i.e., the catharsis explanation; porn as a harmless outlet). However, the opposite has also been claimed, i.e., that violent porn would stimulate actual rape.

16 Michael Heatley, *Ricky Gervais: The Story So Far . . .* , p. 33.

17 B. C. Postow, "Pornography, Indirect Harm, and Feminist Analysis," *Journal of Value Inquiry*, 31 (1997): 354.

18 This idea was most famously defended by Catharine MacKinnon, *Only Words* (Cambridge, MA: Harvard University Press, 1993).

19 Emrys Westacott, "The Rights and Wrongs of Rudeness," *International Journal of Applied Philosophy*, 20(1) (2006): 15–16.

20 Sexist jokes and remarks *à la* Chris Finch might be construed as a case of sexual harassment on the work floor.

21 Brent's social ineptness in this regard clearly shows in his assumed "snappy comeback" to Finch when he says that, with regard to The Corrs, "I'd push the brother out of the room, I'd get the other three, and I'd bend them all over [he mimes the bending over part] and I'd do

the drummer, the lead singer, and the one who plays the violin" (and he mimes violently shagging *The Corrs*, making people look at him in horror).

22 Brent: "I'm a friend first, boss second, and probably an entertainer third" (1/1:59); "When people say, 'Oh, would you rather be thought of as a funny man or a great boss?' my answer is always the same: to me they're not mutually exclusive. There's a weight of intellect behind my comedy, yeah?" (1/2:69).

16

The Hostile *Office*: Michael as a Sexual Harasser

Keith Dromm

"That is the law according to the rules." (Dwight)

Michael has a difficult time balancing the roles of boss, friend, and comedian. For example, in the episode "Sexual Harassment," his nemesis Toby, the human resources representative, advises him to refrain from telling inappropriate jokes. Michael responds: "There is no such thing as an appropriate joke, that's why it's a joke." After he is advised by Jan and the company's lawyer, Michael reluctantly informs the staff of the new situation:

> *Michael*: Attention, everyone. Hello. Yes, I just want you to know that—this is not my decision—but from here on out, we can no longer be friends. And when we talk about things here, we must only discuss work-associated things. And you can consider this my retirement from comedy. And in the future if I want to say something funny, or witty, or do an impression, I will no longer ever do any of those things.
>
> *Jim*: Does that include "that's what she said"?
>
> *Michael*: Yes.
>
> *Jim*: Wow, that is really hard . . . You really think you can go all day long? . . . Well, you always left me satisfied and smiling, so . . .
>
> *Michael*: That's what she said!

Michael's "retirement from comedy" lasted only a few seconds. Except for Kevin and Dwight, who seem to enjoy Michael's humor, the rest of the staff has a low opinion of Michael's comedic skills and would have been glad if he remained in retirement. They have all been targets of Michael's humor, as well as his insensitive remarks and his simple insults. His offensive behavior has prompted warnings from Jan and Toby, a visit by a diversity consultant, a large file of complaints against him in Toby's desk, and a three-month paid vacation and company car for Oscar in exchange for agreeing not to sue Dunder-Mifflin.

Michael's real talent is his ability to offend everyone and for every possible reason. He can be racist, sexist, and homophobic. He can be insulting of a person's age, physical appearance, intelligence, social skills, knowledge of cultural fads, and so on. He can even be several of these at once, for example when in "Diversity Day" he requires each employee to "say a race that you are attracted to sexually." While all of this behavior is deplorable, this chapter will focus specifically on Michael's sexual harassment.

Not only are the women, most often Pam, subject to Michael's innuendos, vague and probably insincere come-ons, provocative remarks, uninvited touching, and the like, so are some of the men. Despite Michael's repeated and unsolicited assertions of his heterosexuality, Ryan the Temp became a focus of his attention soon after arriving at the office. Michael rewarded him with "The Hottest in the Office" Dundie, which he conferred with a slap on Ryan's rear. He also demonstrated an unusual amount of affection for Ryan when he got him a Video i-Pod as his "Secret Santa," despite the twenty-dollar limit. Oscar has had to endure Michael's numerous racist remarks, but in "Gay Witch Hunt" Michael kissed Oscar in a clumsy attempt to prove that he wasn't homophobic. This led to the company's generous settlement with Oscar.

Ryan, Pam, and many others in the office could threaten similar lawsuits. If they ever do, however, Michael could turn to the talents of his lawyer, James P. Albini, to whom we are introduced in "Sexual Harassment." Albini (whose face we might recognize from the billboards) specializes in "free speech issues" and, as he helpfully informs the camera, "motorcycle head injuries, worker's comp, and diet pill lawsuits." In his defense of Michael, Albini could rely on a loophole that many believe exists in United States sexual harassment law. This law arises out of anti-discrimination law, in particular, Title VII of the Civil Rights Act of 1964. In 1986, the Supreme Court ruled that workplace sexual harassment constituted sex discrimination in violation of that Act.[1] However, an indiscriminating harasser, like Michael, would seem to escape the scope of federal sexual harassment law. Both genders are victims of his offensive behavior. He's what's been called an "equal-opportunity harasser." Since Michael harasses both women and men, Albini could argue that Michael has not committed sex discrimination.[2]

But the law is not our only moral authority (if it's a moral authority at all).[3] The law enforces some of our moral principles, but not all of them. There are some behaviors that most of us would consider immoral, but which are not illegal. Angela's snobbish and rude behavior towards others is immoral, but few would think that it should be illegal. So, whether or not Michael's behavior is illegal, it is clearly wrong. But if it is not discrimination, what is wrong with Michael's behavior?

In attempting to answer this question, we will be doing *applied ethics*. Applied ethics is the attempt to use the tools of philosophy to solve particular moral problems or dilemmas. Most of the time, we know how to behave morally. We don't always act according to our principles, but we usually know what it is we *should* do. For example, in "Drug Testing," Dwight knows that it would be wrong to give Michael his urine, but he does so anyway. However, there are situations in which our moral obligations are not as clear (should Pam be planning her wedding during company time?). In other cases, we might believe that an action is immoral, but not know why it is (if Pam shouldn't be planning her wedding at work, why not? Is it because it's a misuse of company time or because it's liable to upset Jim? Or both?). Applied ethics uses all the resources and techniques of philosophy to help us answer such questions. When it comes to Michael's behavior, many of us might believe that it's wrong but we're unable to say exactly why it's wrong. But it's not enough simply to believe that behavior like Michael's is wrong. We might be confusing what we find unpleasant or distasteful with what is immoral. Dwight's hairstyle is unpleasant, but there's nothing immoral about it. Understanding the reasons why Michael's behavior is wrong can also help us challenge such behavior when we are victims or witnesses of it, and it can reinforce our opposition to it, so we're less likely to be perpetrators or facilitators of it.

Filthy Emails and Inappropriate Jokes: Sexual Harassment as Wrongful Communication

In order to decide what is wrong with sexual harassment, we also need to define it. Courts in the United States have distinguished between two types of sexual harassment: *quid pro quo* and "hostile environment." The former occurs when an employer demands sexual attention from an employee in exchange for some job-related benefit, such as simply keeping his or her job. Except, perhaps, for his attempt to kiss Pam in "Diwali," Michael has never been seen committing this form of sexual harassment. While he has been capricious in his hiring and firing decisions, as well as in other work-related matters (for example, in his unwarranted disdain of Toby), he has never demanded sexual favors from an employee—though he has made Dwight do his laundry.

The other type of harassment occurs when an employer is responsible for a workplace environment that is threatening or offensive to an employee.[4] The employer need not be the direct cause of such a workplace. The harassers could be the employee's co-workers. If the boss is aware of the harassment but does nothing to correct it, then he or she can be found negligent. If Michael were to be sued for sexual harassment, it would likely be for creating a hostile environment. Such things as his email forwards (and his constant refrain "That's what she said") could easily be construed as creating a workplace that is offensive to many. But the "king of forwards," as he describes himself, also does nothing to stop the offensive behavior of his workers. In "Conflict Resolution," his proposed resolution to a dispute between Kevin and Angela would actually increase the offensive behavior in the office. Angela complains that Kevin makes sexually suggestive remarks that make her uncomfortable. Michael's solution: "Angela, you are to make sexually suggestive remarks to Kevin that will make him uncomfortable."

But, as we have discussed, since Michael subjects everyone in the office, regardless of gender, to his offensive behavior, US courts would have difficulty finding anything discriminatory, thus illegal, about Michael's behavior. To remedy this kind of problem, Edmund Wall, a contemporary philosopher, has provided a definition of sexual harassment that avoids any connection with discrimination.[5] According to

Wall's definition, Michael's behavior is wrong because it amounts to what he calls "wrongful communication." Wall offers four conditions that must be satisfied for sexual harassment to occur: first, someone—say, Michael—successfully communicates a message to another person—say, Pam—that has sexual content. Second, Pam does not consent to receive such a message. Third, Michael nevertheless repeats a message of this sort to Pam. Fourth, Pam "feels emotionally distressed" either because of Michael's disregard of her refusal to receive such messages or by their sexual content, or both (Wall, 531).

Wall describes these conditions as necessary and jointly sufficient: they all need to be true in order for sexual harassment to have occurred (their necessity), and if they are all true, that is enough for sexual harassment to have occurred (their sufficiency). The sexual content of the message can take a variety of forms. For example, it can express a sexual interest in the receiver of the message, or it can be a dirty joke. The message doesn't need to be communicated verbally. It could be made with a gesture, a drawing, a photograph, an email, or some other form of written communication. Wall makes it clear that the harassment doesn't need to be intentional. The harasser might not be aware that his behavior amounts to harassment, but he persists in it either because of insensitivity or ignorance. This agrees with what Toby says during his review of the company's sexual harassment policy: "Intent is irrelevant" ("Sexual Harassment"). Even if the harasser intends only to make the victim laugh, not feel embarrassed or offended, his behavior can still count as sexual harassment. The victim of the harassment can fail to consent to the sexual messages in a variety of ways. He or she can explicitly say that she doesn't want to receive such messages, or she can refuse these messages through, as Wall puts it, a "suggestive silence" (Wall, 532).

So, sexual harassment occurs when a person subjects another to communication that he or she does not want to receive, and when he or she has made the harasser aware of this refusal. This way of understanding sexual harassment allows us to see what's wrong with Michael's behavior towards both Pam and Ryan. The gender of either the harasser or the victim does not matter. The problem with the harasser's behavior is not that it is discriminatory, but that it violates the privacy and autonomy of its victim. According to Wall, the victim's privacy is being violated insofar as they are being coerced to discuss highly personal sexual matters. The victim's autonomy is breached because their refusal to engage in such a conversation is being ignored. When Michael sends Angela "these filthy emails" he is subjecting her to messages that she finds inappropriate, and he is not respecting her right to refuse them.

While this definition succeeds in showing at least some of what's wrong with Michael's behavior, it has some problems. First of all, the definition seems adaptable to any topic—not just sex—that a person would find offensive or be disinclined to talk about. For example, in "Benihana Christmas," Dwight's discussions of how to slaughter a goose, or just the goose, were offensive to many (even though it was a Christmas miracle!). We need only make the necessary substitutions in Wall's definition and we will have another instance of wrongful communication (for example, "someone successfully communicates to another person a message that is about *how to slaughter a goose*," and so on). So, while it might identify what is wrong with such behavior, Wall's definition fails to pick out anything especially egregious in the case of *sexual* harassment. There is more to sexual harassment than just forcing someone to discuss matters that they are disinclined to discuss. For example, in "The Fire," Michael compels Ryan to listen to his business advice. He also admits (during the "Who would you do?" game) that he would want to have sex with Ryan. These two cases seem to be importantly different both in the kind of offensive message being communicated and the degree of its offensiveness.

But do the messages even need to have a sexual content in order for sexual harassment to occur? US courts, at least, have begun to recognize, as Sandra M. Tomkowicz explains, "that a workplace can be made hostile or abusive not only by overt sexual conduct or conduct tinged with sexual overtones, but also by conduct that demeans, derides, denigrates or otherwise deprives an individual of opportunities because of that individual's gender."[6] In "Alliance," Michael calls the party-planning committee his "party-planning bitches." In "Boys and Girls," Michael interrupts Jan's "women in the workplace" meeting to plead with them against doing anything like what was done in the Albany office, namely turn the break room into a lactation room; "which is disgusting," he says. These remarks are not sexual, at least not in the sense meant by Wall, but they are nonetheless offensive, and seem to be perfect examples of sexual harassment. But since Wall does not see any connection between sexual harassment and the disparate treatment of genders, his definition cannot identify what, if anything, is wrong with remarks like these.

There's another problem with the definition we've been discussing. People's level of tolerance for offensive behavior varies. Contrast Meredith and Angela, for example. An employee might also become hardened to offensive behavior after being subjected to it for a very long time.[7] Couldn't there still be something wrong with communicating sexual messages to these employees, even if they do not feel offended by them? And what if an employee has good reason for not objecting to behavior that she finds offensive (perhaps the fear of retaliation by her co-workers or boss)?

"That's what she said": Sexual Harassment as Sex Discrimination

The legal scholar Catherine A. MacKinnon has been an influential advocate of the view that sexual harassment is wrong because it *discriminates*. According to this view, Michael doing such things as saying of Angela in "The Dundies" that she has a "great caboose" or encouraging Pam in "The Convention" to unbutton the top button of her blouse so as to, as he puts it, "let those things breathe," is not wrong simply because he is telling people things they'd rather not hear from him. Rather, MacKinnon would say that such behavior is wrong because it "perpetuates the interlocked structure by which women have been kept sexually in thrall to men at the bottom of the labor market."[8] Michael's treatment of the women in the office has the cumulative effect of maintaining this structure. By constantly calling attention to their physical appearance and sexual characteristics, he is implying the particular role women are to play in society, namely, to be objects of men's sexual attention. Any ambitions that are independent of that role are being discouraged. In the episode "Basketball," Michael asks Pam to be a cheerleader for their team in the basketball game against the warehouse. He suggests she wear a halter-top and her hair in pig-tails; "something youthful for a change," as he puts it. When she declines, Phyllis volunteers. Michael automatically responds: "Oh Yuck! That's worse than you playing."

These insults take on an added dimension because of the power asymmetry between Michael—as not only their boss but also a man—and the women: "It is a reminder of that image of a deprived reality in which sexuality and attractiveness to men were all a woman had to offer—and she had very little control over either" (MacKinnon, 45). Michael treats the women in his office as if all that matters is their looks. In doing this, he is discriminating against them. He is not treating them as equals to men, as persons capable of doing more than being the objects of male heterosexual attention.[9]

Jan Crosthwaite and Graham Priest offer a similar way of understanding Michael's behavior. They argue that it amounts to "a form of oppressive behavior."[10] They define oppression as "a relation between social groups which involves one group wielding power which is illegitimate, in some sense, over another group in the society" (Crosthwaite and Priest, 66). Sexual harassment is behavior that maintains or contributes to the subordinate position of one gender in society. It does this primarily through the psychological effect it has on its victims, causing the members of the oppressed group "to experience their complete powerlessness as a member of that group" (Crosthwaite and Priest, 66). Various types of behaviors can have this effect. Crosthwaite and Priest make it clear that the behaviors need not be sexual. Sexual harassment is "not best understood as harassment of a sexual nature" (Crosthwaite and Priest, 65). Calling a group of women "bitches" is not only to subject them to a word they might not want to hear (perhaps they have no problem with the word in itself or similar ones; Angela, after all, doesn't mind using the word "hussy" to describe her co-workers); it is to treat them as members of a subordinate group. As such, it is a form of oppression.

This view of sexual harassment identifies what is especially egregious about sexual remarks. It also shows how the same harm can be caused by remarks and other behaviors that are not sexual in nature, but which nevertheless call unwarranted attention to a person's gender. Whereas viewing sexual harassment as a kind of wrongful communication requires that the recipient of the unwelcome messages express her objection to them, this alternative account of sexual harassment allows us to see harassment in circumstances even when the victim does not actively oppose it. While Michael's employees often express their displeasure at his behavior, more often they seem just to tolerate it. Pam might object more if she weren't, like all the members of the office, afraid of losing her job. This or other repercussions might be the result of informing your boss that you object to his or her behavior. The difference in power between them makes it difficult for employees to oppose the harassment of their superiors (and this is a good reason to reject Wall's second condition).

Viewing sexual harassment as a kind of discrimination also allows us to see that the victims of it can extend beyond the immediate recipient of the harassing behavior. As MacKinnon puts it, sexual harassment is a "group injury."[11] Since it reinforces the subordination of women in society, all women are injured by it, even if the immediate recipient of the behavior does not feel injured.

Finally, this view identifies the different effects that Michael's offensive behavior can have on men and women. Ryan is certainly bothered by Michael's attentions. Consider his reply when asked what he will do with his Dundie for "The Hottest in the Office": "That's the least of my concerns right now." But Michael cannot cause him to be reminded of his "powerlessness" in society. Both the psychological and other effects of Michael's harassment will be very different for him than for the female victims of it. However, there still seems to be something wrong with Michael's behavior towards Ryan—something our discussion has not yet been able to identify. Crosthwaite and Priest contend that "women cannot commit [sexual harassment], nor men be victims" (Crosthwaite and Priest, 68). Only if women were the dominant group in society could Oscar or Ryan be victims of sexual harassment, and then only if their harasser was a woman.

Sandra Levitsky tries to broaden her account of sexual harassment to include cases in which a male is the victim of harassment.[12] While she also sees sexual harassment as a kind of discrimination, she says that its central harm is its tendency to reinforce gender stereotypes. These stereotypes benefit men. They characterize men as capable of assuming dominant roles in society and deny that women have such a capability. Stereotypes have the power to influence how we treat other people, and gender stereotypes have the specific effect of causing us to treat men and women unequally. So, any reinforcement of a gender stereotype will add to men's power over women. As Levitsky explains, "Preserving gender distinctions goes hand in hand with preserving the rewards men derive from these distinctions" (Levitsky, 219). Michael's behavior towards Ryan and Oscar counts as sexual harassment because it reinforces these stereotypes: "When a person sexually harasses a man, the harasser both feminizes him and reinforces the idea that those qualities associated with women are subordinate to the qualities associated with men" (Levitsky, 219). However, according to this view, while Ryan and Oscar might be sexually harassed by Michael, they are not really the victims of his harassment. Since they are men, they actually benefit from these stereotypes. Instead, all women are the real victims of his behavior.

The Dundie Award Goes To . . .

So, which view of sexual harassment is correct? They both are. They each identify morally egregious behavior and their different effects on their victims. It would be simply incorrect to deny that Ryan and Oscar are harassed by Michael. But it would also be wrong not to notice the different effects his harassment has on Pam and the other women in the office. When Ryan is harassed, he is not reminded of his subordinate position in society. When Oscar is harassed, he might be reminded of something like this, but what he feels is still different from what is felt by the female victims of Michael's harassment. Everyone subjected to Michael's behavior is harmed in some way, though not all in the same way. Some of his victims are harassed when they are treated as objects of sexual attraction by Michael; others are harassed when he treats them differently because of their gender. So, by sexual harassment we can mean two things: harassment that is sexual in nature or harassment that is directed towards one sex in particular. At most, what is in dispute between these two views is which type of behavior best deserves the label "sexual harassment." I will not try to settle this. Instead, I want to consider whether these two views of sexual harassment are enough for understanding what's wrong with Michael's behavior.

"Crossing the Line": Harassment in the Workplace

While we need both views of sexual harassment to understand what's wrong with Michael's behavior, they each miss something important. Both definitions fail to capture the particular effects that harassment can have in the workplace. MacKinnon comes close to identifying this when she writes that "A man who is allowed to measure a woman's work by sexual standards cannot be said to employ her on the basis of merit" (MacKinnon, 45). But the same can be said of any employee in Michael's office who is a victim of his harassment, especially when that harassment is of a sexual nature, but equally when it attacks the victim's gender, race, age, physical appearance, and so on. When Michael expresses a sexual attraction to an employee, whether male or female, or when he calls unwarranted attention to her gender, he is undermining her expectation that she will be assessed only on her skills or other qualities that are relevant to the performance of her job. If employees lose this expectation, not only will their productivity likely decrease, but they will be wronged: they are entitled to be judged solely on the merits of their work.

People work for a paycheck. Many people would say that, in exchange for that check, workers have an obligation to do all the work that is expected of them by their employers. They shouldn't be playing "Office Olympics" while the boss is away. Instead, they should be performing their duties as well and as completely as they possibly can. But many workers often do more than what is expected from them. In exchange for such things as bonuses, raises, promotions, letters of recommendation, and other job-related benefits besides a paycheck, they will do more than the minimum that is required in order to fulfill their obligations to their employers. Dwight is a perfect example. He often takes on duties that aren't assigned to him (like investigating who wrote something about Michael on a wall in the women's restroom) and the duties he is assigned are performed with an enthusiasm and intensity that would exceed most employers' expectations (for example, as the elf in "Christmas Party" or the "supervisor of security," and consider the risks he assumes, ineffectual as his efforts might be, in "The Fire," both to put out the fire and to retrieve Michael's phone from the building). In doing these things, he is doing more than is required of him in order to receive a paycheck. But he is not doing them for free. He reasonably expects some recognition for all the extra effort he puts into doing his job. Even Michael recognizes this when, in "The Return," he hires Dwight back after coming to believe, though mistakenly, that Dwight made that early morning trip to New York City in order to help the office. More often, however, Michael ignores such dedication, or his behavior towards his employees implies, at least, that it is irrelevant to how he will judge them (just think of how Michael conducts his employee reviews!). But if a boss does not take such extra effort into consideration, if he is only judging his employees on their physical appearance or their gender, or their willingness to tolerate his jokes and insults, then it is all being done for nothing, and the employer is, in essence, getting this extra labor for free.[13]

There are certainly some employees who will use irrelevant characteristics to get ahead in a job. For example, a person might use her sexuality to keep or advance in her position. She might try to seduce her boss or make insincere sexual advances towards him. Or an employee might try to ingratiate himself with the boss in other ways, as Andy does, by pretending to be Michael's friend or to find his jokes funny. But in doing these things, such employees are taking advantage of some characteristics that their co-workers might not possess. And since these characteristics are irrelevant to how well a person can perform his or her job, they are being unfair to their co-workers when they exploit them in this way. But it is ultimately Michael, when he takes such irrelevant characteristics into account, who is responsible for the harm done to his employees.

When Michael sexually harasses, he is undermining the legitimate expectation of his workers that they be judged fairly and only on those things relevant to the performance of their duties. They might also be discriminated against, "wrongfully communicated" to, and simply annoyed. Some harms might be worse than others, both in their scope and degree, but they are all equally real, no matter which most deserves the label "sexual harassment."

NOTES

1   *Meritor Savings Bank v. Vinson* (1986).
2   This loophole appears to be closing. In a recent decision, the Supreme Court ruled that sexual harassment can occur when the harasser and the harassed are of the same gender, and even when there is no sexual attraction for the harassed by the harasser. The harassment just needs to be "because of sex" (*Oncale v. Sundowner Offshore Services, Inc.*, 1998).

3 See Mark D. White, "Respect My Authorita! Is Cartman 'The Law,' and Even If He Is, Why Should We Obey Him?" in *South Park and Philosophy*, ed. by Robert Arp (Oxford: Blackwell, 2007).

4 The Equal Employment Opportunity Commission (EEOC), the government body commissioned with bringing sexual harassment suits on behalf of employees, describes both forms of sexual harassment in the following way: "Unwelcome sexual advances, requests for sexual favors, and other verbal or physical conduct of a sexual nature constitute sexual harassment when this conduct explicitly or implicitly affects an individual's employment, unreasonably interferes with an individual's work performance, or creates an intimidating, hostile, or offensive work environment" (www.eeoc.gov/types/sexual_harassment.html).

5 Edmund Wall, "Sexual Harassment and Wrongful Communication," *Philosophy of the Social Sciences* 31 (2001): 525–537. Hereafter cited parenthetically as (Wall, page number) in the text.

6 Sandra M. Tomkowicz, "Hostile Work Environments: It's About The Discrimination, Not 'The Sex,'" *Labor Law Journal* 55 (2004): 99–111.

7 The Supreme Court has ruled that Title VII is violated even if the plaintiff does not suffer psychological harm from a hostile environment (*Harris v. Forklift Sys., Inc.*, 1993).

8 Catherine A. MacKinnon, "Sexual Harassment of Working Women: A Case of Sex Discrimination," in *Sexual Harassment: Issues and Answers*, ed. by Linda LeMoncheck and James P. Sterba (Oxford: Oxford University Press, 2001), p. 43. Hereafter cited parenthetically as (Mackinnon, page number) in the text. The LeMoncheck and Sterba anthology will hereafter be cited as SH in the notes.

9 Even Jan is treated in this way by Michael, but it is a good question—one I don't have the space here to explore—whether that can count as sexual harassment, since Jan is his boss. But while their relationship—what there is of one—is voluntary, could Jan be sexually harassing Michael, her subordinate? Some advocates of the present view, as we will soon see, would say no.

10 Jan Crosthwaite and Graham Priest, "The Definition of Sexual Harassment," in SH, p. 65. Hereafter cited as (Crosthwaite and Priest, page number) in the text.

11 Catherine MacKinnon, "Sexual Harassment as Sex Discrimination," in *Sexual Harassment: Confrontations and Decisions*, ed. by Edmund Wall (Buffalo, NY: Prometheus Books, 1992), p. 145.

12 Sandra Levitsky, "Closing the 'Bisexual Defense' Loophole in Title VII Sexual Harassment Cases" in SH. Hereafter cited as (Levitsky, page number) in the text.

13 It might be said that workers in such a workplace simply shouldn't put in this extra effort. If they know that the boss is not going to take it into account, then they are just wasting their time and energy. But among the benefits that workers seek when they work harder at their jobs than expected is simply continual employment. With the threat of downsizing, this has been an important motivation for the workers in *The Office*. But the employment relationship is always a tenuous one. Most of the workers at Dunder-Mifflin seem to be *at-will* employees. That means that their employment can end at any time. As it is often explained, the *at-will* employee can be fired for a good reason, a bad reason, or no reason at all.

Both US courts and legislation have made some exceptions to the *at-will* doctrine. For example, courts have recognized a "public policy" exception to the doctrine, such as when an employee is fired for refusing to do something illegal. And there is US legislation that protects employees from being fired for certain reasons, such as supporting a union.

17

The Obscene Watermark: Corporate Responsibility at Dunder-Mifflin

David Kyle Johnson

Ryan's about to attend the Michael Scott School of Business. I'm like Mr. Miyagi and Yoda rolled into one . . . There are 10 rules of business that you need to learn. Number one. You need to play to win . . . but . . . you also have to . . . win to play. Got it? And . . . I will give you the rest of the 10 at lunch.
(Michael Scott, "Fire")

In "Product Recall," the Scranton branch of the Dunder-Mifflin paper company faced a crisis. Michael described it best:

Apparently a disgruntled employee at the paper mill decided that it would be funny to put an obscene watermark on our 24 pound cream letter stock. Five hundred boxes has [*sic*] gone out with the image of a beloved cartoon duck performing unspeakable acts upon a certain cartoon mouse that a lot of people like . . . I've never been a fan. ("Product Recall")

The watermark was so obscene that NBC had to "black bar" it. The backlash was huge. Dunmore High School (a "keystone account" holder) sent their prom invitations out on the obscenely watermarked paper, and Barbara Allen (one of Dunder-Mifflin's oldest clients) nearly lost business and found the watermark "horrifying" and "disgusting" (despite Dwight pointing out that the sex was apparently consensual, since both animals were smiling). It put the branch at "threat level midnight"[1] and the entire day (so said Kelly) was "bananas . . . B.A.N.A.N.A.S.!"

Business ethics, the branch of philosophy that deals with moral obligations of the business world, raises two very important questions regarding what we shall call (as Michael did) "the watermark boner." First, is the company morally obligated to "make amends" for its mistake or is it only morally obligated to minimize the resulting "profit loss"? Second, if Dunder-Mifflin is responsible, who should bear the brunt of the responsibility for the incident: the disgruntled employee, the paper mill floor manager, quality assurance, Michael Scott, Jan, David Wallace . . . ?

The Business of Businesses

What is the single most important thing for a company? Is it the building? Is it the stock? Is it the turnover? It's the people. The people. My proudest moment here wasn't when I increased profits by 17 percent, or cut expenditure without losing a single member of staff. No, no, no, no. It was a young Guatemalan guy, first job in the country, hardly spoke a word of English, but he came to me and he went "Mr. Scott, will you be the Godfather to my child?" Wow. Wow. Didn't work out in the end. We had to let him go. He sucked. (Michael Scott, "Pilot")

In the name of profit, corporations do seemingly immoral things all the time. Power plants won't control their pollutants—dumping them into nearby rivers or releasing them into the air—because the efforts to control the pollutants reduce their profits. Car companies won't recall defective parts if the recall will cost more than the resulting lawsuits. Companies will close plants with short notice, leaving hundreds or thousands of loyal employees out of work with little warning. Oil companies will drill for oil in third world countries, leaving huge environmental messes.[2] Our first reaction is to declare it immoral for companies to do such vile things. But before we rush to judgment let's consider things from "corporate's" point of view.

Corporate might argue along the following lines: when people buy stock in a company, they are—quite literally—handing over their money to the manager of that company. When they do so there is an implied agreement: "I, the stockholder, give you, the manager, my money under the condition that you use it to make as much money as possible." With this agreement a promise is made, and this promise creates a moral obligation for the managers to spend the stockholder's money only in ways that ensure the most profit. Thus, managers—and in fact the companies themselves—do not have "free rein" to do whatever they wish with the company's money—for it is the money of the stockholders. They can only spend that money in ways already approved by the stockholders: the ways that make the most profit. So, on this argument, even though protecting the environment, reducing deaths by recalling defective parts, and ensuring jobs for loyal employees seems nice to us on the outside, managers are *not* morally obligated to do such things. Such things are not profitable. Since the managers are morally obligated to spend the stockholders' money in profitable ways, if they can get away with "vile" things that save them money,[3] not only is it morally permissible for them to do so, it is morally obligatory.[4] We'll call this the "Stockholder Theory" (for it suggests that a company's moral obligations are only to its stockholders).

Although the watermark boner isn't as big a deal as environmental pollution and the death of vehicle drivers and passengers, the Stockholder Theory still entails specific things about how Dunder-Mifflin should handle the incident. Take Barbara Allen, the client who nearly lost business and found the watermark horrifying and disgusting. What Dunder-Mifflin should do is ensure that it retains Barbara's business. This will obviously mean refunding her money for the watermarked paper, and she will probably need other incentives if she is to continue her patronage. The incentives might include some free paper—Michael offers her 6 months' worth (or 25 reams, whichever comes first)—but whatever they offer her can't end up costing the company more money than keeping her business would make them. Bigger clients, like Dunmore High School, could be given greater incentives to stay—since their continued business will generate more profit—but the same rules apply; keeping their business can't cost more than it will make. You've heard the phrase, "It's all about the bottom line." Well, according to the Stockholder Theory, making it all about the bottom line is morally obligatory and—although keeping customer business is preferable—efforts to do so can't cross that line.

That Dunder-Mifflin ascribes to the Stockholder Theory is fairly evident. All the company seems willing to do to make amends for this mistake is "apologize" (except for Angela, who can't seem to apologize to anyone) and make sure it doesn't happen again—two things that clearly only consider the bottom line. Apologies are cheap, and letting it happen again would cause a huge loss in business. There are many other examples of the bottom line having the last word at Dunder-Mifflin—the cheaper health care plan in "Health Care," the downsizing in "Halloween" and "The Merger" . . . and no open bar at The Dundies! (Whether Michael ascribes to the Stockholder Theory is unclear. His attitude towards Barbara is fairly "Stockholderish"—25 reams of paper is pretty cheap. But in "Business School," Michael seems to suggest that business is "all about the people." Of course, he says the same thing in the pilot, when talking about the Guatemalan guy—but then turns around and fires him.)

As you may guess, there are some serious objections to the Stockholder Theory. First, it's unclear that implicit agreements exist, at all, between stockholders and managers.

> . . . a [stock]holder buys shares of a corporation from pervious owners, not from the corporation itself, and even in the case of original purchases of stock, there is no agreement beyond the prospectus . . . [stock]holders expect to be treated as "investors," . . . and expect corporate managers to consider a wide constituency when making corporate decisions . . . the lack of any face to face dealings . . . and . . . any specific representation by management to individual [stock]holders further mitigate against any presumption that an implied contract exists.[5]

So it seems that no "I'll get profit at all costs with your money" promise is ever made by managers to stockholders. It's also unclear that buying stock in a company makes the managers of that company your "agent" whose *moral responsibly is solely to you*. Managers have many other duties—some of which they directly consent to and some of which are defined by law. When these duties conflict with your interests, it seems that you (the stockholder) will—and should— get the short end. Wouldn't the same be true of the manager's moral duties? Additionally, if a manager was really your "agent" in this way, the manager would be able to make your decisions for you—but in normal modern business relations they can't. When it comes to major corporate decisions (like mergers), managers have no say. But, most importantly, your conditional involvement with the company seems to remove the manager's obligations to you. As a stockholder, you don't "own" the company (or even a piece of it); your money isn't forever sunk into the company in such a way that the company's success is inevitably tied to your own. Only if that were so would you *own the company* in such a way that the managers would be morally obligated to you. But you can sell your stock whenever you wish! Accordingly, the managers are not obligated to look after only your interests. If you don't like what they're doing, then you can get out.

As an alternative to Stockholder Theory, let's consider "*Stakeholder Theory*," according to which a company is morally obligated to consider and act in the interests of everyone who has *a stake* in the company: employees, manufacturers, customers, and even society. No one person or group of people owns a company;[6] people simply become involved with it—whether as a stockholder, an employee, or a customer—by their own consent on a conditional basis (all with the hope that it will benefit them). The company's obligations, therefore, are to everyone so involved, that is, the stakeholders. So the managers—acting on behalf of the company—are morally obligated to weigh the interests of all such parties and act accordingly.

Perhaps, a hundred or so years ago when businesses were smaller (or even today with some very small businesses), when ownership was more explicit and direct, this was not the case.[7] But today, Stakeholder Theory seems right. And that being the case, it seems that Dunder-Mifflin needs to do more than simply refund money and apologize for the watermark boner. Ultimately, it would need to repair any damage done by the watermark. Perhaps Dunder-Mifflin should personally call everyone invited to the prom and explain that it wasn't the school's fault. Perhaps it needs to make amends for its mistake to Barbara Allen with much more than 25 reams of paper— even if it cuts into profits. Perhaps, if she calls for Michael's resignation, she should get it (we'll talk about this in a moment.) Most likely, the best way to "make up" for the mistake would be determined on a case-by-case basis. Regardless, Dunder-Mifflin needs to keep in mind the wellbeing of all its stakeholders—and that includes its customers.

Considering the interests of *all* stakeholders, of course, includes the interests of the employees. Dunder-Mifflin can't make amends in such costly ways that it has to start laying off employees. Employees are

211

stakeholders too; a balance must be struck. But simply apologizing and refunding doesn't seem to be enough.

Doesn't Someone Need to be Fired?

> If I could leave you with one thought: remember it wasn't me. They are trying to make me an escape goat. (Michael Scott, "Product Recall")

Usually, when companies make major mistakes, someone loses his or her job. Indeed, this happened in the case of the watermark boner. Although Barbara Allen called for Michael to resign, Creed got Debbie Brown (the floor manager at the paper mill) fired. But should anyone get fired? Maybe whoever is at fault should get fired. But who is that? And after all, couldn't it just simply be the company's fault, not an individual's fault?

Just like the issue of "which bear is best," when it comes to the issue of corporate responsibility, there are two schools of thought. One is that when things like the watermark boner happen, it is the business itself—not any one individual—that is at fault, and it is the business itself that should bear the brunt of the moral and financial responsibility. Let's call this the "corporate responsibility" school of thought. The other school of thought is that the individual(s) responsible for the mistake should be held responsible. Let's call this the "individual responsibility" school of thought. We all know that the black bear is the best, but which school of thought is right?

There are three major problems with the corporate responsibility school of thought. First, we usually think that responsibility for a wrong—especially moral responsibility—can only be attached to something if it intentionally causes the wrong. But only individual persons—not businesses—can form intentions and intentionally do anything. After all, only individual persons have minds, and intentions are mental states. Although businesses are collections of persons that we sometimes describe as having intentions, such talk is metaphorical, not literal—like when we describe a car as "trying" to start. Businesses and cars don't *really* have intentions because they don't have minds.

Second, holding the entire business responsible unduly punishes the blameless. Most Dunder-Mifflin employees didn't have anything to do with the watermark boner, and making the entire company bear the brunt will hurt everyone. This seems unfair—especially if there is someone directly responsible. Third, "spreading around" the responsibility in this way only encourages more irresponsibility. Other disgruntled employees will also pull obscene watermark tricks if they know that the entire corporation will pay for what they have done (instead of them paying personally).[8]

Of course, there will be times when no one is responsible; sometimes business mistakes are just the result of innocent decisions of separate individuals doing their jobs as they should. Perhaps different people choose, independently, different materials that, when combined, don't work properly (Kevin and Oscar don't work properly when they are bored and play Hateball).[9] In those cases, it seems that—since no one person is to blame—the company should shoulder the responsibility. But that was not the case with the watermark boner; clearly, an individual should be held responsible. But who?

The obvious answer might seem to be to assign the blame to the paper mill employee who was directly responsible for the watermark; that employee seemed to play the most direct causal role. Clearly, the paper mill was thinking like this when they fired Debbie Brown, the floor manager, after Creed alleged that she had missed her "quality assurance inspection" meeting with him. The paper mill didn't know who was specifically responsible and simply fired the most causally responsible person they could identify. (Although it should be noted that, in fact, no such meeting was ever scheduled; Creed made it up to save himself from becoming a homeless man . . . again.) But there are two major problems with stopping our investigation there: Dunder-Mifflin is clearly partly responsible for the incident and the paper mill is not a part of Dunder-Mifflin. As was revealed in the episode "Take Your Daughter to Work Day," Dunder-Mifflin is a middleman—buying paper from the paper mill and reselling it at a higher price (the *daughters at work* pointed out that this seems to be unfair). So firing someone at the paper mill does nothing to absolve Dunder-Mifflin or its employees.

So which Dunder-Mifflin employee should bear the brunt of Dunder-Mifflin's moral responsibility? Who is, we might say, "blameworthy"? Maybe the person who is most causally responsible for the incident should be fired, but identifying that person is difficult. Causal relationships are not easy to pin down. Something like, "if one fails to do something that would have prevented an incident, then one is causally responsible (at least in part) for that incident," might work as a criterion for causation. But—regarding the watermark boner—such a thing is true of almost everyone at Dunder-Mifflin. The watermark boner would have been avoided had only the sales staff refused to sell any 24-pound cream letter stock, or had only Angela not written the check to the paper mill for the paper, or had only Devon done a better job of arguing to save his job (getting Creed fired instead) on Halloween 2005, or had only Josh Porter (Stamford Regional Manager) not taken the job at Staples and merged the Scranton branch into his . . . the list could go on. But it doesn't seem right to blame the sales staff, Angela, Devon, Josh, etc., for the watermark boner—so it seems that mere causal responsibility isn't enough for *blameworthiness*.

All is not lost. When it comes to "being blameworthy" for office blunders, a different criterion works better. "If one fails to perform an action that *it is one's job to perform*, and that failure causally contributes to a negative incident, then one is blameworthy for that incident." And this seems right. We *don't* want to blame the sales staff for the incident because they sold the paper—even though selling the paper causally contributed to the occurrence of the incident—because it is their job to sell the paper. But we *do* want to blame Creed. Every week he is supposed to take four hours and do a quality spot check at the paper mill, but Creed chose to blow off that weekly responsibility—all year long! Had he not blown it off—and instead done his job—he might have caught the watermark and prevented the paper from being sent. (Notice also that if we found out that Creed *had been doing his job*, but the disgruntled paper mill employee found a way to "sneak it past" his inspections, we wouldn't be inclined to blame Creed.) If the criterion is right, Creed is blameworthy for the incident.

But we can't stop there. We must ask if anyone else fits the criterion. And it seems that Michael does. Of course, he denies this in his apology video:

> By now you are probably sick of hearing about Dunder-Mifflin and our embarrassing watermark boner. [I have literally apologized an

infinite number of times over this, and still there are calls for me to resign, calls from an annoying woman and possibly over the media a little.] Well let me tell you something. Something from the heart. [I will not resign.] I am not leaving this office. It will take a swat team to remove me from this office and maybe not even then. There is no way I will resign. It wouldn't be fair. Not to the good workers I work with. Not to my clients. And especially not to me. Let's not forget who this whole resigning business is about anyway. [I need this job. My mortgage is hundreds of dollars a month. With this job I can barely afford that. I have a company car, but I still have to pay for the gas. Gas prices are high and I have no savings whatsoever. And it wasn't even me. It's not fair that they want me to resign.] If I could leave you with one thought: remember it wasn't me. They are trying to make me an escape goat. If I am fired, I swear to God that every single piece of copier paper in this town is going to have the F-word on it—the F-word. You have one day.[10]

But none of this matters! Granted, he didn't personally put the watermark on the paper, and yes he needs the job, but none of this changes the fact that had he been checking to ensure that the spot checks were being done—something that his job clearly includes—he would likely have prevented the incident. Unless Creed was somehow tricking Michael into thinking that inspections were happening when they were not, Michael is guilty of contributing to the incident by failing to do his job and is thus blameworthy.

The same is true of Jan. She knew that Michael was inept as a manager, but still allowed him to keep his management position—probably she wanted to keep Michael wearing schoolgirl dresses in the bedroom. But since Jan's job involves ensuring the quality of the employees under her (no pun intended), and doing so would have prevented the incident, she is blameworthy as well.

Of course, this line of responsibility might also be tracked all the way back to David Wallace (Chief Financial Officer) and the corporate big wigs. But since they were already planning to fire Jan for gross incompetence, they can be absolved of responsibility. They were doing their job before the incident occurred. So ultimately the morally appropriate response to the watermark boner would be to hold Creed, Michael, and Jan responsible.

But should the responsible individuals be fired? Sometimes less severe punishments (such as a demerit, citation, violation, verbal warning, written warning, disciplinary review, or one of Jim's full disadulations) will do. But the watermark boner was serious enough to warrant firing. Creed, Michael, and Jan should all have been fired.

You might disagree. If one willfully avoids doing one's job (like Creed), one should be fired. But what if one *doesn't willfully* slack off ? Michael's problem is ineptitude, not laziness. He *intends* to be a good manager, he just doesn't pull it off. Is this enough to save his job? Well, *I* can't keep my job on good intentions. If I can't teach philosophy, I should be let go—even if I *intend* to teach philosophy (and try really hard). The same is true of office work. If someone *intends* to do his job, but simply cannot do it, then he should be fired.

Just intending to do their jobs doesn't let Michael and Jan off the hook. Taking the management position away from Michael was something Jan knew should've been done, but she willfully avoided it. Making sure the inspections were happening was part of Michael's job, but he willfully avoided it. He even let Creed talk him out of doing his job when Michael was forced to let someone go.

The only real difference between Creed, Michael, and Jan is this: Creed failed to do a bigger portion of his job. Checking up on Creed is only one of Michael's many responsibilities. Checking up on Michael is only one of Jan's many responsibilities. But one of Creed's main responsibilities is the mill inspection (he is, after all, quality assurance). So if "the amount" of your job you willfully ignored makes a difference, then perhaps only Creed should be fired. But, then again, ensuring the quality of employees is one of Michael's main responsibilities; ensuring the presence of competent managers is a main part of Jan's responsibilities.

Much more could be said. All in all, if you think only Creed should be fired you need to point out what is different about what he did and show how that difference is relevant to "firing decisions." I can see no such difference and thus conclude—since Creed, Michael, and Jan are all equally blameworthy for a fire-worthy incident—they should all be fired.

A Boss is Like a Teacher, and I am Like the Cool Teacher

Dunder-Mifflin is morally and socially responsible for making amends for the harm they caused their customers by the watermark boner—even if it cuts into company profits. It should not cause all the employees to lose their job, but if some of the higher ups have to take a bit of a pay cut, so be it. The company has moral and social obligations beyond the bottom line. But since this was not just an "anonymous mistake" for which no one was to blame, someone should be held directly responsible. Since the incident was big enough to call for firing, I guess that Michael and Jan have Creed to thank for shifting the blame to Debbie Brown—well, maybe not Jan; she got fired anyway.

NOTES

1   Which, if you don't recall, is the title of the movie screenplay Michael wrote and the employees read in "The Client."

2   For specifics and more such examples, see Tom Beauchamp and Norman Bowie (eds.), *Ethical Theory and Business*, 7th edn. (Upper Saddle River, NJ: Prentice-Hall, 2004).

3   Now, of course, sometimes such things won't turn out to be profitable. If your company pollutes and everyone finds out about it, people might stop buying your product—and that will cut into profit. If that is the case, on the Stockholder Theory, the managers are obligated to do something about the pollution. But it would not be because polluting is wrong; it would be because polluting is cutting into profits and the managers are obligated to seek the highest profits.

4   For a classic rendition of this argument see Milton Friedman's article "The Social Responsibility of Business Is to Increase Its Profits," and John Hasnas, "Two Normative Theories of Business Ethics: A Critique" (pp. 50 and 65 of the aforementioned Beauchamp and Bowie).

5   John Boatright, "What's So Special About Shareholders," p. 76 in Beauchamp and Bowie.

6   There are obviously exceptions in the case of very small businesses—but we aren't really concerned with those here.

7   Of course, when ownership is so direct, the manager and owner are often one and the same. Personal moral obligations more readily apply in such cases.

8   For more on such arguments see Manuel Velasquez's article "Debunking Corporate Moral Responsibility" in Beauchamp and Bowie (pp. 109–121).

9   They call it that because of how much Angela hates it. See "Office Olympics."
10 The pieces of this quote in brackets were not spoken by Michael in the original airing of the episode, but were on the cue cards that Dwight was holding for him. I suspect they were edited from the episode for time.

MEMO 5

PHILOSOPHY AT THE WATER COOLER . . .

18

For *L'Amour*: Love and Friendship in *The Office*

Robert Arp and Jamie Watson

Office Loving

It's Valentine's Day. Pam, the ever-hopeful receptionist, has been signing for flower and gift deliveries for *other* people all day long. At the end of the day, Roy walks in, smiling and empty-handed, to take her home. Obviously frustrated, Pam tells him that she was "kind of hoping" that he got her something for Valentine's Day. Roy gleefully responds: "Well, Valentine's Day isn't over. Let's get you home, and you are going to get the best sex of your life" ("Valentine's Day"). Needless to say, Pam is not impressed.

Love is a surprisingly complex concept. It is sometimes regarded as animalistic, erotic passion that one finds in sexual relationships (as Roy seems to think). But it is also sometimes seen as a kind of cosmic force that binds the world together—the very thing Pam hopes will be expressed in romantic gestures, perhaps. Love can also be associated with a general care and concern for the welfare of human beings, but also sometimes reserved for intimate friendships and family members. And, of course, sometimes "love" is just the name we give to physiological processes having to do with blood rushing to specific parts of our bodies.

Oh, *l'amour*! You are so very confusing! And you can make us do unbelievable things: cut off our ears (Van Gogh), take our own lives (Cleopatra), die for the sins of humanity (Jesus), or—gasp—even get married (the authors . . . although, we're not married to each other)! How can we ever understand you, *l'amour*? Can philosophy help?

Can *The Office* help? Can the two things really help each other? Oh *l'amour*, we shall have to see.

"Who would you 'do'?" Erotic Loving

The ancient Greek philosopher Empedocles (492–424 BCE) envisioned Love and its opposite, Strife, as cosmic principles at work in the cycle of the universe. Love is the source of all that is generative, unified, harmonious, and good; while Strife is the source of all that is destructive, disunified, chaotic, and evil. The cosmos is held in tension between the forces of Love and Strife, and at various times either Love is dominant, or Strife is dominant.[1] Here, love is not just something that affects human relationships—love literally "makes the world go round" as a cosmological principle! Think of those hippies from the 1960s who claimed, "All you need is love" or "Give peace a chance." Many people can think that love and hate take on lives of their own—leading people to peace, harmony, and respect, or to war, chaos, and violence.

But the Empedoclean view has been attacked as being too vague or inaccurate concerning the nature of love. Most people associate love with some kind of *human*, passionate emotion where one desires someone or something with a great deal of intensity. This association has a long history in Western philosophy that begins with the ancient Greeks who had a conception of love understood as *eros*. In Greek mythology, Eros was a god who seemed to have a great power over mortals, causing them to do crazy things like lie, steal, and murder—mostly for some kind of sexual payoff. Hesiod (eighth century BCE) characterizes Eros as the enemy of reason in his *Theogony*, and this erotic conception of love continued to be influential in the Golden Age of Greek philosophers who envisioned human beings as having a rational, controlled, prudent part of their personality (or soul) that must keep this erotic, irrational, animalistic part of their personality in check. The irrational part of one's personality that is shared with animals—and that normally gets people into trouble—often times has to do with sex. After all, humans are rational *animals* with basic needs. In Greek mythology, when mortals and gods weren't trying to screw each other over, they were trying to screw each other! So, *eros* came to be associated with sexual desire. That's why, today, erotic desire is so closely linked with sex and sexual relationships.[2]

In *The Office*, we see that Roy has this kind of loving in mind for Pam when he comes to pick her up on Valentine's Day. Roy is not concerned with Pam's desires or needs insofar as they differ from his own. He merely projects—in an appropriately Freudian fashion—his own desires onto Pam, and thereby assumes that she wants only what he does for Valentine's Day: "the best sex of your life." Oh *l'amour*, you can be such a bitch.

In the episode "The Fire," when everyone is outside waiting to be cleared by the fire department to go back into the building, Jim gets everyone to play the game "Who Would You Do?" This has obviously erotic overtones, and virtually all the men present name Pam as the object of their *eros*. (And ironically, we find Roy claiming that he would "do" Angela, that "tight-ass Christian chick," instead of Pam.) We also see glimpses of how erotic loving is at work when Todd Packer says inappropriately sexual things in "Sexual Harassment," or, especially in the episode "Hot Girl," how erotic loving for Katy "motivates" Michael and Dwight to break office rules and manipulate one another (maybe even more than usual). After all, in that same episode when Michael asks, "What motivates people more than anything else?" Dwight's response is quickly and decisively: "Sex." Dwight may not be too off the mark.

"The perfect mate": Ideal Philial Loving

In contrast to the irrational and animalistic *eros*, the Greeks had another conception of love that they called *philia*, which can be understood as an appreciation of another's beauty or goodness. This "philial" form of love is present in Plato's (427–347 BCE) writings—especially in the dialogue *Symposium*—where he ultimately conceives of love as a contact with an intellectual "Form" of Beauty Itself in which all beautiful things we experience through our senses share.[3]

Plato believed that reality could be broken up into two basic realms: (1) the less-than-ideal, corruptible, changeable, "visible" realm of things around us we recognize through sense experiences; and (2) the ideal, incorruptible, unchanging, "intelligible" realm of ideas, concepts, or "Forms" we can only know through the use of reason. There is one, ideal, eternal, unchanging, specific Form in the intelligible realm for each kind of object, event, thing, or action that one experiences in the visible realm, as is represented in the figure below. A Form is like the ideal essence, core, or fundamental "nature" of something. So, for example, all of the different people, office desks, trees, and cats—as well as the more or less good actions and beautiful things—that we experience around us in our visible, sensible world have a corresponding ideal Form found in another realm of reality that can only be known or "accessed," ultimately, through our minds.

For Plato, the Forms are what humans should be striving to know, as these ideal universals fulfill the twofold purpose of (a) making the things in the visible realm *be known as* what they are as well as (b) making the things in the visible realm actually *be* what they are. Plato expressed this by saying that things in the visible world "participate" in the Forms. So, if you want to be able to recognize and understand objects and events around you in the visible realm of sense experience—as well as be able to explain how it is that these objects and events come to be—Plato suggests that you get to know the Forms. After all, to be able to know and understand the essence or fundamental nature of something is good, as it will help you avoid bad reasoning and poor decisions.[4]

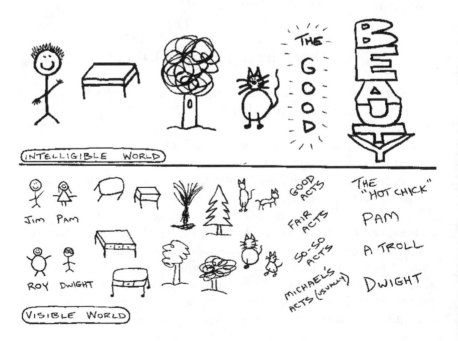

The idea behind Plato's conception of *philia* is that one will be led from the changeable and imperfect beautiful (and not-so-beautiful) things of this world to the unchanging and perfect universal Form of Beauty. And unlike any erotic experience, this philial form of love will be satisfying to the mind, rather than the body. In erotic encounters, physical pleasure is produced when our bodies make contact with beautiful objects in the visible realm. In philial encounters, our minds make contact with the Form of Beauty in the intelligible realm, and mental pleasure is produced. Philial love is concerned with a desire for the Beauty that underlies persons, places, and things—and it is concerned with this *for Beauty's sake.*[5]

Plato conceived of love as a contact with an "ideal" or "perfect" Beauty, and there is a sense in which people are used as conduits or channels to that Beauty. We hear people talk about "the ideal soul mate" or "the perfect person for me." In *The Office*, Angela and Dwight seem to aspire to this idealization more than any of the other characters. In certain respects, they just deserve each other. With their strict legalism and righteous indignation, Angela and Dwight attempt to raise the employees of Dunder-Mifflin to a higher plane of goodness (or so they would claim, at any rate). Recall "The Fire," when, as the alarm bell sounds and other Dunder-Mifflin employees grudgingly leave their desks, Angela and Dwight personify procedure, directing people with "Do not panic!" "This is not a drill!" "Keep your arms to your side!" "Take your stockings off!" . . . Well, maybe "personify" is too strong. But that they strive for a Platonic ideal is clear.

Angela comes across as "holier than thou," as if she is the only person who knows what perfection is, and this attitude is reflected in her interpersonal relationships (the poster conflict with Oscar in "Conflict Resolution"; her kibosh on office romance talk in "Performance Review"; her "excessive" preparation on the Christmas party planning committee, her initial complacency when Dwight was about to lose his job over going to New York for her), her personal relationship (the ever-chastising looks at Dwight), and her comments about herself (as she puts it in "Performance Review": "I really enjoy being judged"). And why the hell is she interested in Dwight? Angela is looking for the ideal mate, not for the mate's sake, or even seemingly for her own pleasure, but to satisfy her own idealized conception of what she takes beauty and goodness to be. Dwight becomes the object of her affection probably because he reminds her of all that is right, good, and beautiful with his attentiveness to strict laws (he was, after all, a volunteer Sheriff's Deputy) and "ideal" working conditions. Although it's true that they have an erotic relationship (for example, we see them entangled in each other's legs in "Email Surveillance"), Angela and Dwight's relationship is more channeled in the Platonic direction of love for "ideal's" sake.

"I'm friends with everybody in this office": Friendly Loving

Aristotle (384–322 BCE) was Plato's student, and criticized his teacher for having divided reality into two separate realms. Why complicate things by thinking that there are multiple realities? Why not just have *one* realm and simply think and talk about the two features of the one realm—the visible and the intelligible—in different ways? Aristotle disagreed with Plato that philial love should be concerned with some Form of Beauty that ultimately *transcends* beautiful things. Loving the Form of Beauty in which a person participates rather than the person him or herself is using or bypassing that person in order to get to some abstract, intangible goal.[6] This didn't make sense to Aristotle. When we love someone, we appreciate *that person's* beautiful characteristics. Love is not some ideal, "intelligible," universal Form of the Beautiful in some other realm found *beyond* beautiful things in this realm. Rather, love entails an appreciation of the beautiful and good qualities of another person standing before you right here and right now, as well as an interaction between lover and beloved. Thus, love is best understood as a relationship of friendship between two people in which mutual awareness of each other's good is kept in mind.

So, various forms of *friendship* best capture what Aristotle means by love. Friendship comes in three kinds. *Friendships of utility* are those relationships where mutual benefit is to be gained from each other's services, as in a business relationship. Obvious examples from *The Office* would be Jim and Dwight developing friendly relationships with their clients so as to supply them with paper, or officemates forming "alliances" with one another to protect their jobs or investments.

Friendships of pleasure are those relationships where pleasure is to be gained from engaging in mutually enjoyable experiences. So *if* it were the case that everyone from the office went drinking, bowling, eating, gambling, or participated in the Dundies—and *actually enjoyed hanging out with one another while doing these things*—then they *would* be friends of pleasure. Part of the humor of the show has to do with the fact that most of the officemates detest one another, so their friendships rarely rise above utility. Although, there are moments where the officemates take much pleasure in making fun of Michael or Dwight, for example, reading Michael's movie script or making up diseases for Dwight to read out loud. Or, remember "Office Olympics," where the office mice play—and compete in events—while the managerial cats are away.

Friendships of virtue are the best and most noble friendships, and are found between those who are most wise, virtuous, and good. In this kind of friendship, as Aristotle so poetically puts it, "two bodies share one soul"—two lovers have the common desire for one another's good.[7]

Jim and Pam sometimes have this kind of relationship, especially when it comes to thinking about one another's good. It's not just that Jim and Pam communicate thoughts, goals, aspirations, and emotions with one another, or that they share music, dinner, and a "show" as in "The Client." In the "Halloween" episode Pam recognizes that Jim is a "talented" salesperson and wants what is best for him in terms of his working career. In "Christmas Party," Pam eventually sacrifices her desire for an iPod to take the tea pot that Jim bought for her. Pam's selflessness for the benefit of Jim and his feelings leads her to see the deeper nature of Jim's affection for her. Jim is concerned for Pam's good when he encourages her to pursue the possibility of utilizing her artwork talents for Dunder-Mifflin or when he sees how poorly Roy treats her on a regular basis. Jim not only finds Pam physically attractive, but he obviously finds her pleasurable to be around and seems to have her general welfare in mind. This general welfare is probably the main reason why Pam claims in "Hot Girl" that: "Jim's a great guy. We're like best friends. He's like a brother to me."

We can contrast Jim's deep friendship love with Roy's obvious erotic, *non*-virtuous love for Pam. Roy not only keeps Pam on engagement hold for three years, never makes her dinner, and discourages her from pursuing her artistic dreams, but he also forgets about her, stranding her at a hockey game, and getting her absolutely nothing for Valentine's Day. He doesn't enjoy hearing about her day or her interests, telling Jim that he's glad she has someone to talk to all day so "she's not all, 'bap, bap, bap, bap,' you know, when she gets home" ("Boys and Girls"). In fact, he apparently doesn't even find her all that sexually attractive since Angela is his "doee" ("The Fire") and he would "be all over that [Katy] if I wasn't dating Pam" ("Hot Girl").

"I love everybody here": Equal Loving

The ancient Greek Stoics, whose founder was Zeno of Citium (344–262 BCE), had a conception of love as a kind of universal respect for all of humankind that we'll call *equal loving*. This equal loving requires that one should be detached enough from this world and its pleasures to appreciate the beauty and goodness of all of humanity. Such a detachment would bring about a universal harmony and peace, which is the ultimate goal of a happy life. Stoic love treats all humans *equally* as "Citizens of the World," as opposed to being concerned only with your own family or the citizens in your specific community.[8] The Stoic conception of love is similar to Immanuel Kant's (1724–1804) call for general respect for persons as "ends in themselves." For both the Stoics and Kant, this kind of universal equalizing love is something that manifests itself in moral actions and needs to be fostered if peace, both within and among communities, is ever to be achieved.[9]

Although it's hilariously absurd, when Michael claims in the pilot episode that Bob Hope, Abe Lincoln, Bono, and God have "helped the world in so many ways"—and that he sees *himself* as being like them—he is talking about this kind of Stoic-Kantian equal loving. These famous figures can be viewed as having a general respect, care, and concern for the welfare of others—not as friends or family members—but simply because they're human beings. If Michael were *truly* concerned about the impact that downsizing will have upon the members of his office or the kids like Oscar's nephew with cerebral palsy then, again, these would be instances of equal loving. Celebrating "Diversity Day" is another way of showing equal loving to all people, regardless of race, creed, or color. In fact, on the equal loving view, you treat another person with respect—and thereby care for them or help them in some way—even if that person is a total jerk the way that Michael is most all of the time! Thus, Jim and Pam show equal loving to Michael during the Dundies at Chili's (after bullies silence him by hurling insults *and* food) by calling for "More Dundies! More Dundies!"

"We're like family": Family Loving

Finally, there is a Christian idea of love known as *agape* (ä-'gä-pä) that emphasizes the unconditional love like one finds in a family. For Christians (and many other religions), God is seen as a kind of Father who loves His creation with a deep and profound bond that nothing can ever break.[10] Likewise, earthly parents are supposed to show unconditional love to their own children. Families stay together through good times and bad times, while also treating each other badly and taking each other for granted. We've all seen commitment to family taken to mind-bending extremes. Think of the psychopath's family members who claim "He's still my son, and I love him" or "He'll always be my brother, and I'll stick by his side to the bitter end." This kind of loyalty and devotion is typical of familial love, even among those of us who are not psychopaths.

Further, in families there is usually someone who is spoiled, someone who takes charge of things, someone who fixes things, someone who lays down the law, someone who's an alcoholic, someone who's a religious zealot, someone who steals, someone who is overweight, someone who gets walked all over, someone who's a sexual deviant . . . Hey! This sounds just like the characters on *The Office*. As with any dysfunctional family, the workers at Dunder-Mifflin keep coming back for more abuse from each other; they bicker, they fight, they laugh, they lie, and they *love* one another like family members. Thus, Michael claims in the pilot episode that "I'm the head of this family, and you ain't gonna be messin' with my children."

And then there's Mr. Schrute. Dwight seems to love Michael with the kind of loyalty and devotion only a son could have. In most episodes, Dwight looks to Michael as his role model, confidant, and, unfortunately, moral compass. "Michael and I have a very special connection. He's like Batman, I'm like Robin. He's like the Lone Ranger, and I'm like Tonto" ("The Fire"). A particularly obvious example of this kind of family-type devotion occurs in the episode "Drug Testing," where Dwight agrees to pee in a cup and let Michael use it as his own sample claiming, "I want him to have all the urine he needs." Michael had been to an Alicia Keys concert that previous weekend and had smoked some pot. Even though it's obvious that this is a moral conflict for Dwight, loyalty ultimately trumps justice; the obligation to one's family outweighs the obligation to the law.

"I love you this many dollars worth": Michael Scott and Love

It is an interesting fact of Western philosophy that it has no term for selfish love. Love has almost always meant affection for another. Perhaps it was the shift toward individualism led by Descartes, or the shoulder-shrugging skepticism of Hume, or maybe it was the "death of God" movement that led to thinking of selfishness as a kind of love. But whatever brought us to this idea, it has not been the traditional view; and it is very difficult to figure out just why we should think of our self-centered motivations as "love." But regardless of what you want to call it, no one on *The Office* better exemplifies selfishness than Michael Scott.

In certain ways, he's much worse than Roy. Michael *pretends* to care about the good of his employees, all the time masking a deep insecurity or personal agenda (Roy doesn't bother with such pretense during his engagement to Pam). In the pilot episode he claims that he is a "friend first"—but his actions show us he's no such thing. He's so self-absorbed that we want to pity him as some kind of overgrown child. When Michael is the first out of the building in "The Fire," he defends his actions against the adage "women and children first," by arguing, "We do not employ children. We are not a sweat-shop, thankfully. And women are equal in the workplace, by law. So, I let them out first, I have a lawsuit on my hands." On "Diversity Day," Michael dons his best PC tone in order to build his reputation as a representative of diversity, while failing at every turn to show any sensitivity at all . . . to anyone. He confuses "colored greens" for collard greens, because collard greens "doesn't make any sense," and asks Oscar if there's anything less offensive than "Mexican" that he would prefer to be called.

There is no doubt that Michael lacks friendships of virtue, but even his attempts at friendships of pleasure and utility get distorted into relationships of abuse and misery. He's the quintessential egotist, consistently failing to provide enjoyment for his employees (as a friend of pleasure might do) or even do the minimal work needed to keep the branch open (as a friend of utility might do). He feigns several attempts at Stoic-Kantian love through charities, he attempts erotic love with Katy, Jan Levinson, and Carol, he attempts philial love with Todd Packer, with Dwight, with Ryan, and at one time with Jim. But, of course, all these pursuits are undermined by his self-imposed blindness to the needs of others. Is Michael *incapable* of love? Hopefully love is something intrinsic to human nature, which cannot be lost. But only the next few seasons will tell for our anti-hero. And if the British version of *The Office* offers any indication, we might be pleasantly surprised.

"You need to have that crazy sexual tension to keep things interesting"

There's much truth in the quotation from Michael that heads this final section, as *The Office* is undoubtedly a popular show because of the sexual relationships presented that are either taboo, kept under wraps, tainted, or re-kindled. But, it's really *all* of the different kinds of loving relationships mentioned in this chapter—held in some kind of tension—that keep us coming back to watch the show again and again. The show's central concern really is love, in all its forms, and all its strange evolutions. Consider how the introduction of Karen's character in the third season added "spice" to Jim and Pam's relationship, or the look on Roy's face when he sees Pam happily dancing, or how Michael tries to kiss Pam (both occurring in the episode "Diwali"), or the love triangle that develops between Michael, Carol, and Jan at the end of season 2. In "Sexual Harassment," HR Representative Toby claims, "office relationships are never a good idea." *Au contraire, mon aime*, they are a great idea—perhaps the very life-blood of *The Office*.

NOTES

1 Empedocles, *Fragments*. In *The First Philosophers of Greece*, translated by Arthur Fairbanks (London: K. Paul, Trench, Trubner, 1898), pp. 157–234.

2 See *Hesiod's Theogeny*, translated by Norman Brown (New York: Liberal Arts Press, 1953), pp. 56–59, lines 120–122; also, Bruce Thornton, *Eros: The Myth of Ancient Greek Sexuality* (Boulder: Westview Press, 1997).

3 Plato, *Symposium*, translated by Robin Waterfield (Oxford: Oxford University Press, 1994), 196B, 201B, 210D.

4 See Plato, *The Republic*, translated by Desmond Lee (New York: Penguin Books, 1955). For an introductory commentary on Plato's thought, including the Forms, see Julia Annas, *An Introduction to Plato's Republic* (Oxford: Oxford University Press, 1981).

5 We find remnants of this idea today in the concept of a *Platonic relationship*, where two people have a relationship that does not involve sex. The original idea involved not merely a friendship that lacked sex, but that also included loftier, intellectual pursuits, though contemporary use has lost this aspect. Of course, the original idea also involved a relationship only between two men, since certain misogynistic tendencies led philosophers to believe that women were not capable of such "divine" love. Interestingly, the philosopher who introduced the term "Platonic love" in 1484, Italian Marsilio Ficino, thought that Plato's conception of love must involve a sexual relationship between the men in order to transcend the physical and achieve the divine. See Marsilio Ficino, *Commentary on Plato's Symposium on Love*, translated by Sears Jayne (New York: Spring Publications, 2000).

6 For Aristotle's criticism of Plato's Forms, see his *Metaphysics*. In *The Complete Works of Aristotle*, edited by Jonathan Barnes (Princeton: Princeton University Press, 1984), Books I–V.

7 Aristotle, *Nicomachean Ethics*. In *The Complete Works of Aristotle*, edited by Jonathan Barnes (Princeton: Princeton University Press, 1984), Books VIII and IX.

8 See A. A. Long, *Epictetus: A Stoic and Socratic Guide to Life* (Oxford: Oxford University Press, 2002); also Martha Nussbaum, *The Therapy of Desire* (Princeton: Princeton University Press, 1994).

9 See Immanuel Kant, *The Metaphysics of Morals*, edited by Mary Gregor (Cambridge: Cambridge University Press, 1996), particularly Ak 6:449–59; Immanuel Kant, *Groundwork for the Metaphysics of Morals*, edited by Alan Wood and Jerome Schneewind (New Haven,

CT: Yale University Press, 2001), Third Section, Ak. 4:438; Immanuel Kant, *Perpetual Peace, and Other Essays on Politics, History, and Morals,* translated by Theodore Humphrey (Indianapolis: Hackett, 1983); James Bohman and Matthias Lutz-Bachmann (eds.), *Perpetual Peace: Essays on Kant's Cosmopolitan Ideal* (Cambridge, MA: MIT Press). Kant was a Christian who most assuredly rooted his respect for persons in biblical passages such as "You shall love the Lord your God with all your heart, and with all your soul, and with all your might" (Deuteronomy 6:5); "love your neighbor as yourself" (Leviticus 19:18; also Matthew 22:37); and "love your enemies" (Matthew 5:44–5). Also, sisterly/brotherly love among all members of humanity is reflective of God's love (Psalms 91:14; 1 John 4:16), and will be the way in which to bring about peace and harmony in communities (1 Corinthians; 1 John 4:16–20; James 2:9).

10 See Cyril G. Williams (ed.), *Contemporary Conceptions of God: Interdisciplinary Essays* (New York: Edwin Mellen Press, 2003).

19

Look at the Ears! The Problem of Natural Kinds

Thomas Nys

Philosophy has a reputation for being difficult. Yet, despite philosophers congratulating themselves on the fact that they are able to handle such difficulty, it also has a reputation for being utterly pointless and boring. Both features are linked. It's difficult because it's often hard to see what the philosophical problem is. In fact, it's not only difficult to solve philosophical problems, but also to understand philosophical questions. It's boring to the extent that these problems are often so far-fetched or so out-of-this-world that we wonder what all the fuss is about. Philosophy is just much ado about nothing.

This should make us wonder why anybody would ever choose to study philosophy. At least Ricky Gervais' reasons were clear. Although his initial interest was in biology,

> within two weeks of arriving at University College London he changed his course to philosophy when he realized how few lectures he would be obliged to attend for the latter subject. "I thought, 'Why am I still doing this? I didn't come here to study. This is ridiculous.'"[1]

Apparently, London philosophy students have a lot of free time, and Ricky was eager to use this time to make it in the music business. So his decision to study philosophy was not entirely wholehearted: like David Brent, he only did the job because of the perks. The extra benefits were not conceived as extra, but as essential.

Nevertheless, as this book proves, these philosophy courses, few as they may have been, have still rubbed off on the work of Ricky Gervais. Many hidden philosophical themes have been dealt with in previous chapters and will be explored in chapters to come. In this

particular chapter, however, I want to focus on a philosophical discussion that fully bears the marks of brain-sizzling difficulty and real-
world irrelevance (and, at the same time, it harks back to Ricky's
initial field of interest: biology). It is the problem of natural kinds.

This problem is very difficult and obscure, but two of the most
hilarious scenes from *The Office* can introduce it like no professional
philosopher ever could. Let's start with the first. Remember episode
three of the first series—the one with the quiz? In one of the talking
head cut-scenes, Brent muses on what must have been one of his
finest moments:

> We've been quiz champions for six years now. We nearly lost it two
> years ago, unjustly, because Gareth was quizmaster then and the
> question was, "What type of alien is Mr. Spock?," and everyone
> put "Vulcan," which is incorrect! Mr. Spock is half-Vulcan, half-
> human, ok? And Gareth went, "Oh, look, everyone gets one point."
> "No, no, everyone does not get one point. Carpet Munchers don't get
> a point, Dr. Wankenstein doesn't get a point, Stephen Hawking's
> Football Boots don't get a point. I do." I had to go home to get a book to
> prove it. And he went, "Oh yeah, oh yeah, you're right again, well
> done, you've won, sorry." "No apologies necessary, let's go on with the
> quiz. But remember. Learn . . ." (1/3:134)

Apparently, Brent cares a lot about correct classification, and to illustrate just how important this is he draws a revealing parallel with the
annual British dog show Crufts:

> People say, "Why is it important, a question about Mr. Spock?" I go,
> "Oh, it's like saying, ooh, I've got a new pedigree dog breed, it's half-
> alsation, half-labrador." I go along to Crufts. I go, "Oh, can I enter
> this dog in the labrador section?" "No." "Why?" "'Cos it's not a
> labrador." "Correct." "Can I enter it in the alsation section?" "No,
> for the same reasons. Now get that dog outta my sight." "Thanks.
> I will. You've proved my point." And that's Crufts. Alright? (1/3:136)

Brent's point is that alsations are alsations, and labradors are
labradors, and Mr. Spock is half-Vulcan, half-human and that people
who believe that when it comes to classification we do not have to
be so strict, are just wrong. There is some truth about the matter.
Mr. Spock is not that *kind* of alien; he's something else. And if you
were a real Trekkie you would know that!

So the issue here is about kinds and the truth about them. Now, "the problem of natural kinds" (as we'll call it) is about whether any of the kinds we know are in fact *natural*. This may sound odd, so let me explain. First of all, we know quite well what a kind is, so in that sense all kinds seem natural to us. We say things like "an armoire is a kind of chest," or "an office chair is a kind of chair" (or "Gareth is a kind of dork"). There are more chests than armoires, and not all chairs are office chairs. What we say is that these specific types of chairs and chests belong to larger categories, and that these categories are different from each other (no chair could ever be a chest or vice versa). Now, the philosophical problem is whether some kinds are *natural kinds*, that is, whether they are part of nature—part of the objective world "out there," instead of mere constructs of our imagination.

Are there really chests and chairs in the world? Of course, you will say, "They are right there!" But that's no answer to my question because the things you are pointing to are just things that *we* call *chests* and *chairs*, but is there anything in these objects that makes them either this or that? Suppose that someone says that an armoire is a kind of chair, does she make a mistake? And again, your answer will be quite straightforward: "Yes, she's obviously mental and needs to go to primary school again, or watch reruns of *Sesame Street*." But what exactly is her mistake? Is it just that she has not learned how to speak properly (like a Dutchman who, when asked his profession, answers "I fuck horses" although what he meant to say was that he bred horses—*fokken* is Dutch for breeding)? Or is it that she fails to make a distinction between chairs and chests that is natural?

Perhaps now you understand what I meant about philosophy being difficult and boring. All this talk about chests and chairs and nature . . . What's the bloody problem? Perhaps you want to cry out in Brentish fashion: "Let's not go there, shall we? Let's all hop on the Beer Express. Next stop: drunkenness!" But before you reach for the bottle, let's give the philosopher in ourselves another chance. It's not just about names. Of course, there are many different languages and they all use different words for different things: what the English call *vegetables*, the French call *légumes*. And it's also true that the same word can have radically different meanings across the globe. A *fanny*, to take one of Keith's favorite examples, means something different in Britain than it does in the US . . . But these differences are not the problem. If we think of names as labels that we put on jars (where some of these jars are kinds) then it doesn't matter that the labels are different, but that there are indeed *different* jars. If natural kinds exist, then although the labels may be of our own making, the jars are not.

Secondly, what might be confusing is that chairs and chests do not seem natural at all because they're artifacts—products of our labor. Chairs don't grow on trees, and neither do chests. But the question is not whether *all* kinds are natural, but whether at least *some* are. Water, for example, seems to be a much better candidate. Water is water and not something else, and if the French say *l'eau* then that's just another name for the same thing. In fact, water was water long before there even was a name for it. Saul Kripke,[2] a contemporary philosopher, believes that water is indeed a natural kind because there is something that makes water water, and this something is revealed in its atomic structure: H_2O. If some substance does not have this atomic structure then it is not water. Someone who does call it water makes a mistake, not just because he has his labels mixed up, but because once this label is fixed and we have agreed that this is water (because we could easily have called it differently), this label only applies to water because there really is something "out there" which is water and not something else. There really is a specific jar to be labeled. This is different from when we say that something is funny, because funny means different things to different people. Even if we all agree that *The Office* is very funny and that Brent's jokes are not, this could easily change over time. It's just a matter of convention and opinion. We cannot strip it down to some basic structure which is assessable to all and then say, "Look, you're wrong you see. It *is* funny, and this is what *makes* it funny."

From David to Davidson

So far, we have taken the notion of "kind" for granted. But why do we group things into kinds? Well, we say of two things that they belong to the same kind when they are somehow *similar*. For example, a parrot and a sparrow are both birds because they both have feathers, and beaks, and they are both able to fly, and they lay eggs, and so on. Since they share these commonalities to a sufficient degree, they belong to the class of birds. And this is indeed a matter of degree, because there are birds that cannot fly, or cannot fly very well (like chickens, for example) but which are nevertheless still birds. But there are no birds with lips (except for the proverbial "birds"). If a creature has lips it cannot claim membership in the bird group. The presence of lips puts it into a whole new—and scary—category ("If only my auntie had bollocks, she'd be my uncle!," 2/3:123). But perhaps this need not be the case. Perhaps this new creature shares so many of the other bird-features that it's still a bird. It's a lippy lark, or something. So, it seems that there are criteria for kinds. This is not merely a matter of convention: things have to be *similar*.

But this doesn't get us very far, because the question returns. Are those standards of similarity determined by the nature of things, or are they contributed by us?

> At one extreme in the traditional debate about kinds is the view that the world is intrinsically structured into kinds. In this view, reality provides an objective standard of similarity against which the standards of similarity built into our concepts can be measured. . . . At the other extreme in the traditional debate is the constructivist view that the world itself is a bare, unstructured mass of stuff. In picking things out, and in classifying them as similar to or different from one another, we are carving up the world—imposing structure on an intrinsically unstructured reality.[3]

So, the discussion is between realists—who think that reality calls the shots—and conventionalists. The first group believes that nature is (naturally) carved up into kinds so that the truth about kinds lies in reality and that we have to discover the relevant differences in studying nature. The second group thinks this is impossible and therefore absurd. *We* perform the carving up, and we can do so any way we like. There is no question of "getting it right." It's just a matter of convention and convenience.

Imagine that there is a part of the world that has not yet been discovered. On the constructivist view, there are no cows on this *terra incognita* even though there might be other things living there—unbeknownst to us—which are similar to our cows. These animals are only cows from the moment they are discovered and we agree that this bunch of creatures belongs to the category we denote as cows. We put labels on reality; the labels are not dictated directly by the world.

Admittedly, the question of whether some particular group of animals are cows is not totally up for grabs. Or, at least, it is *no longer* up for grabs. Constructivists might hold that once we have agreed on the criteria for cowness this question is settled by reality. They either fit the description or they don't. But the category cow is a human construct, and different cultures might do that differently—for example, they might group them together with bears and ugly women into one single category—and that would be fine too. They would not make a mistake.

Nevertheless, the philosopher Donald Davidson (1917–2003) rejects the constructivist view for two reasons. First, "it reduce[s] reality to so much less than we believe there is."[4] Even if we are convinced that some sentence is true, it might still be false. Reality might still be different. Secondly, Davidson thinks that the idea of a neutral, structureless world makes no sense to us at all. The only world we can imagine is the one that is already carved up into chairs, and cows, and airplanes. However, Davidson also rejects the other extreme. Chairs and cows are only natural kinds in the sense that the classification into chairs and cows seems natural *to us*, not natural *tout court*. So the realist's idea that the world is already naturally structured is as incomprehensible as the constructivist's fantasy about a structureless mass of stuff.

Children and Fear

Perhaps the whole problem is still blurry to you, so let's return to something familiar. You probably noticed that the animals pictured in children's books are quite different from their real-life counterparts. In general, they're a whole lot cuter. I, for example, have never seen a smiling pig or a happy hippo in my whole life, except in children's books. Still, they do resemble them in some important respects. These key features allow kids to learn how to categorize correctly on the basis of relevant resemblances. We teach them how to pick out the right stuff. Not all yellow things are ducklings, and not all ducklings are yellow (and, as I've come to learn the hard way, not all doggy-woggies are nice . . .).

In the Mr. Spock example, Gareth is confident that he has his categories straight and that he knows exactly what makes Spock a Vulcan: "I don't want to go through all that again about, you know, whether he's a Vulcan or a human or vice versa. All I will say is what

I said at the time, ok? Look at his ears" (1/3:135). The distinguishing feature of Vulcans is their pointy ears. Nuff said.

However, there are some troubling cases that seem to withstand categorization, and that are difficult even for adults. Take the platypus, for example. A platypus is "a semi-aquatic mammal" that has a duck-like beak and lays eggs. When it was discovered in the late eighteenth century, people thought it was a hoax, a fictitious animal crafted by an Asian taxidermist with a sense of humor.[5] But the platypus is no puppet; he is very real. The problem, however, is that he shares different features, and *typical* features we should say, with different kinds. As a result, he is neither here nor there. Still, we have managed to "fit him in": apparently he belongs to a very small family of creatures of which he is now the only survivor.

This brings us to the question why this process of "fitting things in" is so important. Why all this fuss about names and kinds? Why bother? Classification is not just a tedious hobby of scientists with too much time on their hands. In fact, what something is and where it belongs is something that concerns us all, because if we *don't* know what something is then this is truly scary. I already mentioned the uncomfortable image of birds with lips (and if this is still not disturbing enough, just imagine that they also have teeth . . .). If we know what "it" is, then we know what "it" does and this comes in handy if we want to survive. If we know that Godzilla is actually just an oversized lizard, then we know how to kill it. It's the unclassifiable that is really frightening. It is *The Thing*, or *The Blob*, or *The Darkness*— something general and unspecified, something shapeless, formless, and nameless—that triggers our deepest fears. So it's no coincidence that many creatures in horror and fantasy fiction are hybrids, that is, combinations of creatures like werewolves and vampires, beings that defy our neat system of classification.

All this suggests that the constructivists are right. We lay down the soothing blanket of classification on a burning and brooding reality—we establish order out of chaos. And we teach our children how to use this system of language by telling them which labels fit on which jars, and we don't bother with the tiresome question whether the jars are really out there. We just teach them the rules of a game, a language game.

The term *language game* (*Sprachspiel*) comes from the famous Austrian philosopher Ludwig Wittgenstein (1889–1951). Wittgenstein is one of those philosophers whose career has been split up into two parts (Martin Heidegger, for example, is another). So we have the early Wittgenstein and the later Wittgenstein. In his major work *Tractatus Logico-Philosophicus*, published when he was 32 years old, Wittgenstein held that "meaning is reference [representation]." This means that reality consists of states of affairs and that language is a device that allows us to picture this reality by representing these states "as they are." But this, of course, doesn't always happen. Sometimes people speak as if they are talking about some state of affairs, while actually, there is nothing in the world that corresponds to their talk. They say things about God, for instance, while we don't know what this word *God* refers to. Such talk, the early Wittgenstein says, is meaningless, and people who just talk without concerning themselves about the question of whether or not their speech has any such correspondence are just purveyors of bullshit. David Brent is a shining example of such a purveyor.[6]

In his *Philosophical Investigations*, however, the later Wittgenstein takes a different approach. What we call language, he says, is actually a set of many different language games. The analogy with a game points out that there are certain rules, but that these rules are not objective, or universal. Rather, they only apply to the players as they are engaged in the game. These players know—although they may not be consciously aware of this—which moves are allowed, and which moves don't make any sense at all. (Consider, for example, the moves on a chessboard.) Therefore, "meaning is use." This means that whether or not a sentence is true depends on whether it satisfies the criteria implicit in the particular language game one is playing. One is talking nonsense if one confuses the criteria of one game with those of another, that is, if one doesn't recognize the context-dependence of these rules. So the later Wittgenstein is much more approving of ordinary language because it has a right of its own (whereas formerly he thought it had to conform to the rules of empirical science: only talk about what can be verified by the senses!).

To realize the context-dependence of language, consider the jokes that Tim and Dawn pull on Gareth. They like to ask him questions about his army experience, but not because they are actually interested in this stuff, but because they like to poke fun at Gareth's unnatural *machismo*. With highly ambiguous questions they try to trick

Gareth into saying things he does not want to say. They ask, for example, "Could you give a man a lethal *blow*?" and Gareth—not realizing the homoerotic subtext—answers "If I was forced to, I could" (1/3:122). The term *blow* has a very different meaning depending on the context in which it is used, and those who don't realize that their conversation partners are engaged in a different language game can make serious mistakes.

Whether or not something is a kind depends on what game you are playing, and the games we need to consider are those of science and ordinary language.

Leopards

When it comes to leopards, for example, science can still teach us a thing or two. Recently, a number of websites reported the discovery of a new species of a cat, the so-called "Bornean clouded leopard." One such website reported under the title *Spot the Difference!* that "genetic and skin tests on the creature show it's almost as different from clouded leopards found on the Asian mainland as lions are from tigers." These differences show that it belongs to a different species (originally, they thought it was the same species living elsewhere). But if it's that different, why is it called a clouded leopard in the first place? On a micro level they're apparently worlds apart (40 differences on DNA level) and that's probably why they added the "Bornean"—to make clear that it's from Borneo and not from the mainland. But at first sight it's indeed hard to spot the difference. In fact, the idea that it was the same species carried on for hundreds of years because no one noticed that the shade and pattern of their fur was actually different from their mainland brethren.

Different as they may be, however, it has also been established that both kinds of leopard evolved from one and the same species which lived during the Pleistocene Epoch. But if they have the same forefathers, at what point exactly did they become entirely different species? How many genetic differences does it take? Although these differences may be real, objective and measurable, it still seems to be up to us when it comes to drawing the line. Science has nothing to say about *that*.

In Search of Essences

Clearly, categorization is something we need to learn. The division into different kinds can be quite complex and confusing. Consider Brent's struggle with the difference between dwarves and midgets, a discussion that quickly derails when Gareth decides to join the debate:

Brent: What's the difference?
Alex: Well, a dwarf is someone who has disproportionately short arms and legs.
Brent: Oh, I know the ones.
[He does a crass impression of a dwarf.]
Alex: It's caused by a hormone deficiency.
Brent: Bloody hormones.
Alex: A midget is still a dwarf but their arms and legs are in proportion.
Brent: Sure.
Gareth: So, what's an elf?
Brent: Do you wanna answer that?
[Brent and Gareth look at Alex, who sighs.]
Alex: An elf is a supernatural being. Sometimes they're invisible. They're like fairies.
Brent: They don't actually exist, do they? In real life . . .
[Some time further . . .]
Gareth: So is a pixie the same thing as an elf?
Brent: Hold on, Gareth.
Gareth: What? I just want to know how come he knows so much about midgets.
[They all look at Alex]
Alex: It's called an education.
[He storms out]
Workman: So what's a goblin?
Brent: How long you gonna be, mate?

Brent and his gang are obviously confused about all these different kinds of little people, and Alex rightfully blames their education (or the lack thereof). Still, the questions they ask are insightful. They're looking for essences: What makes an elf an elf? What makes a pixie a pixie? What makes a thing *this* thing, and not another thing?

This question has been on the philosophical agenda ever since Aristotle (384–322 BCE). Plato, Aristotle's teacher, believed that reality as we know it—the things we see, hear, smell, taste, and feel around us—is just a poor copy of the Realm of Ideas. There is no perfect circle in our world, but we can conceive of the pure, mathematical idea of a circle through contemplation. Hence, the world around us is just *mimesis*, a shoddy imitation.[7] Therefore, in order to arrive at truth, we should break away from the grip of our empirical senses and we should look inwardly in order to ascend to the Realm of Ideas.

Aristotle, however, criticized his instructor for unnecessarily duplicating the world.[8] According to Aristotle, we should distinguish between *matter* and *form*. Matter is just stuff, just raw material, but the form is the working principle that is present in every substance, making it into *what it is*. A house, for example, consists of bricks, and wood, and metal, but if you just pile these things up, then this doesn't make a house—it's just a *potential* house. What makes it an *actual* house is when these raw materials are constructed or shaped in such a way that there is an idea behind it; that it has a certain purpose or goal. This idea is not to be located elsewhere (in some mysterious Realm of Ideas). It only shows itself in the particular objects, and we can recognize it through a process of *abstraction*. We can peel away the contingencies and particularities and discover what is essential. Science should do just that: it should map these differences and commonalities in order to arrive at a full classification of being. Such a map would look like a giant tree with an incredibly large base—all the particular individuals (birds, plants, houses, staplers, and so on)—and gradually narrowing down towards the top, until, finally, the top level would spell *BEING* (as shorthand for "all that is").

We still have the idea that science should tell us something about the way reality actually works—how it operates independently of our preferences and fantasies. Scientists therefore should lend their ears to Mother Nature. Their theories should capture her story (they should explain it and predict it), and not the other way around. Nature doesn't obey the theory; it doesn't bow down to people scribbling on paper. If anything, it falsifies the theory and then we have to come up with a new one in order to account for these anomalies. The stubbornness of reality warrants its objectivity. So, if the jars are really out there—which is the realist's claim—then science should reveal them; it should lay bare the natural kinds.

Indeed, the example of the clouded leopard shows that the similarities should be sought on DNA level, something that cannot be established on sight. Ricky Gervais might have learned this if he had stuck with biology. Science tells us that a Bornean clouded leopard is as different from his mainland look-a-likes as a tiger is from a lion. And that is a fact, something you can quantify. But it still seems to be a human decision at what point these differences become relevant. So, although the differences are inscribed in nature, nature does not carve itself up into kinds.

In fact, Willard Van Orman Quine (1908–2000), Donald Davidson's teacher, made us understand that science is the doorway to natural kinds. Science showed us that our ways of classification were arbitrary, or naïve, or at least not very accurate:

> Living as he does by bread and basic science both, man is torn. Things about his innate similarity sense that are helpful in one sphere can be a hindrance in the other. Credit is due man's inveterate ingenuity, or human sapience, for having worked around the blinding dazzle of color vision and found the more significant regularities elsewhere. Evidently natural selection has dealt with the conflict by endowing man doubly: with both a color-slanted quality space and the ingenuity to rise above it.[9]

Science provided us with a new and disenchanted vision, it revealed a world that was cold, colorless, and indifferent. In *The Matrix*, Morpheus says to Neo: "Welcome to the desert of the Real." The "desert of the real" is what reality becomes once you strip away the rosy goggles. It's a world of DNA, atoms, quarks, and strings. However, this new perspective, no matter how uncomfortable it may be, is also more real. Science can provide a foothold, a firm basis for our classifications; it can revive the Aristotelian quest for essences and perhaps even bring it to completion. Water *is* H_2O, and there is no way around it.

But the problem with nature is that, besides being stubborn, it is also terribly mute. Our scientists pry and discover ever-more basic particles, and they show us the complex tapestry of our world. But with all these particles before us, the work of classification is not finished: it hasn't even started yet. Classification into kinds is a difficult matter. It all seems very natural and very solid, but it isn't. Philosophers, once again, have opened up a can of worms.

Still, if you're ever in doubt as to what creature crosses your path during your late-night escapades, don't bother with science or

Thomas Nys

philosophy, just follow Gareth's advice: "Look at the ears." And as to the question of which body parts count as "ears," I leave that entirely up to you . . .

NOTES

1 Michael Heatley, *Ricky Gervais: The Story So Far . . .* (London: Michael O'Mara Books, 2006), p. 28.
2 There is a cool story about Kripke. At the age of sixteen he solved a famous problem in modal logic. Princeton University, however, was unaware of his age when, after they read his brilliant paper, they decided to offer him a job. Allegedly, Kripke's answer to the invitation was: "I'm honoured by your proposal, but my mom says I have to finish high-school first."
3 William Child, "Triangulation: Davidson, Realism and Natural Kinds," *Dialectica* 55 (2001): 30. My discussion of the problem of natural kinds owes a lot to this paper.
4 Donald Davidson, "The Structure and Content of Truth," *Journal of Philosophy* 87 (1990): 298–299
5 In fact, now that we know that the platypus is real, some people have suggested that this proves that God has a sense of humor . . .
6 Harry Frankfurt, in his work on bullshit, refers explicitly to Wittgenstein as someone who hated inaccurate speech. The story goes that when Fania Pascal had her tonsils removed, Wittgenstein called her to see how she was doing. She said that she felt "like a dog that has been run over." Allegedly, Wittgenstein responded in anger, saying: "You don't know what a dog that has been run over feels like!" In: Harry Frankfurt, *On Bullshit* (Princeton: Princeton University Press, 2005), p. 24.
7 Plato had a great contempt for art because, as it tries to represent reality, it is just a copy of a copy.
8 If you're ever in the Vatican Museum and you take a look at the famous painting by Raphael, *The School of Athens* (a painting often used on the over of philosophy textbooks and available for viewing on the Internet), then you'll see that, of the two central figures walking side-by-side, Plato is pointing up—away from this world—while Aristotle gestures downwards.
9 Willard V. O. Quine, "Natural Kinds," in Stephen Schwartz (ed.), *Naming, Necessity, and Natural Kinds* (Ithaca: Cornell University Press, 1977), p. 166.

20

Gareth Keenan Investigates Paraconsistent Logic: The Case of the Missing Tim and the Redundancy Paradox

Morgan Luck

Team leader, health and safety officer, military tactician, survival expert, kung-fu master, corporate detective, and assistant (to the) regional manager, Gareth Keenan is the quintessential Renaissance man. Yet despite the obvious caliber of the Keenan mind, there remain those who continue to trifle with Gareth, doubting, of all things, his ability to reason. According to Keenan dissenters, Gareth is guilty of committing a number of logical blunders. In this chapter we'll focus on one alleged error, an error supposedly committed during an incident known in Keenan scholarship as the Case of the Missing Tim. A closer examination of this case will demonstrate that Gareth was in fact making a sophisticated argument for the legitimacy of paraconsistent logic. We shall begin our evaluation of Gareth's argument by first examining the case in question.

The Case of the Missing Tim

The Case of the Missing Tim begins with Tim erecting a wall of files between himself and Gareth. In addition to the fact that such an erection obviously constitutes a health and safety hazard (blocking out valuable light and constituting a misuse of company files), it also makes it impossible for Gareth to see Tim. Tim uses this obfuscation to "muck about" (something that would not be allowed in the army).

Once the wall is in place, Tim lures Gareth into conversation, only to sneak away mid-chat. Tim's plan was to trick Gareth into committing the irrational act of "talking to no one." Yet, as we shall see, Gareth's mind is too highly trained to be taken in by such a schoolyard prank.

Gareth deduces that Tim may no longer be present, and promptly announces that he knows no one is there. Keenan detractors argue that, rather than allowing Gareth to save face, the announcement is itself irrational. If Keenan really believed no one was present, the detractors argue, to whom was he communicating this fact? In Gareth's defense, I will argue that his announcement was in fact the most rational act he could perform. Let's take a look at the arguments.

The Argument Against Gareth's Rationality

The argument against Gareth's rationality is based upon two premises that we generally accept as true. The first involves the idea that if you believe that no one is present to say anything to, it would be irrational to say anything at all. For instance, if you are trapped alone on a desert island it would be completely irrational to say, for example, "Pass me that coconut, would you Daley." The second premise proceeds from the principle that it is irrational to declare something you do not believe. So in this case, if Gareth did actually believe Tim was present to talk to, then he should not have declared otherwise. These two premises fit together to form the following argument:

> If you believe there is no one present, then it would be irrational to say anything.
> If you believe there is someone present, then it would be irrational to say, "No one is present."
> Therefore,
> It is always irrational to say, "No one is present."

This argument seems quite straightforward. Keenan apologists such as myself, however, can defeat this trifling reasoning with an appeal to the Redundancy Paradox.

The Redundancy Paradox

The Redundancy Paradox (also known in some circles as the lottery paradox)[1] is best illustrated as follows. Imagine that David Brent has been forced by head office to make at least one redundancy.[2] In order to avoid actually making a decision (and therefore attracting blame), David elects to draw the name of the hapless employee from a hat. Let's assume that the hat contains thirty names in total, one for each employee in the office. Given that the name is chosen at random, there will be a one in thirty chance that any single employee will be given the flick. The question on everyone's mind now is—who will be made redundant?

To see if we can determine who will be packing their bags, let's establish a rule concerning when it is rational to believe something is true. We shall refer to this rule as the Rule of Acceptance. The Rule of Acceptance states that, at the very least, it is only rational to believe something if it is likely. Let's define something as likely if it has more than half a chance of being true. So, for example, it would only be rational to believe Gareth could catch a monkey if, at the very least, there was more than half a chance this were true. With such a rule in place, let's now consider who will be made redundant.

To help us answer this question let's take a systematic approach and consider each employee in turn. First, we'll consider the fate of Monkey Alan. Is it rational to believe Monkey Alan will be the employee who is made redundant? Well, since it is unlikely his name will be drawn from the hat (there being only a one in thirty chance of this occurring), and as the Rule of Acceptance states that we should only believe those things that are at least likely to be true, it would seem irrational to believe Monkey Alan will be made redundant. Likewise, we shouldn't believe that Big Keith will be made redundant either, as it is similarly unlikely that his name will be drawn from the hat. The same can be said of each of the thirty employees of the office.

If it is not rational to believe that, for example, Big Keith will be made redundant, and it also isn't rational to believe that Monkey Alan will be made redundant, then it stands to reason we should believe that neither employee is going to lose his job. This follows from what is known as the Conjunction Principle, which states that if it is rational to believe proposition *p* and it rational to believe in proposition *q*, then it is also rational to believe in proposition *p & q*. However, as the argument below illustrates, if the Rule of Acceptance and the Conjunction Principle are both correct then it would be irrational to believe that anyone at all in the office will be made redundant:

> Since it is unlikely that Monkey Alan will be made redundant, it is irrational to believe he will be made redundant.
> Since it is unlikely that Big Keith will be made redundant, it is irrational to believe he will be made redundant.
> And so on for all thirty employees.
> Therefore,
> It is irrational to believe anyone will be made redundant.

Such a conclusion seems inconsistent with our belief that David will make one person redundant.

Normally, we would accuse anyone who holds inconsistent beliefs of irrationality. However, Keenan apologists may claim that in circumstances such as the Redundancy Paradox it does seem perfectly rational to hold inconsistent beliefs. And we are not alone in this assertion. A small band of philosophers, led most notably by Graham Priest,[3] have also championed this cause, the cause of paraconsistency.

Paraconsistency

Although the Redundancy Paradox itself provides some indication of when it might be considered rational to hold inconsistent beliefs, such a possibility is highly contentious. This is chiefly because classical logic operates on the assumption that a proposition and its negation cannot both be true. For example, the proposition, "There is a boy who can swim faster than a shark," and its negation, "There is *not* a boy who can swim faster than a shark," cannot both be true according to classical logic. This assumption is referred to as the Law of Non-contradiction.

Without the Law of Non-contradiction in place, chaos seems to ensue. This is largely because it is possible to argue anything from a contradiction. For example, from the premises, "A good idea is a good idea forever" and "A good idea is *not* a good idea forever," we could infer within classical logic that "the price of Opti-Bright Laser copy paper is £2.98 a kg," which is of course ridiculous (it is £2.40 a kg). This utterly anarchic outcome is based upon what is known as the Principle of Explosion. In order to avoid the consequences of this principle, a new system of logic, known as paraconsistent logic, has been championed.

Paraconsistent logic is a branch of logic that allows people to proceed rationally from inconsistent premises. In other words, paraconsistent logic denies the legitimacy of both the Law of Non-contradiction and the Principle of Explosion. As we'll see, Gareth's actions during the Case of the Missing Tim are evidence of the fact that he is working within a paraconsistent framework. Furthermore, given such a conclusion, Gareth's actions should be interpreted, not as the bumblings of a weasel-faced fool, but rather as the terribly clever actions of a Blockbuster grand finalist.

The Argument for Gareth's Rationality

Although Keenan apologists accept that, during the Case of the Missing Tim, Gareth was indeed expressing inconsistent beliefs, they reject the notion that holding such an inconsistent set of beliefs, and acting on them in the manner in which he did, was actually irrational. Let's review the case. Since Gareth had no real way of determining whether Tim was behind the wall of files, it seems perfectly reasonable that he place even odds upon each possibility. Therefore:

Possibility 1 (Tim is present behind the wall) has a 0.5 chance of being true.
Possibility 2 (Tim is absent behind the wall) has a 0.5 chance of being true.

The Rule of Acceptance suggests that it is only rational to believe a possibility is true if it is likely, where a likely possibility has *more* than half a chance of being true. So in this case it seems it is neither rational for Gareth to believe Tim is present (possibility 1), nor that he is absent (possibility 2). Yet since the two possibilities are mutually exclusive (either Tim is present or he is not), one must be true. In which case, because Gareth does not believe Tim to be present, he is committed to the belief that Tim is absent. However, as Gareth also has reason to not believe Tim is absent, he must likewise believe Tim is present. In other words, if the Rule of Acceptance and Conjunction Principle are correct, it seems rational for Gareth to believe the proposition, "Tim is present and absent."

Given such a result, Gareth's declaration that he knows no one is present behind the wall is a completely rational utterance. Indeed, it is the only rational course of action open to Gareth, given his beliefs. For if Gareth were to say nothing, given his belief that Tim was still present to talk to, this would be irrational. Yet to talk to Tim would also be irrational given his belief that Tim was not present. Consequently, the only reasonable action for Gareth is to announce that Tim is not present, since the act of announcing is consistent with his belief that Tim was present to be announced to, while the content of the announcement is coherent with his belief that Tim was absent. So, rather than the Case of the Missing Tim entailing a logical blunder on Gareth's part, Keenan's actions are actually a shining example of what is fast becoming the new buzz within middle management—paraconsistent logic.

NOTES

1   H. Kyburg, "Conjunctivitis" in *Probability and the Logic of Rational Belief* (Middletown, CT: Wesleyan University Press, 1961).
2   The yanks across the pond call this "downsizing," or something equally strange.
3   G. Priest, "Logic of Paradox," *Journal of Philosophical Logic*, 8 (1979): 219–241.

21

Being Your Self in *The Office*

Rick Mayock

"I never smile if I can help it," Dwight says to the camera. "Showing one's teeth is a submission signal in primates. When someone smiles at me all I see is a chimpanzee begging for its life" ("Conflict Resolution"). When Dwight and his *Office*mates speak directly to the camera they reveal the private side of themselves. For better or worse, our workplace, or "office," often splits us into two spheres: an official self and a private self. Since most of us spend a large portion of our time working, the official or public self becomes a significant part of who we are. Yet we think we know someone better when they reveal their private "self."

But what does it mean to know someone, and what exactly are we referring to when we speak of our "selves?" Philosophers have been discussing the problem of personal identity for centuries, yet there is no conclusive theory or definition of the "self" that satisfies everyone. Michael, Jim, Pam, Dwight, and the other characters of *The Office* struggle to define themselves in an artificial and often alienating environment. An examination of this cast of characters, this dysfunctional family of sorts, can yield valuable insights into the most noteworthy philosophical theories of the self.

Michael's Materialism

In the episode called "The Injury," Michael accidentally steps on his "George Foreman" grill, burning his foot. Although it's a minor injury, Michael completely identifies himself with his injured body.

The change in the condition of his foot changes his perception of himself from that of a healthy, able-bodied person to that of a disabled person.

Michael appears to embrace a materialist theory of personal identity—a theory that maintains personal identity, or the self, is identical to the physical body. In general, materialists believe that the world and everything in it, including the self, is composed of physical matter. There is no self other than the body and bodily processes, so if the body changes, the self changes. Michael is thinking like a materialist when he assumes that a minor change to his body changes his personal identity. He exploits this change by defining himself as disabled and believing he is entitled to enjoy certain benefits that the able-bodied do not enjoy.

But Aristotle's (384–322 BCE) distinction between "substances" and "accidents" might help convince Michael that he has not really changed.[1] Substances are unique and independent things, for example, a man, like Michael Scott. Accidents are things that can be said about a substance, like the fact that Michael has dark hair, or works for Dunder-Mifflin, or has burned his foot. Influenced by Aristotle, Thomas Aquinas (1225–1274) adopts this distinction and claims that there is a fundamental difference between accidental and substantial changes. An accidental change occurs when a physical object undergoes a change, but despite the change, the object remains essentially what it is. None of its essential characteristics have changed. For instance, if a tree undergoes a change to one of its limbs, it remains a tree. It does not become some other physical object just because its branch is broken. If, however, the tree were to be chopped down, ground into wood pulp, pressed into a ream of paper, and stored at the Dunder-Mifflin warehouse, it would no longer be a tree, but a ream of paper. This is an example of a substantial change.

So we might conclude that someone with a debilitating injury, whether temporary or permanent, is still a person, and such changes to the body are only accidental changes. The person is not damaged essentially and still remains the same substance. Michael, or anyone else, is still the same person despite any injuries or accidental changes to the physical body. In defining himself as disabled, Michael adopts a materialist attitude, but distorts the concept of disability by equating his relatively minor injury with more serious physical disabilities (like being made into a ream of paper).

In the same episode, Michael calls the office to ask Pam to drive him to work, but Dwight volunteers to pick him up and dashes out to the rescue. While driving his car out of the parking lot, Dwight hits something, apparently injuring his head. Later, Dwight behaves even more strangely than usual. His speech is odd; he calls Pam "Pan," and he stops mid-sentence in describing his office responsibilities. His self-awareness is diminished; Dwight doesn't even realize his hand is raised at the disabilities awareness meeting. His perception is off; he mistakenly thinks that Creed is related to him, calling him "Dad." And his disposition becomes sweeter; he starts being nice to Pam.

For the reductive materialist there is a scientific (that is, physical) explanation for Dwight's behavior. Reductive materialists believe that mental states and processes can be reduced to physical states and processes. Mental activity, or lack of activity, can be explained in terms of brain activity. Dwight's odd behavior, accordingly, is due to a change in his brain, likely the result of his auto accident. According to the philosopher René Descartes (1596–1650), what distinguishes us from "beasts" is the linguistic ability to express thoughts accurately and the capacity to act with rational deliberation.[2] By these standards, a strict materialist might conclude, at least during the time that his speech and motor control are impaired, that Dwight may be no more than a beast (Dwight does, after all, think of humans as primates). According to Aquinas' distinction, however, Dwight does not undergo a substantial change, but merely an accidental change. As if to confirm this, he types his name on the computer repeatedly, making Aquinas' point—he is still essentially "Dwight." There has been no substantial change to his personhood.

Jim's Dualism

Michael has been given the order to fire someone by the end of the day in the "Halloween" episode, but he's having a hard time making a decision. So to prepare himself, Michael does some role-playing with Jim and has Jim "fire" him. Jim plays along but suggests that he should sit behind the desk in Michael's chair. Jim then tries to confuse Michael by not relinquishing the chair and taking Michael's phone call, pretending to be Michael. Jim "becomes" Michael, and even fields a call from a prospective employer inquiring about Dwight.

(Jim had sent out some fake resumes on Dwight's behalf.) Michael, of course, is not fooled by Jim's role-playing. Even though Jim takes over Michael's chair and desk and simulates his voice on the phone, he is not Michael. No matter how much Jim, who has a talent for imitating voices, talks or sounds like Michael, he can never *be* Michael.

We can distinguish between two sorts of identity: qualitative identity and numerical identity. If two things (or people) share qualitative identity they may look or sound the same (for example, two copies of the book *The Office and Philosophy*). But two things (or people) who share numerical identity are, in fact, one and the same thing (for example, the man who plays Michael Scott and the actor Steve Carell). Michael knows that even if Jim looks or sounds like him, they only share an incomplete qualitative identity; they are not numerically identical. For example, in "Product Recall" Jim dresses like Dwight and adopts his mannerisms. "Identity theft is not a joke, Jim," Dwight responds, "millions of families suffer every year." At the end of the episode, Dwight enters the office and does his best imitation of Jim. But Michael, Jim, and Dwight can never be deluded into thinking they are anyone else, despite any physical similarities.

Descartes imagined all sorts of things that we could be deluded about, but he said we can be sure of one thing: our identity. Descartes reasoned that it is possible to doubt everything—the senses, the physical world, even the truths of mathematics (since an evil demon may be deceiving us about such truths—well, it's possible!). But the one thing we cannot be deceived about is our own existence. I know that as long as I am thinking, I exist. Even if my body is an illusion, my mind exists, that is, my thinking, questioning, reasoning, and doubting mind must exist in order for me to think, question, reason, and doubt. So Dwight can be assured that no matter how much Jim resembles or imitates him, he is not Jim, and Jim is not him.

Dualism is the theory that the person is a combination of mind and body. Descartes explains dualism by arguing that the mind is a separate substance from the body. This allows us to conceive of ourselves as a mind, or spirit, occupying the body. A person is a non-physical substance, a spirit or ghost, which resides in a material body. Jim is a kind of dualist because he seems to believe the mind or soul is something that is separate from but resides in or is connected to the physical body. He plays mind games with his co-workers, especially with Dwight, and acts as if personal identity is not dependent upon the body alone.

Jim practices his deceptive role-playing with Dwight in the "Drug Testing" episode. Because half of a marijuana joint was found in the parking lot, Dwight appoints himself to the role of questioner and begins an inquisition of the office employees. During his drug interview, Jim switches roles and begins to accuse Dwight of smoking pot: "Marijuana is a memory loss drug, so maybe you just don't remember." "I would remember," Dwight replies. "Well, how could you if it just erased your memory?" says Jim. Dwight can't be sure he never smoked pot, Jim argues, because if he had, the pot may have erased his memory of having smoked it.

Dwight's Identity Crisis

Dwight's self-image is tied to his title: "Assistant (to the) Regional Manager." This title designates him as wholly dependent upon the manager, Michael, who has his own reasons to control him. Dwight desperately wants to change his title to "Assistant Regional Manager," perhaps because this would give him some independence from Michael. As Assistant Regional Manager he would climb not just the corporate ladder, but the ladder of existence. He would gain in ontological status.[3] Anything that has existence or comes into being has ontological status, and to question the existence of anything is to question its ontological status. As the Assistant *to the* Regional Manager, Dwight's reason for existence is dependent upon the Regional Manager. That is, if the Regional Manager were to cease to exist, there would be no need for an Assistant *to the* Regional Manager. There would, however, still be need for an Assistant Regional Manager. Dwight wishes to concretize himself, as an independently existing entity. He wants to improve his ontological status. Otherwise he has a crisis of identity.

Dwight's crisis is nothing new. According to the philosopher Friedrich Nietzsche (1844–1900), we all share an identity crisis. Nietzsche questions the very idea of a subjective self, and rejects Descartes' famous *cogito* argument (*cogito ergo sum*, "I think, therefore, I am") whereby we know with certainty that we exist, because we can think. Descartes argues that it is not possible to doubt one's existence. In fact doubting my existence only affirms it, because I must exist (at least as a thinking thing, or mind) in order to do the doubting. So the very fact that I am capable of thinking means I must exist.

Nietzsche takes issue with Descartes' argument by suggesting that we posit the word "I" in "I think . . ." because of a grammatical habit.[4] Nietzsche says that there is no reason to assume an "I" behind the "thinking." It's merely the constructions of language that deceive us into assuming there is a subject, or ego, that must be responsible for thought. Descartes insists that the mind exists as a substance that accounts for thought, but Nietzsche deconstructs this concept and shows that it is the result of a confusion of language. So Dwight's identity crisis is due to an error in thinking, since the self, according to Nietzsche, is only a fiction.

The "Diversity Day" episode illustrates a similar issue associated with the problem of personal identity. The purpose of Diversity Day is, presumably, to make the staff sensitive to racial stereotypes. Michael attempts to do this by putting labels on the foreheads of the office staff, designating them as representing particular racial and ethnic groups, such as "Jewish," "Black," "Jamaican," and so on. The result is that each of the office staff is forced to interact with others as representatives of racial stereotypes, rather than as individuals. Kelly, the Indian "valley girl," has no label on her forehead, yet Michael talks to her using an accent. "Welcome to my convenience store . . . would you like some googi googi?" he asks Kelly. She slaps him. Being a materialist, he can only react to physical appearances. He treats her as a racial stereotype even though she does not have a label on her forehead.

When confronting prejudicial thinking, it is tempting to think, like a dualist, of a substance ("soul" or "mind") behind appearances. In fact, one argument against racial stereotyping is that it diminishes the true self or person, the non-physical element that lies behind any outward appearances. But the philosopher David Hume (1711–1776) rejects the theory that the self is an entity or substance that lies behind our perceptions. Hume argues that what we call the self or mind is more accurately a bundle of perceptions, and what we are referring to when we perceive ourselves is just a series of images.[5] The mind, according to Hume, is like a theater where these perceptions successively make their appearances. But we construct this "theater" and call it the "soul" or "self." We bundle our perceptions together into this artificial entity in order to connect them together. Our self, then, is merely a collection of perceptions, and has no ontological status of its own.

Dwight finally gets his title upgrade in "The Fight." After his karate match with Michael, he is informed by Michael that he was only being tested, and that he has been promoted to Assistant Regional Manager. "I told Dwight that there is honor in losing, which, as we all know, is completely ridiculous," Michael later says to the camera. "But there is, however, honor in making a loser feel better, which is what I just did for Dwight." At the end of "The Fight" episode, Dwight is seen changing his title on his business cards and seems to be temporarily placated. Dwight is having a crisis in establishing his identity, but the rejection of the self by Nietzsche and Hume would likely be of little or no comfort to him.

Michael's (Dysfunctional) Family Values

In addition to materialism, Michael can help illustrate the "social construction" theory of the self. For Michael, the family is the social structure that is most meaningful in constructing identity, though oddly we never hear much about his parents or siblings.

Michael sees himself (ironically, since he is in many ways the most childlike and immature) as the father of his office "family." His need to view the staff as his family gives us a glimpse of Michael's loneliness, as revealed in the video of himself as a child in "Take Your Daughter to Work Day." "I want to be married and have one hundred kids so I can have one hundred friends, and no one can say no to being my friend," says the young Michael. But Michael rarely behaves like an adult or parent. In the "Christmas Party" episode, he shows displeasure with his "Secret Santa" gift—a knitted oven mitten. Although he says that "presents are the best way to show someone you care," he childishly manipulates the gift-giving arrangements in order to end up with a different gift.

In "Office Olympics" the characters struggle to establish a sense of personal identity by attempting to define themselves in a competitive environment. The "children" of the (artificial) family play games when Dad's away, giving rise to sibling rivalry and competition.

259

Dwight, for example, sees himself as the preferred sibling, the favored son, and leaves the office with Michael to help him buy a condo. When they return, the "children" feel compelled to give Michael and Dwight the gold and silver medals, even though they didn't participate in the Olympics.

The sibling rivalry theme is illustrated in "The Fire" when Dwight displays his jealousy of Ryan, whom he sees as a lesser, younger, yet favored son. "Michael's in there right now evaluating the temp . . . he hasn't evaluated me in years," he says to the camera. During the fire drill, Dwight grabs Ryan in a headlock. Michael yells at Dwight: "He's not your five-year-old brother, Dwight . . . he's a valued member of this company and . . . you know what? He knows more about business than you ever will." Dwight's ego is wounded, but he later takes delight in discovering that Ryan had inadvertently started the fire, and hopes to prove to Michael his moral superiority over Ryan.

In the parable of the "Prodigal Son," the older brother is jealous of the younger, prodigal son, who gets into trouble through carelessness yet is accepted back into the family by the father. Ryan is not castigated by Michael for his carelessness with the fire, but accepted back into the family, after a few jokes at his expense. Dwight, who sees himself as the older sibling, is jealous. He is also jealous of Jim, who temporarily goes to work at the Stamford branch. Upon their reunion in Philadelphia in "The Convention" episode, Michael greets Jim with: "the pro-gi-dal son . . . my son returns." Michael can be identified as the father in the parable, who accepts and favors his wayward "son," despite Dwight's resentment and jealousy.

Social constructionism is the theory that the self is defined by social relationships and institutions like the family. According to this theory of personal identity, we try to establish our identities by overcoming alienation and discovering ourselves in our relationships. The philosopher G. W. F. Hegel (1770–1831) claims that the self only exists when it is recognized by others.[6] In other words, for Hegel, other selves are essential to the discovery of our own self, and we, in a sense, produce our selves in relation to others.

In the "Performance Review" episode, Michael seeks the acknowledgment and approval of others to maintain a sense of himself. It is the morning after a romantic evening with Jan, and Michael asks Pam, because she's a woman, to interpret Jan's phone message. In doing so, Michael shows that he needs the recognition of others in order to define himself, particularly as a man who can satisfy women sexually. He wants his "performance" to be reviewed favorably by Jan (and by Pam) and to be approved of. One needs, as Hegel states, acknowledgment from others in order to have a sense of self.

We watch shows like *The Office* because we are concerned with individual characters as they exist in relation to others. What makes them interesting is not a succession of perceptions, as Hume described in his bundle theory, but our desire to know what happens to an enduring personality over time. How will things work out between Jim and Pam? Will Dwight leave the company if he can't achieve his ambitions? How will Michael react if he finds out that Dwight has been talking to Jan about replacing him?

When we care about a character we come to know his or her personality. But we're back to our opening question: What does it mean to know someone? According to the social constructionist, the self is not a metaphysical essence or substance, but something that we construct through our interactions with and acknowledgment by others. Jim is not simply feeling love—he loves Pam. Dwight is not simply jealous, he is jealous of Jim and of Ryan. Personality is a function of the other people we interact with and is determined by the theatrical roles we play. Each person treats the other as an audience, in front of whom he or she forges an identity. There is no "real self" lurking behind these dramatic roles; rather, we are what we make ourselves to be. The most authentic self is the one that we have been acting or portraying the longest and is the most adaptable to our changing situations.

Many of the most engaging characters are victims of their own imagination. For them, the self becomes divided and fragmented, a collection of conflicting forces. Like many of us, they struggle to overcome the public/private split of their personalities. Dwight is a character who catches our attention because he is always in conflict. If he were satisfied and content, he would be less interesting dramatically. His comment to the camera about never smiling shows that he sees himself through the eyes of others. It is his ambition, his jealousy, and his competitive nature that make him an intriguing character.

Defining the self is never an easy task. For the social constructionist, it is our interaction with others that brings our public and private selves into focus, and it is through the acknowledgment of others that we become aware of ourselves.

NOTES

1 Aristotle makes this distinction in his book *Categories*, from *The Basic Works of Aristotle*, trans. R. McKeon (New York: Random House, 1941), p. 9.

2 Descartes is not a materialist but advocates dualism, which will be discussed in the next section. René Descartes, *Discourse on Method*, from *The Philosophical Writings of Descartes*, trans. J. Cottingham, R. Stoothoff, and D. Murdoch (Cambridge: Cambridge University Press, 1985), vol. 1, p. 140.

3 Ontology is the branch of philosophy that is concerned with the nature of being or existence.

4 Nietzsche writes: "For, formerly one believed in 'the soul' as one believed in grammar and the grammatical subject: one said, 'I' is the condition, 'think' is the predicate and conditioned—thinking is an activity to which thought *must* apply a subject as cause." Friedrich Nietzsche, *Beyond Good and Evil*, trans. W. Kaufmann (New York: Random House, 1966), p. 67.

5 Concepts of the mind or self, says Hume, are "nothing but a bundle or collection of different perceptions, which succeed each other with an inconceivable rapidity, and are in perpetual flux and movement." David Hume, *Treatise on Human Nature* (London: Penguin Books, 1969), p. 300.

6 Hegel writes: "Self-consciousness exists in itself and for itself when, and by the fact that, it so exists for another; that is, it exists only in being acknowledged." G. W. F. Hegel, *Phenomenology of Spirit*, trans. A. V. Miller (Oxford: Oxford University Press, 1977), p. 111.

22

Michael Scott is Going to Die

Meg Lonergan and J. Jeremy Wisnewski

Being Hit by an Ed Truck

One fine day in season 3, Michael gets a call with some sad news from Jan ("Grief Counseling"). They "lost Ed Truck." Michael is initially confused and responds by looking for Ed's cell phone number to help with the search and rescue. But there is no rescue from death. What at first looks like Michael's thick-headedness is actually an instance of a very common phenomenon: the denial of death. Michael is so unwilling (or unable?) to consider death that a common euphemism for death ("we lost so-and-so") is completely lost on him. Yet it's true. Ed Truck, the previous Regional Manager of Dunder-Mifflin Scranton and Michael's former boss, is dead.

When Jan drops the euphemism, Michael is forced to realize what has happened: Ed Truck is dead. Michael is surprised, but has no idea how to respond. Michael's denial is so deep that he doesn't even know how to react once he realizes that Ed isn't missing, but dead. He doesn't show any strong reaction until Kelly unwittingly alerts him to an appropriate response:

Michael: Attention everybody, I just received a call from corporate with some news that they felt that I should know first. My old boss, Ed Truck, has died.
Kelly: Oh, Michael that's such terrible news. You must feel so sad.
[Kelly hugs Michael]
Michael: Yes, I am. It's very sad. Because he was my boss.

Creed then lets Michael know that Ed died gruesomely:

> *Creed*:   It's a real shame about Ed, huh?
> *Michael*:   Must really have you thinking.
> *Creed*:   About what?
> *Michael*:   The older you get, the bigger the chance is you're gonna die.
>   You knew that.
> *Creed*:   Ed was decapitated.
> *Michael*:   What??

Michael is shocked that Ed didn't die of old age. Michael is well aware that, at the end of life, death comes to everyone. What he manages to deny, though, is that death can come at *any* time—in the middle of a sentence, in between two syllables, while closing a deal on a condo—even while doing mediocre impressions of Bill Cosby. Death happens in *the middle of life*, not merely at its end. Creed's comments force Michael to realize that he could die anytime, he may not have years stretching out in front of him—he could be decapitated on his drive home!

The philosopher and anthropologist Ernest Becker (1924–1974) argues that everything people do is motivated by the terror of death.[1] While this may or may not be true for every human being, it's certainly true for Michael Scott. Michael is living in denial of death. While he recognizes death as a fact of life—as something that "happens," he refuses to recognize it as a fact of *his* life. The shock of Ed Truck's death jerks him out of his inauthentic understanding of death—forcing him to recognize that death is not like shit. It doesn't just happen. It happens *to me*.

This duplicitous attitude toward death is a centerpiece of the philosopher Martin Heidegger's (1889–1976) analysis of human existence.[2] Heidegger contends that very few people manage to authentically realize and comprehend the meaning of their own mortality—that our death is "not to be outstripped"—that there is nothing we can do to escape it, despite our ever-present efforts to be more than bags of flesh and bones that are destined to decay. We construct an average, everyday conception of death that enables us to chatter about it, and to file it away in fatuous categories when we are confronted with it. All of this enables us to *avoid* looking honestly at our own existence. Rather than acknowledging that *we* will die, we simply note that "death is a part of life," and remain totally unaffected. When others die, we can tell ourselves little stories that make contemplating *our own death* utterly pointless: the dead person is "in a better place," "it was his time to go," "God works in mysterious ways," "she was too good for this world," "he has moved on to the next life."

Our ways of describing death allow us to deal with it without confronting it. We (inauthentically) regard death as a fact of life, but not as a fact of *our* individual lives. To confront our own mortality is to stop telling ourselves stories about another world, or a better place; it is to realize that we are decaying flesh, and that all we do will ultimately end in rot and decay. It is this that Michael is confronted with when he is hit by Ed Truck's decapitation. Like Ed, Michael loses his head (figuratively, that is).

Good (and Not So Good) Grief

Once Michael figures out that he's supposed to be sad (thanks to Kelly!), he decides that the rest of the office isn't grieving properly. To "help" them, he drags them all into the conference room for some grief counseling, mostly so he can express his newly confronted feelings of horror at death:

> I lost Ed Truck, and it feels like somebody took my heart and dropped it into a bucket of boiling tears and at the same time somebody else is hitting my soul in the crotch with a frozen sledgehammer. And then a third guy walks in and starts punching me in the grief bone, and I am crying, and nobody can hear me because I am terribly, terribly . . . terribly alone. ("Grief Counseling")

Michael uses Elizabeth Kubler-Ross's five stages of grieving to explain to the camera crew how he's going to facilitate the grieving of his staff:

> There are five stages to grief. Which are [reads from computer] denial, anger, bargaining, depression, and acceptance. And right now, out there, they are all denying the fact that they're sad. And . . . that's hard. And that's making them all angry. And it is my job to get them all the way through to acceptance. And if not acceptance, then just depression. If I can get them depressed, then I will have done my job. ("Grief Counseling")

So, in what looks like an attempt to confront his own mortality honestly, Michael attempts to conduct some grief counseling. Like most

of Michael's management efforts, this one proves pretty ineffective—
either because Michael is a total goofball, or because the rest of his
staff is as death-denying as he is (or maybe both!). Michael asks
everyone to talk about an experience that they've had with death, and
Pam starts out by reworking the plot of *Million Dollar Baby* to suit
those purposes:

> *Pam*:   Let's see . . . I had an aunt that I was really close to; she was this
> amazing female boxer. Anyway, she was injured in a fight, and
> she was paralyzed. So, you can imagine how sad I was . . . when
> I found out that she asked her manager to remove her breathing
> tube, so she could die.
>
> *Michael*:   Wow. If you wanna cry, that's ok. ("Grief Counseling")

Ryan catches on and chooses *The Lion King*, and Kevin unsuccess-
fully tries *Weekend at Bernie's*. Death denial is not isolated to individual persons at individual times: it is as rampant in the office as it is
in the world. Michael's attempt to confront death is met with comedy
and unconcern. Pam, Ryan, Kevin, and the rest of the office clan can't
even acknowledge death enough to indulge Michael. They use examples of death that are fictionalized and distant from them, as if they
didn't know anyone who has died. At this point, Toby has to step in
to console Michael:

> *Toby*:   Michael, look, I know this is hard for you but that's just a part
> of life. Just this morning I saw a little bird fly into the glass doors
> downstairs and die. And I had to keep going.
>
> *Michael*:   How do you know?
>
> *Toby*:   What?
>
> *Michael*:   That that bird was dead. Did you check its breathing?
>
> *Toby*:   It's obvious.
>
> *Michael*:   Was its heart beating, Toby? Did you check it? No, of
> course you didn't. You're not a veterinarian. You don't know
> anything!! ("Grief Counseling")

According to Becker, "there is nothing like shocks in the real world to
jar loose repressions" (21). Michael has been denying death subconsciously, but Ed Truck's nasty demise and a little dead bird successfully remind Michael that he, too, will eventually die (just like you
will, reader!). Becker's discussion of how children deal with death
unsurprisingly applies perfectly to Michael, who is less than mature:

Recently psychiatrists reported an increase in anxiety neuroses in children as a result of the earth tremors in Southern California. For these children the discovery that life really includes cataclysmic danger was too much for their still-imperfect denial systems—hence open outbursts of anxiety. (21)

Michael's ability to repress is obviously weak, so a catastrophe like Ed's decapitation reminds him of his own finitude—the fundamental limitations imposed on him by being finite, mortal, and a plain piece of *biology*. Like a little kid after an earthquake, Michael spends the whole day in an open outburst of anxiety.

For the Bird

Michael's death-denying is in full view when he insists on a funeral procession for the bird that Toby saw die. Ryan immediately recognizes this as at least a little odd:

When I was five, my mom told me that my fish went to the hospital. In the toilet. And it never came back, so we had a funeral for it. And I remember thinking, I'm a little too old for this. And I was five. ("Grief Counseling")

Ryan can see that having a full-blown funeral for the bird is juvenile and unnecessary. What he *doesn't* see, though, is the *function* of the funeral service for Michael in particular, and perhaps for society in general. The funeral allows us to give meaning to an otherwise absurd existence. It enables us to *know what we're supposed to do* in the face of an unbearable confrontation with mortality. Like other rituals, the funeral provides us with something to do, something to hold onto, when we must confront the brutal reality of our existence. As the philosopher Robert Pogue Harrison has argued, it is through a shared symbolic language of grief and ritual that "the work of separation begins to take place. It is essential that this work fulfill its purpose, for if and when it fails, instead of the dead dying with me, I die with the dead"[3]—even when that dead is just a bird. So, the funeral is by no means a pointless exercise. It is a means of making our confrontation with our own biological existence a little less horrifying. "Mourning rituals would be feckless if they did not provide

267

the means, or language, to cope with one's own mortality even as they help one cope with the death of others" (Harrison, 70).

In fact, Ernest Becker argues that *all* of our activities—the practical jokes of the office, the ambition that drives us to become Assistant Regional Manager (or better), or our desire to find true love, are the result of an inability to openly and honestly acknowledge the fact of our inevitable death. "All culture, all man's creative life-ways, are in some basic part of them a fabricated protest against natural reality, a denial of the truth of the human condition, and an attempt to forget the pathetic creature that man is" (Becker, 32–33).

Michael doesn't want the bird's life and death to be meaningless, much as he doesn't want his own existence to be meaningless. He assigns greater significance to the bird in an attempt to deny his own insignificance, his own finitude. Luckily for Michael, Pam realizes that the real problem here isn't Ed's shuffling off of this mortal coil. It's Michael being terrified of *his own* death, and the isolation that his death accentuates. So Pam makes the bird's funeral more about Michael than about the little bird. Pam takes the death of the bird seriously as a means of taking Michael's death-anxiety seriously, making a casket and saying things in the eulogy that will comfort Michael:

Pam: What do we know about this bird? You might think, not much, it's just a bird. But we do know some things. We know it was a local bird. Maybe it's that same bird that surprised Oscar that one morning with a special present from above.
Kevin: I remember that, that was so funny.
Pam: And we know how he died. Flying into the glass doors. But you know what, I don't think he was being stupid. I think he just really, really wanted to come inside our building. To spread his cheer and lift our spirits with a song.
Dwight: It's not a songbird.
Michael: Shhhh.
Pam: An impression then. Lastly, we can't help but notice that he was by himself when he died. But, of course, we all know that doesn't mean he was alone. Because I'm sure that there were lots of other birds out there who cared for him very much. He will not be forgotten.

The main theme here, as elsewhere, is the thing that no one will talk about—the fact that Michael will one day die (a fact that Michael is just realizing). Everyone dances around the reality of the human condition, making the conversation about Ed Truck, or the little bird, or death in general. Michael especially tries to make the day about Ed, who is a good representative of Michael, saying things like: "That is just not the way a Dunder-Mifflin manager should go, I'm sorry . . . alone, out of the blue . . . not even have his own head to comfort him" ("Grief Counseling"). Although Michael is scarcely aware of it, he's talking about himself here—about how he doesn't want to die alone. In making his words about Ed Truck, Michael tries to repress his fear of death, as well as his fear that his life will be insignificant—two fears that, if not identical, are at least complementary. "The guy who had my job has died, and nobody cares . . . and he sat at my desk" ("Grief Counseling"). Confronting mortality is a deeply depressing, if not outright offensive, event. "What kind of deity would create such a complex and fancy worm food?" (Becker, 87)

Final Thoughts

In "Safety Training," Michael confronts death again, although in a different way. As every viewer knows, Michael is of the opinion that he's a fairly important guy who will go on to do great things, and be remembered. This is one version of what the philosopher Søren Kierkegaard (1813–1855) calls living in the world-historical. To live in the world-historical is to live as though the significance of one's life depended on something external to one's own individuality. One's life is devoted to something that is not really one's own. A person's life takes on significance if that person plays some role, however minor, in the world-historical process: one is an important person by being a volunteer sheriff, or by being a soldier, or by being an admired manager who brought comedy to the lives of his workers. This is why Michael wants hospital wings named after him, why he donates to Oscar's nephew's charity, why he does so many of the things that he does—he wants to be remembered. Kierkegaard called "living in the world-historical" a defense mechanism for the ego.[4] It is yet another form of death-denying. A person "living in the world-historical" believes that they can live on through their work, that what they create or influence will still be there after they die and in that way, they become significant for having created or influenced it. Kierkegaard says:

> When a headstrong person is battling with his contemporaries and endures it all but also shouts, "Posterity, history will surely make manifest that I spoke the truth," then people believe that he is inspired. Alas, no, he is just a bit smarter than the utterly obtuse people. He does not choose money and the prettiest girl or the like; he chooses world-historical importance.[5]

The world-historical life, it turns out, isn't much more than the life of a nitwit—one who hasn't the courage to be himself. If this is true, then it is almost certainly better to take the subjective course—to live "subjectively," as Kierkegaard puts it, rather than "world-historically." How one is to do this, however, is a mystery to all of us.

Even though he's committed to the world-historical task of being a beloved office manager, Michael's not that thrilled about his life. He admits this only when he forgets the cameras are there. For instance, when he is contemplating jumping off the office building in "Safety Training" to demonstrate that his life *is* a life of danger, Michael becomes quite depressed about his circumstances. His playing at being suicidal brings him quite close to his own death, and Darryl tries to talk him down from the roof:

> *Darryl*: Mike, this is the opposite of safety. You jump, you're going to seriously hurt yourself.
> *Michael*: You told me that I lead a cushy . . . wimpy . . . nerf-life.
> *Darryl*: Yeah, but I never said you have nothing to live for.
> *Michael*: What do I have to live for?
> *Darryl*: A lot . . . of things . . . uh . . . you . . . What about Jan? Lovely, lovely, lovely Jan, man. It's going good, right?
> *Michael*: It's complicated with Jan. I don't know where I stand or what I want; the sex isn't near as good as it used to be.
> *Darryl*: Mike, you're a very brave man. I mean, it takes courage just to be you. To get out of bed every single day, knowing full-well you gotta be you.
> *Michael*: Do you really mean that?
> *Darryl*: I couldn't do it! I ain't that strong. And I ain't that brave.
> *Michael*: I'm braver than you?
> *Darryl*: Way braver. You Brave Heart, man.
> *Michael*: I Brave Heart. I am.

Michael's not happy with his nerfy life. He's not positive he has anything to live for at all. (He also doesn't realize he's at the wrong end of the little backhanded compliments in Darryl's pep-talk.) Up on the rooftop (and when he learns about Ed's death), Michael is feeling something that Becker describes amazingly well when examining the knowledge of one's own death: "This is the terror, to have emerged from nothing, to have a name, consciousness and self, deep inner feelings, an excruciating inner yearning for life and self-expression—and with all this yet to die" (87). Michael returns to his old death-denying ways at the end of this episode, when he states that he saved his own life: "I saved a life . . . my own. Am I a hero? I can't really say, but . . . yes" ("Safety Training"). Surely someone who's saved a life has done something significant and will therefore be remembered!

And the rest of the office staff are no better. They too deny death. Only once does Michael's staff even mention death, and it's just a joke. Jim says "He's going to kill himself pretending to kill himself," but it's just a silly pun—the kind we love Jim for—not an expression of an actual confrontation with mortality. In a more serious moment, Jim drops talk of death, opting instead to talk about Michael being "seriously injured" if he jumps off the roof. Darryl uses the same kind of language when he says Michael is going to "seriously hurt" himself ("Safety Training"). They use such phrases because, even when confronted with the prospect of death, they don't see it—or, better, they *refuse to see it*. Sometimes what we do *kills us*—and death is not just another injury!

The Office is not a show that will teach you how to confront your own mortality. No show will. Even this chapter won't. At most, philosophy (the discipline) and *The Office* (the show) might force us to rethink some of our assumptions about human existence. The rest is up to us. You will die. And so will Michael Scott.

NOTES

1 See Ernest Becker, *The Denial of Death* (New York: Simon & Schuster, 1973). All citations from Becker are from this text.
2 Martin Heidegger, *Being and Time* (New York: Harper Collins, 1962).
3 Robert Pogue Harrison, *The Dominion of the Dead* (Chicago: University of Chicago Press, 2003), p. 58.
4 See Søren Kierkegaard, *Concluding Unscientific Postscript to Philosophical Fragments* (Princeton: Princeton University Press, 1992), pp. 136–137.
5 Kierkegaard, *Concluding Unscientific Postscript to Philosophical Fragments*, pp. 136–137.

Appendix A

From Our Office to Yours: The University of Scranton and *The Office*

From: Joseph Kraus
To: Maria Johnson
Re: The Office Proposal

Hey Maria

I just got the word that Blackwell Press is bringing out a collection called *The Office and Philosophy*. I think maybe it would be funny if a group of us got together and wrote an essay for it. After all, we are doctors of philosophy, and we work in an office in Scranton. In a way, we even "sell paper," don't we? We try to get our students to appreciate the books they've already bought and, if grading counts, then we deal in more paper than most of us ever bargained for. Maybe we could even do something that was a kind of a mock-umentary of an essay, something in writing that still gets across that funny feeling in the show where you aren't always certain that it's a joke.

   Do you think it would be a good idea to pitch this to Stephen and Michael? At times like this, I feel a lot like Ryan from the first two seasons; we untenured assistant professors are a little bit like temps, don't you think? There's just that vague uncertainty in the air. You're an associate professor; maybe it would make more sense coming from you so that I'm not stepping on anyone's toes.

Joe

From: Maria Johnson
To: Joseph Kraus
Re: Your proposal

272

Joe

I must say I rather admire your nerve, proposing a collaborative project to three senior colleagues. I'll raise it with Michael and Stephen, if that's what you really want; I trust they won't see it as too pushy.

But go ahead, tell us what you have in mind.

Maria

From: Maria Johnson
To: Stephen Whittaker, Michael Friedman
Re: Joe Kraus

Gentlemen

I am attaching a message I received from your junior colleague. I find the untenured rather endearing at times. Heavens knows why he chose to run it by me first—probably thinks I'm the motherly sort. He'll learn. However, Blackwell is a good press; no harm doing it. Not sure I want to work with Beaver Cleaver, though.

Maria

From: Stephen Whittaker
To: Maria Johnson
Re: Joe Kraus

Maria

Good lord, he is touchingly clueless, isn't he? The idea's intriguing, though. I suggest we let him get the ball rolling, and then see if we want to keep him around.

Stephen

From: Joe Kraus
To: Maria Johnson
Re: Proposal

Maria

Do you really think I'm being pushy? I hadn't thought of it that way. It was probably a bad idea, and we should probably just forget about it. Thanks for your wise counsel—it's good to have a mentor as I figure out how things work around here.

Joe

273

From: Maria Johnson
To: Joe Kraus
Re: Proposal

Joe

Well, you should have thought of that yourself. I've already spoken to Stephen, as I thought that's what you wanted, and he's waiting—we both are—to see what you can produce. So I think you would be well-advised to come up fairly quickly with something more concrete than lame jokes about "selling paper." I assume you do have an idea?

Maria

From: Joe Kraus
To: Maria Johnson, Stephen Whittaker
Re: Proposal

Maria and Stephen

Thank you for taking an interest in my proposal. The way the essay has to work is that it explains some aspect of philosophy in terms of the characters and situations from *The Office*. I was thinking that since we live in Scranton, it would be fitting for us to reflect on the way our town is represented in the show, and to move from there to a consideration of theories of representation.

I got the idea from the experience I have every morning when I drive down the Central Scranton Expressway off of Interstate 81 and pass the sign from the opening credits of the show. "Scranton Welcomes You," it says, and what's funny is that I barely noticed it before the show came on the air. It was just there, just one of those things you pass, like billboards, mounds of old mining culm, or abandoned railroad cars. At some level it didn't even exist until I began to see it on television; then it turned into one of the landmarks of my commute. I see it every day and, sometimes, if it's a sunny day or the nearby leaves are dramatically colored, I do a double take because it no longer exactly resembles itself from television.

What makes it strange, then, is that the sign didn't become "real" until it was turned into an image broadcast back to me. Now, when I do notice the sign, I realize that I am recognizing the real sign as a reflection of the television image. That's backwards, but it's just the way it seems to work. The sign itself seems somehow less real than the Thursday television image of it.

I see that dynamic as an illustration of what the late philosopher Jean Baudrillard called a simulacrum, an image reprinted or rebroadcast so widely that it no longer refers to what it originally represented. Instead of serving as an image of some actual thing, it becomes an image that refers to the idea of images. A standard example would be an Andy Warhol soup-painting, a work that takes something that once meant soup and turns it into something that we are simply supposed to look at for its own sake.

That's my take. Do you think we can build a clever article on these ideas?

Joe

From: Maria Johnson
To: Joseph Kraus
cc: Stephen Whittaker
Subject: Proposal

Joe
You could build rather a clever house of cards on quicksand too, if you were so minded. And you evidently are. Baudrillard and Warhol . . . I take it you think it a cutting-edge, ironic, exclusively postmodern idea that signs and images function and interact in complex ways and can take on a life of their own? Honestly, you lit. theory types. I hate to burst your bubble, but these ideas are very very old. We've dealt with them in theology for more than two millennia, but I can't expect a wet-behind-the-ears sort like yourself to know that.

By the way, was that you I saw in Farley's the other night? I was passing the window on my way back from the library (I usually stop work around 9 on a Friday, but I was working late this evening). I'm glad you have sufficient confidence in your productivity that you can spend time in bars, but don't forget that your tenure review is coming up.

Maria Johnson

From: Maria Johnson
To: Stephen Whittaker
Re: Joe Kraus

Stephen
I've softened him up a bit. How about you have a go at it?

M

From: Stephen Whittaker
To: Maria Johnson
Re: Joe Kraus

Maria
I think the key to Joe's idea is that he's new. He has impressions. He wants to write about his impressions of his impressions. God, can you imagine having to try to make tenure off of postmodernism? I'd rather spend my time translating Milton back into Latin.
　　Leave him to me.

S

From: Stephen Whittaker
To: Joe Kraus
cc: Maria Johnson

Joe
Maria has passed on to me your rather unusual proposal. It's nice to have someone around who is as *au courant* as you evidently are with the most up-to-the minute trends. But I must ask, are you acquainted with Plato? He was a "literary critic," though perhaps before your time. His dialogue *Ion* gives us an uncomfortable intersection of light comedy and terrible embarrassment, wherein the main character, like Ricky Gervais' David Brent or Steve Carell's Michael Scott, imagines himself as knowing everything when in fact he is, as the children say, clueless. Ion's business is selling not paper but spoken words; he recites Homer. In the dialogue Socrates plays all the supporting characters who, mixing flattery and contempt, allow the title character to reveal his gorgeous and spectacular incompetence.
　　Socrates' questioning of the rhapsode Ion allows us to see a particular picture of *poesis*, or making. According to Socrates, the muses are the real makers of the Homeric material, and Ion just one in a long sequence of performers who imitate the original. Socrates

276

takes pains to demonstrate that Ion, though capable of an affecting performance of Homer, in fact knows nothing of the real content, nothing of being a great leader in battle or an intrepid sailor in heavy weather.

Socrates concludes famously that the real maker is like a lodestone or magnet, and each subsequent performer like a piece of iron, capable of transmitting the force of the original, but not of generating it. And the transmissions undergo an ever-increasing diminishment. In the end, Socrates makes it clear that Ion's performance is in fact full of sound and fury, but without significance. Ion, like the British David and the American Michael, exhibits a wonderful capacity not to see that he has been utterly humiliated. Plato's deeper point seems to be twofold: to be really good, art has to be made by people who actually know something; and well made art can be engaged by rigorous intelligence without blowing away like cheap paper.

Might I suggest that you use some of your spare time (Maria tells me you have been hanging out in Farley's) to deepen your acquaintance with the tradition as a whole? You may have been hired to teach minority literature, as a nod toward political correctness, but someone who operates exclusively in the last 50 years is unlikely to find a long-term home in our department.

From: Joe Kraus
To: Stephen Whittaker
cc: Maria Johnson
Re: Proposal

Stephen
Thank you for your advice. You are of course quite right that this is a topic with a long history (you may have forgotten—quite understandably, given all you have to do—that my MA thesis was on Plato; my interest in critical theory is of more recent date) and it was probably foolish of me to start the discussion with something so recent. I do appreciate your suggestions.

By the way, I got some good news this morning. University of Stamford Press has accepted my manuscript. I hope a book from them will help my tenure case.

Joe

From: Stephen Whittaker
To: Joe Kraus
Re: Proposal

Joe

It seems there's nothing I can tell you about Plato that you don't already know. What about Aristotle, or did you skip 2,500 years and go straight to Baudrillard? Aristotle had rather a different take on mimesis, or the art of imitation. He had quite a lot to say about tragedy and, it is supposed, on comedy as well, though the latter treatise has not survived. But as regards *The Office* that is perhaps not such a great loss. I say this because it seems to me that the leading characteristic of both versions of the TV show depend, for their peculiar effect, upon an alloying of conventional comedic moves with elements of tragedy. For Aristotle, our experience of tragedy depends upon our identification with the human frailty of the tragic figure, and our being suspended between pity and terror. That pretty well sums up the intense discomfort one feels watching either David Brent or Michael Scott: a sympathy for the delusions and insensitivities, poised by a terror, itself rising both from disgust with the character and recognition of oneself within the character. For Aristotle, the value of the particular mimesis was the intensity with which we were brought to a catharsis by the show. By catharsis Aristotle seems to have meant a kind of purification of the very emotions, pity and fear, which the depiction has aroused.

Hope this helps.

By the way, Stamford's acceptance of your monograph does do a bit to mitigate Scranton Press's passing on it.

Stephen

From: Maria Johnson
To: Joe Kraus
cc: Stephen Whittaker
Re: Proposal

Joe

I see that Stephen has kindly offered you week one of a tutorial on philosophies of representation. Here's week two: fast-forward a few hundred years to the start of the Christian era. Within a couple hundred years AD there were two thoroughly established Christian schools with complex systems for understanding how texts relate to themselves, to each other, to things in the world, and to things beyond the world.

The kind of exegesis centered around Antioch concentrated on the historical and moral significance of texts. If an Antiochene exegete of *The Office* looked Scranton up on a map and read up on its history, he'd learn that the city is named after the local coal magnate William Scranton, who was so afraid of potential violence from the exploited miners on whose labor his fortune was built that he had a tunnel dug directly from his house (where the faculty dining room and the Admissions Office is right now) to the railway station in case he needed to make a quick getaway. He'd also learn that Scranton was very proud of his athletic abilities and is recorded as having, at the age of 36, lifted a dead weight of 2,000 pounds in the presence of several witnesses. He'd link such an obviously spurious legend to the deluded self-promotion of Michael Scott, draw the edifying conclusion that those who seek to elevate themselves in fact only dig themselves a tunnel and earn the hatred of those who love justice, and wrap up with an exhortation to humility. It would not have mattered to Antioch that the producers of *The Office* knew none of that local background. To him, God was the real author of all texts, and such deep background was His doing.

Alexandrian theologians, on the other hand, moved past the literal and historical meanings as quickly as possible, in search of elevated, spiritual meanings. An Alexandrian exegete of *The Office* would take as his starting point the derivation of the name Scranton from the Dutch *schrantsen* meaning to split, tear or shred. He'd refer this to the division between management and clerical staff, and then go on to construct an elaborate system in which the paper that Dunder-Mifflin sells is the vehicle of earthly knowledge, which ignorant men like Scott blindly seek to possess and manipulate to their own material ends. Such knowledge must be torn or shredded, he would argue, so that the soul can be liberated from earthly bondage and ascend to the higher knowledge of spiritual essences which are not written on paper.

I hope we are starting to help you build a more complete picture of the field. I have to attend a Tenure Board meeting now. You walk the plank next year, right?

Maria

From: Joe Kraus
To: Maria Johnson
Re: Proposal

Maria

Many thanks. As much as I appreciate your thoughts on this I hate to trouble you: I know you are very busy, particularly during tenure season, so maybe we should just drop the idea for *The Office* essay?

You know, the only reason I spend any time at Farley's is that—as the producers of *The Office* seem not to know—we don't have a good Hooters around here.

Joe

From: Maria Johnson
To: Joe Kraus
Re: Proposal

Joe

I'm glad to be of service: as busy as senior faculty are, it is an important duty to work with our junior colleagues. My service on the Tenure Board makes me acutely aware of how much additional work we make for ourselves whenever we turn someone down.

To pick up where we left off, the Antiochene and Alexandrian schools were eventually consolidated into a system of scriptural interpretation that was embraced by Augustine and widely accepted through the Middle Ages. According to this system, every word or event in scripture has four meanings. There is the literal meaning—the word means just what it appears on the surface to mean. There is the allegorical meaning—the word is a reference to Christ and the Christian covenant. The tropological meaning relates to morality and the duty of the Christian, and the anagogical to the eschaton, the end of the world. So when there is a reference in the Bible to Jerusalem, the literal meaning is the Israelite city, the allegorical meaning is the Church, the tropological meaning is the human soul, and the anagogical meaning is heaven. Any or all of these meanings can be called on in interpreting a particular passage which refers to Jerusalem.

A medieval interpreter of *The Office* would see in Scranton references to, literally, the town in Pennsylvania that we work in:

allegorically, a typical American blue collar town: tropologically, the distortion and darkness of the soul given over to material aims and, anagogically, the inevitable collapse of Western civilization under the soul-crushing bleakness of a commercial culture.

Is this picture becoming a little clearer? I hope this isn't too difficult for you to follow.

Incidentally, Stephen and I were discussing your little project with Michael Friedman the other day. He was concerned, as we all are, about the direction in which your scholarship is going. You'll be hearing from him.

And, really, Hooters? You can't be serious.

Maria

From: Joe Kraus
To: Maria Johnson
Re: Proposal

Maria

You have been very clear indeed, thank you. It is good to be reminded of some of the work I did in my graduate seminar on Augustine. I used him quite extensively in the third chapter of my book.

I do appreciate your time and concern—really, it's very kind of you. But you needn't have troubled Michael. I don't want to cause him any extra work. *The Office* idea was just a passing thought, that I never should have mentioned.

Oh, and the Hooters reference? In case I wasn't clear, I was just joking.

Joe

From: Michael Friedman
To: Joe Kraus
cc: Stephen Whittaker, Maria Johnson
Re: Proposal

Joe

Stephen and Maria have told me about this notion of yours to write on *The Office*. I am, of course, just a simple country Shakespearean scholar, so I can't quote Faulkner and Baudrillard and all them other highfalutin' Greeks, but I do possess the advantage of actually having watched the show, which ought to count for something, as none of the rest of you appear to have more than a passing acquaintance with it.

Michael

From: Stephen Whittaker
To Michael Friedman
cc: Joe Kraus, Maria Johnson
Re: Proposal

Michael
Naturally, I spend little time watching television. You, of course, are free to spend your time as you wish, though I am surprised that Joe, untenured as he is, watches sitcoms. But as regards *The Office*, you will not be surprised to hear that I prefer the British version.

Stephen

From: Michael Friedman
To: Joe Kraus
cc: Stephen Whittaker, Maria Johnson
Re: Proposal

Stephen
Unlike you, I vastly prefer the American version of *The Office*. I tried to watch the opening episode of the British version a long time ago, and I found it so intensely uncomfortable that I had to turn it off after about ten minutes. Since the American version strives to give viewers the same unnerving experience, there must be some other aspect of the show that allows me to keep watching. I've come to believe that the Scranton setting is that decisive element.

Part of my pleasure in watching *The Office* derives from the fact that I have to pay pretty close attention to catch all of the local color. And unlike other TV shows that hit you over the head with obvious gags, *The Office* demands a higher level of engagement, since a great deal of the meaning is expressed through subtext and gesture rather than dialogue. But it's more than just Pam's nervous glances at the camera or Jim's goofy grins that share with the viewer exactly what he's thinking. Did you see the episode in which Pam gives a eulogy for a bird that has died because it flew into the glass doors at Dunder-Mifflin? Pam's eulogy speaks of the bird, but subtextually it refers to Michael himself, who fears that he too will die alone and unloved, like his old boss. As Pam speaks, we can see on her face that her words are designed to comfort Michael, and that his cathartic release of tears represents a combination of self-pity and oddly humorous reassurance that he will not meet the same desolate end. In its reliance on what goes unsaid, *The Office* more closely resembles a Chekhov play than it does any of the other sitcoms on TV today.

Michael

From: Stephen Whittaker
To: Michael Friedman
cc: Joe Kraus, Maria Johnson
Re: Proposal

Michael
My favorite thing about this great chain of being funny is that the American version of the show credits itself as created by Ricky Gervais and Stephen Merchant. So the Michael Scott of the American version is performed by Steve Carell, who performs a script by whomever wrote the particular episode. And the entire American version is said to be created by the two guys who wrote and directed the British version, one of whom not only performed David Brent, but himself directed himself, from a script he himself wrote. Now, if you follow the Socratic genealogy, if Ricky Gervais conceived, wrote, and then directed himself acting David Brent, then, while embodying David Brent, Ricky Gervais is his own grandfather, creatively speaking. If, by the same logic, David Brent and Michael Scott are brothers, then it follows that Michael Scott is his own great-great uncle. Take that, Jean Baudrillard (with apologies to James Joyce and Stephen Dedalus).

What Plato would enjoy in all this is that the TV show defies genre classifications, such as comic or tragic, which he considered to be the hallmark of shallow imitation. He might even see the American show as somehow an authentic poesis. Though, as I say, I consider the British the worthier candidate.

Stephen

From: Michael Friedman
To: Stephen Whittaker
cc: Joe Kraus, Maria Johnson

Stephen

That's all well and good, but why did the creators of the show choose to locate a branch of Dunder-Mifflin in Scranton in the first place? Clearly, they saw Scranton as the equivalent of the British version's location, Slough, which Wikipedia calls a "depressing industrial wasteland." In 1937, John Betjeman wrote a poem that begins, "Come, friendly bombs, and fall on Slough/It isn't fit for humans now/There isn't grass to graze a cow./Swarm over, death!"

Scranton has, in the minds of those Americans who have never been here, a similar reputation for being an abandoned coal-mining town, devoid of beauty, culture, and interest of any kind, which makes it the perfect setting for the soul-crushing, mundane workplace setting of *The Office*. Now of course, those of us who live and work here know that Scranton is actually a charming, pleasant, and vibrant city undergoing a civic revival, but in the minds of its residents, it still hasn't quite recovered from the decline of anthracite in the 1950s. We still make excuses about residing here to our friends and relatives in other parts of the country and tell them how easy it is to get from Scranton to other, more exciting cities along the east coast.

For me, the program's symbol of Scranton's decrepitude in the public imagination appears briefly, before the "Welcome to Scranton" sign, in the show's opening credits. For a moment, we see a crumbling brick building featuring a tall tower with a circular emblem at the top that reads, unintelligibly, "Pen Pa." I suppose that, for most people, this brief glimpse of dreary architecture merely designates Scranton as a decaying hell-hole, but I have to confess, it gives me a thrill every time I see it. As I'm sure you know, that building is the headquarters of the Pennsylvania Paper Company, which is located only a few blocks from my house, and to the great annoyance of my family, I point it out to them every time we pass by it. When I see that image on TV on Thursday nights, I get the inside joke that this real, inglorious paper company building sheds lackluster light on the fictional Dunder-Mifflin office. And for some reason, that makes me proud.

Although *The Office* clearly holds Scranton up for ridicule, we Scranton residents have embraced the show as an elevation of our community into the upper-echelon of American cities. Like New York, Los Angeles, and Las Vegas, Scranton is now the type of place where hit television programs are set. Although the episodes aren't filmed here, the show's writers pepper the dialogue with references to local landmarks like the Steamtown Mall, and the office itself contains various objects, such as Dwight's Froggy 101 bumper sticker, that leap out at the initiated as genuine reminders that this famous dysfunctional workplace exists *here*, in *our town*. Did you know that local bars now advertise that they have *The Office* on big-screen TVs so that aficionados can gather to do their civic duty by cheering these local references? Are you aware that the *Scranton Times-Tribune* reports on these allusions and indignantly corrects them when they are inaccurate? (Having Michael and Dwight travel from Scranton to Philly by train was a particularly egregious error.) Have you heard that there is a movement afoot to invite the stars of the show to our fair community and offer them the key to the city? Like Michael Scott himself, we have steadfastly refused to accept that we are being ridiculed, and we have managed to take each insult as a compliment of the highest order.

Michael

From: Joe Kraus
To: Michael Friedman
cc: Stephen Whittaker, Maria Johnson

Michael
Thank you for taking the time. Your observations are very interesting indeed. Do I take it you are interested in collaborating on a contribution to the volume?

Joe

From: Michael Friedman
To: Joe Kraus
Re: Proposal

Joe
Aw, hell no! I was merely putting in my two cents. Is this what passes for philosophy these days? And do you really think that this is what the Tenure Board means by scholarship?

Michael

From: Michael Friedman
To: Stephen Whittaker, Maria Johnson
Re: Joe Kraus

Stephen and Maria
You know the Dean and Provost are getting very keen on faculty "publishing beyond conventional scholarly parameters" blah blah blah, "addressing a broader audience" yada yada yada. They'd probably be all over this pop culture nonsense. Shall we do it? If so, do we cut Joe out of the project?

M

From: Stephen Whittaker
To: Maria Johnson, Michael Friedman
Re: Joe Kraus

Good idea, Michael. It might be a notch on the gradebook towards a merit raise, you never know. I don't really want to be bothered with that postmodern puppy, though. I doubt he'd ever find out and if he does, well, what's he going to do about it? Maria, get rid of him, will you?

S

From: Maria Johnson
To: Joe Kraus
Bcc: Stephen Whittaker, Michael Friedman

Joe
I'm sorry to disappoint, but Stephen, Michael, and I discussed the situation and agreed that we can't spare any more time to discuss your *Office* proposal. Of course, it is important that you pursue your own interests, even if those interests are in television sitcoms. Let me give you a friendly warning, however, that the Dean and Provost are likely to take a rather dim view of the sort of project you are proposing. I would strongly advise you to concentrate your efforts on serious scholarly publication.

I hope this conversation has been useful to you—I'm sure I speak for all of us when I say that it has been gratifying to be able to contribute to your intellectual development. I trust we have helped you to place the trendy theories of representation which you find so fascinating in the context of the broader intellectual tradition. Maybe we can discuss them more when you have had time for a little more reading in the area. For now, however, I must bring our conversation to a close, and I hope that you will focus your energies on the kind of work likely to win you a favorable decision from the Tenure Board.

Maria

From: Joe Kraus
To: Maria Johnson, Stephen Whittaker, Michael Friedman
Re: The Office

Thank you all for your thoughtful replies to an idea I now regret putting forward at all. May I follow up with a request for a personal favor: I've applied for a position at the University of Stamford, and I was hoping that you three might write letters of recommendation on my behalf.

Joe

Appendix B

Question: What Do You Need to Know About Dwight K. Schrute?

Fact: Dwight K. Schrute keeps his desk drawers locked, and keeps his phone in a locked drawer when not working. (Pilot)

Fact: Dwight K. Schrute has no problem with downsizing. He's been recommending it since he first got to Dunder-Mifflin; he even brought it up in his interview. (Pilot)

Fact: Dwight K. Schrute used to drive a 1978 2802. (Pilot)

Fact: Dwight K. Schrute is a Lackawanna County Volunteer Sheriff's Deputy on the weekends. (Diversity Day)

Fact: Dwight K. Schrute has knowledge of the characteristics of superheroes. (A hero kills people who wish him harm. A hero is part human, part supernatural. A hero is born out of a childhood trauma or disaster and must be avenged. We all have a hero in our heart.) (Diversity Day)

Fact: Dwight K. Schrute has never been sick. He has a perfect immune system and superior brain power. (Health Care)

Fact: Through concentration, Dwight K. Schrute can raise or lower his blood pressure at will. Why would he want to raise it? So he can lower it again. (Health Care)

Fact: Dwight K. Schrute loves Count Chocula. (Health Care)

Fact: Dwight K. Schrute brings his own water to work, which puts him at a real disadvantage for hearing the gossip at the water cooler. (The Alliance)

Fact: Dwight K. Schrute is a deer hunter; he goes with his dad. Dwight K. Schrute is better at hiding than deer are at vision. (The Alliance)

Fact: Dwight K. Schrute has dyed his hair to go undercover and spy on the Stamford branch. (The Alliance)

Fact: Dwight K. Schrute believes in protecting his face when engaged in athletic activities. (He wears one of those plastic masks when playing basketball. (Basketball)

Fact: The Schrutes produce very thirsty babies. (Hot Girl)

Fact: Dwight K. Schrute owns a purse. (Hot Girl)

Fact: Dwight K. Schrute keeps his Dundies in a display case above his bed. (The Dundies)

Fact: Dwight K. Schrute can play "Mambo #5" on his recorder. (The Dundies)

Fact: Dwight K. Schrute's grandfather left him a 10-acre working beet farm. He runs it with his cousin Mose. They sell beets to local stores and restaurants. His grandparents also left him a large number of armoires. (Office Olympics)

Fact: Dwight K. Schrute has his own crossbow range. (Office Olympics)

Fact: Dwight K. Schrute's bathroom is under his porch. (Office Olympics)

Fact: Dwight K. Schrute enjoys the song "Everybody Hurts" by REM. (The Fire)

Fact: Dwight K. Schrute's all-time favorite movie is *The Crow*. (The Fire)

Fact: Dwight K. Schrute is a practitioner of Goju-Ryu karate in Scranton. He is a sempai, which is assistant (to the) Sensei. (The Fight)

Fact: Dwight K. Schrute has a purple belt, which is not a toy. (The Fight)

Fact: Dwight K. Schrute's maternal grandfather was a World War II Veteran. He killed 20 men and then spent the rest of the war in an Allied prison camp. Dwight K. Schrute's father battled blood pressure and obesity his whole life, which is a different kind of battle. (The Fight)

Fact: Dwight K. Schrute was secretly promoted from Assistant to the Regional Manager to Assistant Regional Manager. (The Fight)

Fact: Dwight K. Schrute played "Mutey the Mailman" in a 7th grade production of *Oklahoma!* They had to make up parts so all the kids could participate. (The Client)

Fact: Dwight K. Schrute used a fitness orb, which changed his whole life. (The Client)

Fact: Dwight K. Schrute brought in deer jerky for the whole office. (The Client)

Fact: Dwight K. Schrute thinks that one of the greatest things about modern America is the computerization of medical records. (Email Surveillance)

Fact: Dwight K. Schrute is the Christmas Elf. (Christmas Party)

Fact: Dwight K. Schrute was the youngest pilot in Pan-Am history—when he was four, the pilot let him ride in the cockpit and steer the plane. (Booze Cruise)

Fact: Dwight K. Schrute has a bobble head of himself, which he received for Valentine's Day. (Valentine's Day)

Fact: Dwight K. Schrute was Top Salesman of the Year at the company, which is "literally the highest honor that a Northeastern Pennsylvania-based mid-sized paper company regional salesman can attain." (Dwight's Speech)

Fact: Dwight K. Schrute has given a speech originally given by Benito Mussolini. (Dwight's Speech)

Fact: Dwight K. Schrute can play "Greensleeves" on the recorder. (Take Your Daughter to Work Day)

Fact: Dwight K. Schrute's grandmutter read him a story from 1864—a cautionary tale for kids. (Take Your Daughter to Work Day)

Fact: Dwight K. Schrute can play the guitar for, and sing, "Teach Your Children Well." (Take Your Daughter to Work Day)

Fact: The Schrutes consider children very valuable; they would bear as many children as possible so they would have enough laborers to work the fields. And if it was an especially cold winter, and there weren't enough grains or vegetables, they would eat the youngest of the brood. They didn't eat the children—it never came to that. (Take Your Daughter to Work Day)

Fact: Dwight K. Schrute can play "For the Longest Time" by William Joel on the recorder. (Michael's Birthday)

Fact: Dwight K. Schrute will not tip someone for doing a job he could do himself. (Michael's Birthday)

Fact: Dwight K. Schrute likes the people he works with, with four exceptions. (Drug Testing)

Fact: Dwight K. Schrute did not become a sheriff's deputy to make friends. (And, by the way, he hasn't.) (Drug Testing)

Fact: Dwight K. Schrute wants Michael to have all the urine he needs. (Drug Testing)

Fact: Dwight K. Schrute's father and grandfather's names were both Dwight Schrute. His great-grandfather's name was Dwide Shrude—Amish. (Drug Testing)

Fact: Dwight K. Schrute has a standing appointment with Toby (Fridays at 4) to file grievances against Jim. (Conflict Resolution)

Fact: Dwight K. Schrute never smiles if he can help it. Showing one's teeth is a submission signal in primates. When someone smiles at him, all he sees is a chimpanzee begging for its life. (Conflict Resolution)

Fact: Dwight K. Schrute would never ever serve Jim. Not in a million billion years. (Casino Night)

Fact: Dwight K. Schrute owns and wears the tuxedo his grandfather was buried in. (Casino Night)

Fact: Dwight K. Schrute has been convinced that Jim can move things with his mind. (Casino Night)

Fact: Dwight K. Schrute can tell by looking at someone if they're gay. (Gay Witch-hunt)

Fact: It is Dwight K. Schrute's job to know where Jan Levinson shops. (The Coup)

Fact: Dwight K. Schrute has to do Michael's laundry for a year, although after his re-hiring, they can discuss that. (The Coup)

Fact: Dwight K. Schrute believes that instant death is very smart. (Grief Counseling)

Fact: When Dwight K. Schrute dies, he would like to be frozen. He'll wake up stronger than ever, because he would have used that time to figure out why he died and what hold they had him in. (Grief Counseling)

Fact: Dwight K. Schrute believes that a 2/3-size robot is easier to stop than a full-size robot if it turns on its creators. It is also wise to give a robot a 6-foot extension cord, so it could not chase after people. (Grief Counseling)

Fact: When Dwight K. Schrute's mother was pregnant with him, they did an ultrasound and thought she was having twins. A few weeks later, they checked again and found out that Dwight had "resorbed" the other fetus. Now he has the strength of a grown man *and* a little baby. (Grief Counseling)

Fact: Dwight K. Schrute always has his neon green recorder with him. (Grief Counseling)

Fact: Dwight K. Schrute can almost fit a dead bird into a soda can. (Grief Counseling)

Fact: Dwight K. Schrute's grandfather was reburied in an oil drum. (Grief Counseling)

Fact: Dwight K. Schrute enjoys the metal band Life of Agony. (Initiation)

Fact: Dwight K. Schrute is the leader of the "Dwight Army of Champions." (Initiation)

Fact: Cousin Mose will always be Dwight's best friend, unless things go well with Ryan. (Initiation)

Fact: The greatest danger facing Dunder-Mifflin is flash floods. (Initiation)

Fact: Michael Scott's greatest fear is nothing. But Dwight would accept "snakes" as an answer. (Initiation)

Fact: Dwight K. Schrute possesses a nasty old wheelchair and the coffin his grandfather was originally buried in, and he keeps these in a barn. (Initiation)

Fact: Dwight K. Schrute knows a lot about Diwali. *A lot.* (Diwali)

Fact: Dwight K. Schrute can play "The Hanukah Song" on the guitar. (Diwali)

Fact: Dwight K. Schrute receives faxes from Future Dwight. (Branch Closing)

Fact: Dwight K. Schrute was hazed on his first day by being sprayed with a fire extinguisher by Michael. (Branch Closing)

Fact: Dwight K. Schrute outran a black pepper snake. (The Merger)

Fact: Japanese camp guards in World War II killed one man every time a new batch of prisoners came in. Dwight K. Schrute thinks that he would be good at choosing that person. (The Merger)

Fact: He is older, he is wiser—don't mess with him. (The Merger)

Fact: Dwight K. Schrute knows that the safest place to sit is behind the driver. In the case of an accident, the driver always protects his side. (Traveling Salesmen)

Fact: Dwight K. Schrute never lets anyone walk behind him: 70 percent of attacks come from the rear. (Traveling Salesmen)

Fact: Dwight K. Schrute never takes vacations, never gets sick, and doesn't celebrate any major holidays. (Traveling Salesmen)

Fact: One of Dwight K. Schrute's life goals is to die in his desk chair. (Traveling Salesmen)

Fact: Dwight K. Schrute broke down his resume into three parts: professional resume, athletic and special skills resume, and Dwight Schrute Trivia. (The Return)

Fact: Dwight K. Schrute is ready to face any challenges that might be foolish enough to face him. (The Return)

Fact: Dwight K. Schrute would describe himself in three words as: hardworking, alpha-male, jackhammer, merciless, insatiable. (The Return)

Fact: Dwight K. Schrute password-protects his files with the names of mythical creatures. (The Return)

Fact: Dwight K. Schrute has excellent hand-eye coordination. (The Return)

Fact: Dwight K. Schrute doesn't care what Jim says. He is 99 percent sure that the real Ben Franklin did not visit the office. (Ben Franklin)

Fact: The Schrutes have their own traditions. They usually get married standing in their own graves, which makes the funerals very romantic. But the weddings are a bleak affair. (Phyllis' Wedding)

Fact: That's the thing about bear attacks—they come when you least expect it. (Phyllis' Wedding)

Fact: The most inspiring thing anyone's ever said to Dwight K. Schrute was Michael saying "Don't be an idiot." Whenever he's about to do something, he thinks: would an idiot do that? And if they would, he does not do that thing. (Business School)

Fact: If a vampire bat was in the US, it would make sense for it to come to a—sylvania, like Pennsylvania. (Business School)

Fact: Dwight K. Schrute doesn't have a lot of experience with vampires, but he has hunted werewolves. He shot one once, but by the time he got to it, it had turned back into his neighbor's dog. (Business School)

Fact: Dwight K. Schrute has been controlling animals since he was six. (Business School)

Fact: The line on the top of the shrimp is feces. (Cocktails)

Fact: Dwight K. Schrute is shunning Andy for the next three years. It's an Amish technique; it's like slapping someone with silence. Dwight was shunned from the age of four to his sixth birthday for not saving the excess oil from a can of tuna. (Cocktails)

Fact: Bears can climb faster than they can run. (Product Recall)

Fact: Identity theft is not a joke—millions of families suffer every year. (Product Recall)

Fact: 1st rule in roadside beet sales: put the most attractive beets on top—the ones that make you pull the car over and say wow, I need that beet. (Product Recall)

Fact: Dwight K. Schrute grew up on a farm, has seen animals having sex in every position imaginable. (Product Recall)

Fact: Better a thousand innocent men are locked up than one guilty man go free. (Product Recall)

Fact: Once Dwight K. Schrute becomes Regional Manager, his first order of business will be to demote Jim Halpert. His ideal choice for a new #2 is Jack Bauer, but he is unavailable, fictional, and overqualified. (The Job)

Fact: One thousand Schrute bucks equals an extra five minutes for lunch. One Schrute buck is worth 1/100 of a cent. (The Job)

Fact: Dwight K. Schrute has a Froggy 101 sticker near his desk.

Fact: Dwight K. Schrute grows hemp. ("Money")

Fact: Dwight K. Schrute is a notary. ('Money")

Fact: Dwight K. Schrute keeps many pelts in his trunk, along with a bear horn. ("Dunder-Mifflin Infinity")

Fact: Dwight K. Schrute has been employee of the month 13 out of the last 12 months. ("Dunder-Mifflin Infinity")

Fact: Dwight K. Schrute cannot be defeated by a computer! ("Dunder-Mifflin Infinity")

Fact: Dwight K. Schrute plays "Second Life." Everything about him is the same, except that he can fly. ("Local Ad")

Fact: Agrotourism is a lot more than a bed and breakfast. It consists of tourists coming to a farm, showing them around, giving them a bed, giving them breakfast. ("Money")

Fact: Schrute Farms has three rooms, each with a different theme: America, Irrigation, and Night-Time. ("Money")

Fact: The Schrute Beet Farm, Bed and Breakfast caters to the elderly. ("Money")

Fact: The Schrutes give wild oats to members of the family after they have sex with young women. ("Money")

Fact: Dwight K. Schrute can play "You give love a bad name" on the recorder.

Fact: The eyes are the groin of the head. ("Branch Wars")

Fact: Dwight K. Schrute keeps various weaponry around the office. ("Branch Wars")

Fact: It is better to be hurt by someone you know accidentally than by a stranger on purpose. ("Branch Wars")

Fact: Dwight K. Schrute is an excellent table-tennis player. ("The Deposition")

Facts from Dwight's Blog!

Fact: Dwight K. Schrute hates salmon. Clarification: he doesn't hate salmon, he really, really, really DOESN'T LIKE salmon.

Fact: Salmon don't keep blogs.

Fact: Dwight K. Schrute has over 87 people in his immediate family.

Fact: Halloween is his favorite holiday, even though he doesn't celebrate holidays.

Fact: Dwight K. Schrute loves slēet.

Fact: Over 287 billion dollars were wasted last year by people being late and/or pretending to be sick.

Fact: Sometimes the sun never rises in Canada.

Fact: Valentine's Day was created by the flower companies and the Hallmark Company AND the chocolate companies and companies that create little plastic cupid creatures containing candy and other fluffy what-nots.

Fact: Dwight K. Schrute's favorite words: sniffles, monkey, ass, nebula, corn, Smith & Wesson, Mordor, Starbuck, Salesman of the Year.

Fact: They call it Fall because people fall down a great deal over all the leaves and branches.

Fact: Judge not, lest ye be a judge.

Fact: Grampa Schrute used to say: "Learn to share or I'll eat you."

Fact: Every year in spring, Dwight K. Schrute's mind goes to ninjas.

Fact: Dwight K. Schrute does not believe in Lycanthropes. He puts no credence in the theory that a human can change into anything other than a decomposing human.

Fact: Dwight K. Schrute left himself a time capsule in 1985. It was found in 2007. Here are the contents: a dehydrated beet sculpture of himself, a friendship bracelet, half of a twix bar, a letter to himself, a letter to his wife (he has disappointed his former self), and the carcass of a vole.

Employees of *The Office* and Philosophy

Robert Arp is currently a postdoc researcher through the University at Buffalo working in biomedical ontology. He is the editor of *South Park and Philosophy* (Blackwell, 2007) and has written a good deal more than you're prepared to read about right now. Question: Can a person really tell if another person is gay just by looking at them, or must one buy a gaydar?

Michael Bray is an Assistant Professor of Philosophy at Southwestern University. He has published essays on Thomas Hobbes, C. B. Macpherson, Adam Smith, and Theodor Adorno and is at work on issues in film, technology, and society. Sadly, he currently purchases his paper at Staples but would be happy to discuss, over an Awesome Blossom, his options with a local supplier.

Keith Dromm is an Associate Professor of Philosophy in the Louisiana Scholars' College at Northwestern State University in Natchitoches. FACT: He has written chapters for such books as *The Philosophy of the X-Files* (2007). FACT: He has published articles in journals such as the *Journal of Applied Philosophy*, *History of Philosophy Quarterly*, and the *British Journal for the History of Philosophy*. FACT: He knows more about bears than Dwight.

John Elia is the Therese Murray Goodwin '49 Chair and Assistant Professor in Philosophy at Wilson College. He has special interests in ethics, political philosophy, and the philosophy of law. He uses office paper daily (and he's really great with it); if the philosophy gig doesn't work out, he may be moving to Scranton.

Jonathan Evans is an Assistant Professor of Philosophy at the University of Indianapolis. He has published articles on modality and future contingents in medieval philosophy, on ethics, and sport. His current research is on human agency, modality, and time. On weekends, Evans works as a roadie for the under-publicized Grass Roots reunion tour which is slated to play in six large towns in Canada, western New York, and Pennsylvania; live recordings from the tour will be available for download on Creed's blog-site.

Randall M. Jensen is Associate Professor of Philosophy at Northwestern College in Orange City, Iowa. His philosophical interests include ethics, ancient Greek philosophy, and philosophy of religion. He has also contributed to *South Park and Philosophy*, *24 and Philosophy*, and *Battlestar Galactica and Philosophy* (all Blackwell, 2007). Bears, beets, Battlestar Galactica! There's nothing on his horizon except everything.

David Kyle Johnson is currently an Assistant Professor of Philosophy at King's College in Wilkes-Barre, PA. His philosophical specializations include philosophy of religion, logic, and metaphysics. He also wrote a chapter in Blackwell's *South Park and Philosophy*, and has chapters on *Family Guy*, *Quentin Tarantino*, *Johnny Cash*, *Battlestar Galactica*, and *Batman*. He has taught many classes that focus on the relevance of philosophy to pop culture, including a course devoted to *South Park*. (A class incorporating *The Office* is in the works.) Kyle, for some reason, craves Altoids every time his computer reboots.

Rory E. Kraft, Jr. is an Assistant Professor of Philosophy at York College of Pennsylvania, and co-editor of the journal *Questions: Philosophy for Young People*. His main areas of interest are ethical theory, applied ethics, and philosophy with pre-college students. Unfortunately, he suffers from spontaneous dental hydroplosion, and is concerned that he may be infected with a government-created Killer Nanobot Infection.

Meg Lonergan is a student at Hartwick College, finishing dual degrees in Sociology and Philosophy. She has many papers and books that are not yet written, largely because we are not worthy of her brilliance. A second reason, perhaps equally important, is that her love for Count Chocula keeps her very busy.

297

Morgan Luck is a Lecturer in Philosophy at Charles Sturt University and a fellow of the Centre for Applied Philosophy and Public Ethics (CAPPE). His research areas include philosophy of religion, metaphysics, and epistemology. Morgan could give you a list of fifty things he could beat you at. He once threw a kettle over a pub. What have you ever done?

Russell Manning teaches high school philosophy at Yarra Valley Grammar in Melbourne, Australia. He is the author of "Jean Baudrillard and the Fatal Strategy of the City" (*Cinema-scope Independent Film Journal* Issue 8 May 2007), He is currently completing his Master's thesis at Deakin University (Australia) and is developing a project with the Brentmeister to write "Dead Poets Society, the Musical." He is attracted to entertainer/philosophers.

Sean McAleer is an Assistant Professor of Philosophy (not Assistant to a Professor of Philosophy) at the University of Wisconsin-Eau Claire. His work has appeared in *Film and Philosophy*, *Studies in the History of Ethics*, *Pacific Philosophical Quarterly*, and *Inside Paper*. A part-time motivational speaker for Cooper and Webb, in his spare time he plays guitar in the band Foregone Conclusion and enjoys listening to Hat FM.

Rick Mayock grew up in the Scranton area, and, although his memory is fuzzy, he thinks he may have actually worked at the Dunder-Mifflin Paper Company. Regardless, he is certain that his boss was Michael Scott. He is now employed as the Assistant to the Regional Manager of the Philosophy Department at West Los Angeles College, where he hopes to some day be promoted to Assistant Regional Manager. He has recently contributed to *The Beatles and Philosophy* and continues to visit the Scranton area on a regular basis.

Matthew P. Meyer is a Lecturer in Philosophy at the University of Wisconsin-Eau Claire. He also teaches classes at the University of St. Thomas. He has published in the *International Journal of Listening*. He aspires to someday be a manager of Hotel Hell, where he will preside over guests such as Jim Halpert. He currently enjoys teaching and writing, though his attempts at publishing a book have been sabotaged by the inappropriate watermark on the pages of manuscripts he has sent to publishers.

Peter Murphy is an Assistant Professor of Philosophy at the University of Indianapolis. He has published articles in *Bioethics*, *Dialectica*, and *Synthese*. He buys his beets wholesale from the Schrute farm.

Thomas Nys is a Lecturer in Philosophy at Utrecht University and postdoctoral researcher at the University of Amsterdam. He co-edited *Autonomy and Paternalism: Reflection on the Theory and Practice of Health Care* (2007) and published articles on various topics in moral and political philosophy. He also contributed to the excellent *Metallica and Philosophy* (Blackwell, 2007). It is with pride that Thomas reports that he courageously defended Gareth's foxhole in the territorial army.

Stefanie Rocknak has published articles on David Hume, Edmund Husserl, W. V. O. Quine, Rudolph Carnap, death, art, and epistemology. You can find her at Hartwick College (Oneonta, NY), where she is an Associate Professor of Philosophy. "But that's just my day job," she insists, "and a grueling one at that." She dreams of the day that she can run away to a place as glamorous as Scranton. "Ideally, I'd become a receptionist, just like Pam. I could wile the day away playing Solitaire, and then do my art at night." Rocknak is also an internationally recognized sculptor. Since 1999, her sculpture has been included in over 40 shows, including the Smithsonian and the South Street Seaport Museum (NY, NY). Her work has also been featured in five books and over thirty magazines and newspapers, and can be found in private and public collections throughout the United States.

Gregory J. Schneider is a PhD candidate in the Department of Rhetoric at the University of Minnesota. He studies the rhetoric of science and is writing a dissertation about science museum exhibitions and the way that they construct both science and the public. He has worked to reconcile his philosophic undergraduate experience with his sophisticated graduate training, and he thinks he has a handle on it now. Wait.

Nope, he just lost it again. He is the author of numerous unpublished diatribes and manifestos, and aspires to one day have his picture on the cover of *Inside Paper*. Late at night, you can often find him winning contests by throwing everyday objects over pubs.

Scranton (University of). This is an actual university that has the potential to provide the future workforce of Dunder-Mifflin.

Michael Friedman, Maria Johnson, Joe Kraus, and Stephen Whittaker, PhDs all, are faculty at the University of Scranton, where they teach Shakespeare, Theology, Twentieth-Century American Literature, and Irish Studies, respectively. They have, additionally, clerked in a jewelry store in Kansas City, schlepped in a pharmaceutical factory in Parma, tended Christmas trees in central Ohio, and stocked shelves in Austin. Each is regularly mistaken for a cast member of *The Office*, and the confusion leads to many awkward and unscripted moments.

Andrew Terjesen is a Visiting Assistant Professor of Philosophy at Rhodes College. He has previously taught at Washington and Lee University, Austin College and Duke University. His interest in the ways in which pop culture intersects with philosophy have resulted in the essay in this volume as well as essays in *Family Guy and Philosophy* (Blackwell, 2007) and *Battlestar Galactica and Philosophy* (Blackwell, 2007). It is his hope that everyone become a HERO.

Eva E. Tsahuridu was set for David's chair but couldn't keep her head down. So she went back to university to become Principal Lecturer in Organizational Behaviour at the University of Greenwich Business School, where she has her own chair.

Wim Vandekerckhove is an Assistant Professor of Practical Ethics at Ghent University, Center for Ethics & Value Inquiry. His research and publications cover business ethics, global ethics, whistleblowing, forced labour, social responsible investment and workplace stapler incidents.

Jamie Watson is getting his PhD in philosophy at Florida State University. He shares an office with people who are smarter than he is, so he spends most of his time nodding and repeating, "Absolutely." Of course, brains aren't everything. And yes . . . that's what she said.

Mark D. White is Associate Professor in the Department of Political Science, Economics, and Philosophy at the College of Staten Island in New York City, where he teaches courses combining economics, philosophy, and law. He co-edited the book *Economics and the Mind* (2007), and has written many articles and book chapters on economics and philosophy. But his proudest accomplishment is having written the liner notes for Scrantonicity's upcoming live album, *Scranton Comes Alive*.

J. Jeremy Wisnewski is an Assistant Professor of Philosophy at Hartwick College. He is the author of *Wittgenstein and Ethical Inquiry: A Defense of Ethics as Clarification* (2007) and *The Politics of Agency* (2008), and the editor of *Family Guy and Philosophy* (Blackwell, 2007). He is watching you right now, and wants you to buy his books. Wisnewski has also published a number of articles in such journals as *American Philosophical Quarterly*, *Philosophy of the Social Sciences*, *Continental Philosophy Review*, and *Public Affairs Quarterly*. His next project is to play Michael Scarn in a new production of *Threat Level: Midnight*.

Corporate Filing System